The Craft of Research

Chicago Guides to Writing, Editing, and Publishing

Digital Paper
ANDREW ABBOTT

Tricks of the Trade
HOWARD S. BECKER

Writing for Social Scientists
HOWARD S. BECKER

What Editors Want
PHILIPPA J. BENSON AND SUSAN C. SILVER

The Craft of Translation
JOHN BIGUENET AND RAINER SCHULTE, EDITORS

The Chicago Guide to Grammar, Usage, and Punctuation
BRYAN A. GARNER

Legal Writing in Plain English
BRYAN A. GARNER

From Dissertation to Book
WILLIAM GERMANO

Getting It Published
WILLIAM GERMANO

From Notes to Narrative
KRISTEN GHODSEE

Writing Science in Plain English
ANNE E. GREENE

Cite Right
CHARLES LIPSON

How to Write a BA Thesis
CHARLES LIPSON

The Chicago Guide to Writing about Multivariate Analysis
JANE E. MILLER

The Chicago Guide to Writing about Numbers
JANE E. MILLER

The Subversive Copy Editor
CAROL FISHER SALLER

The Writer's Diet
HELEN SWORD

A Manual for Writers of Research Papers, Theses, and Dissertations
KATE L. TURABIAN

Student's Guide to Writing College Papers
KATE L. TURABIAN

The Craft of Research

FOURTH EDITION

Wayne C. Booth

Gregory G. Colomb

Joseph M. Williams

Joseph Bizup

William T. FitzGerald

THE UNIVERSITY OF CHICAGO PRESS
Chicago & London

Wayne C. Booth (1921–2005) was the George M. Pullman Distinguished Service Professor Emeritus in English Language and Literature at the University of Chicago. His books included *The Rhetoric of Fiction* and *For the Love of It: Amateuring and Its Rivals*, both published by the University of Chicago Press.

Gregory G. Colomb (1951–2011) was professor of English at the University of Virginia and the author of *Designs on Truth: The Poetics of the Augustan Mock-Epic*.

Joseph M. Williams (1933–2008) was professor in the Department of English Language and Literature at the University of Chicago and the author of *Style: Toward Clarity and Grace*.

Joseph Bizup is associate professor in the Department of English at Boston University as well as assistant dean and director of the College of Arts and Sciences Writing Program. He is the author of *Manufacturing Culture: Vindications of Early Victorian Industry*.

William T. FitzGerald is associate professor in the Department of English at Rutgers University. He is the author of *Spiritual Modalities: Prayer as Rhetoric and Performance*.

The University of Chicago Press, Chicago 60637
The University of Chicago Press, Ltd., London

Printed in the United States of America

25 24 23 22 21 20 19 18 17 16 1 2 3 4 5

ISBN-13: 978-0-226-23956-9 (cloth)
ISBN-13: 978-0-226-23973-6 (paper)
ISBN-13: 978-0-226-23987-3 (e-book)
DOI: 10.7208/chicago/9780226239873.001.0001

Library of Congress Cataloging-in-Publication Data

Names: Booth, Wayne C., author. | Colomb, Gregory G., author. | Williams, Joseph M., author. | Bizup, Joseph, 1966– author. | FitzGerald, William T., author.
Title: The craft of research / Wayne C. Booth, Gregory G. Colomb, Joseph M. Williams, Joseph Bizup, William T. FitzGerald.
Other titles: Chicago guides to writing, editing, and publishing.
Description: Fourth edition. | Chicago: The University of Chicago Press, 2016. | Series: Chicago guides to writing, editing, and publishing | Includes bibliographical references and index.
Identifiers: LCCN 2016000143 | ISBN 9780226239569 (cloth: alk. paper) | ISBN 9780226239736 (pbk.: alk. paper) | ISBN 9780226239873 (e-book)
Subjects: LCSH: Research—Methodology. | Technical writing.
Classification: LCC Q180.55.M4 B66 2016 | DDC 001.4/2—dc23 LC record available at http://lccn.loc.gov/2016000143

♾ This paper meets the requirements of ANSI/NISO Z39.48-1992 (Permanence of Paper).

Contents

Preface: The Aims of This Edition xi
Our Debts xv

I Research, Researchers, and Readers 1
Prologue: Becoming a Researcher 3

1 Thinking in Print: The Uses of Research, Public and Private 9
1.1 What Is Research? 10
1.2 Why Write It Up? 11
1.3 Why a Formal Paper? 12
1.4 Writing Is Thinking 14

2 Connecting with Your Reader: Creating a Role for Yourself and Your Readers 16
2.1 Conversing with Your Readers 16
2.2 Understanding Your Role 18
2.3 Imagining Your Readers' Role 20
★ QUICK TIP: A Checklist for Understanding Your Readers 26

II Asking Questions, Finding Answers 27
Prologue: Planning Your Project—An Overview 29
★ QUICK TIP: Creating a Writing Group 32

3 From Topics to Questions 33
3.1 From an Interest to a Topic 34
3.2 From a Broad Topic to a Focused One 37
3.3 From a Focused Topic to Questions 38
3.4 The Most Significant Question: *So What?* 43
★ QUICK TIP: Finding Topics 47

4 From Questions to a Problem 49
4.1 Understanding Research Problems 49
4.2 Understanding the Common Structure of Problems 52
4.3 Finding a Good Research Problem 60
4.4 Learning to Work with Problems 62
★ QUICK TIP: Manage the Unavoidable Problem of Inexperience 64

5 From Problems to Sources 65
5.1 Three Kinds of Sources and Their Uses 65
5.2 Navigating the Twenty-First-Century Library 68
5.3 Locating Sources on the Internet 74
5.4 Evaluating Sources for Relevance and Reliability 76
5.5 Looking Beyond Predictable Sources 80
5.6 Using People to Further Your Research 81
★ QUICK TIP: The Ethics of Using People as Sources of Data 84

6 Engaging Sources 85
6.1 Recording Complete Bibliographical Information 86
6.2 Engaging Sources Actively 88
6.3 Reading for a Problem 89
6.4 Reading for Arguments 92
6.5 Reading for Data and Support 93
6.6 Taking Notes 94
6.7 Annotating Your Sources 101
★ QUICK TIP: Manage Moments of Normal Anxiety 104

III Making an Argument 105
Prologue: Assembling a Research Argument 107

7 Making Good Arguments: An Overview 110
7.1 Argument as a Conversation with Readers 110
7.2 Supporting Your Claim 111
7.3 Acknowledging and Responding to Anticipated Questions and Objections 114
7.4 Connecting Claims and Reasons with Warrants 115
7.5 Building a Complex Argument Out of Simple Ones 117
7.6 Creating an Ethos by Thickening Your Argument 119
★ QUICK TIP: A Common Mistake—Falling Back on What You Know 120

8 Making Claims 122
8.1 Determining the Kind of Claim You Should Make 122
8.2 Evaluating Your Claim 124
8.3 Qualifying Claims to Enhance Your Credibility 129

9 Assembling Reasons and Evidence 132
9.1 Using Reasons to Plan Your Argument 132
9.2 Distinguishing Evidence from Reasons 133
9.3 Distinguishing Evidence from Reports of It 135
9.4 Evaluating Your Evidence 137

10 Acknowledgments and Responses 141
10.1 Questioning Your Argument as Your Readers Will 142
10.2 Imagining Alternatives to Your Argument 144
10.3 Deciding What to Acknowledge 145
10.4 Framing Your Responses as Subordinate Arguments 148
10.5 The Vocabulary of Acknowledgment and Response 149
★ QUICK TIP: Three Predictable Disagreements 153

11 Warrants 155
11.1 Warrants in Everyday Reasoning 156
11.2 Warrants in Academic Arguments 157
11.3 Understanding the Logic of Warrants 159
11.4 Testing Warrants 160
11.5 Knowing When to State a Warrant 164
11.6 Using Warrants to Test Your Argument 165
11.7 Challenging Others' Warrants 168
★ QUICK TIP: Reasons, Evidence, and Warrants 171

IV Writing Your Argument 173
Prologue: Planning Again 175

12 Planning and Drafting 177
12.1 Planning Your Paper 177
12.2 Avoiding Three Common but Flawed Plans 183
12.3 Turning Your Plan into a Draft 185
★ QUICK TIP: Work Through Procrastination and Writer's Block 188

13 Organizing Your Argument 189
13.1 Thinking Like a Reader 189
13.2 Revising Your Frame 190
13.3 Revising Your Argument 191
13.4 Revising the Organization of Your Paper 193
13.5 Checking Your Paragraphs 195
13.6 Letting Your Draft Cool, Then Paraphrasing It 196
★ QUICK TIP: Abstracts 197

14 Incorporating Sources 200
14.1 Quoting, Paraphrasing, and Summarizing Appropriately 200
14.2 Integrating Direct Quotations into Your Text 201
14.3 Showing Readers How Evidence Is Relevant 202
14.4 The Social Importance of Citing Sources 203
14.5 Four Common Citation Styles 204
14.6 Guarding Against Inadvertent Plagiarism 206
★ QUICK TIP: Indicating Citations in Your Paper 211

15 Communicating Evidence Visually 214
15.1 Choosing Visual or Verbal Representations 214
15.2 Choosing the Most Effective Graphic 215
15.3 Designing Tables, Charts, and Graphs 217
15.4 Specific Guidelines for Tables, Bar Charts, and Line Graphs 220
15.5 Communicating Data Ethically 227

16 Introductions and Conclusions 232
16.1 The Common Structure of Introductions 232
16.2 Step 1: Establishing a Context 234
16.3 Step 2: Stating Your Problem 237
16.4 Step 3: Stating Your Response 241
16.5 Setting the Right Pace 242
16.6 Organizing the Whole Introduction 243
16.7 Finding Your First Few Words 244
16.8 Writing Your Conclusion 245
★ QUICK TIP: Titles 247

17 Revising Style: Telling Your Story Clearly 248
17.1 Judging Style 248
17.2 The First Two Principles of Clear Writing 250
17.3 A Third Principle: Old Before New 258
17.4 Choosing between the Active and Passive Voice 260

17.5 A Final Principle: Complexity Last 262
17.6 Spit and Polish 265
★ QUICK TIP: The Quickest Revision Strategy 266

V Some Last Considerations 269
The Ethics of Research 271
A Postscript for Teachers 275
Appendix: Bibliographical Resources 281

Index 313

Preface

THE AIMS OF THIS EDITION

This fourth edition of *The Craft of Research* is the first to appear since the deaths of the book's three original authors, Wayne C. Booth, Gregory G. Colomb, and Joseph M. Williams. In undertaking this revision, we—Joseph Bizup and William T. FitzGerald—faced the pleasurable and challenging task of reworking a book we have both long admired. Our goal has been to update and refine it without appropriating it from its original authors.

The fourth edition has the same main aim as the first three: to meet the needs of all researchers, not just first-year undergraduates and advanced graduate students, but even those in business and government who do and report research on any topic, academic, political, or commercial. The book was written to

- guide you through the complexities of turning a topic or question into a research problem whose significance matches the effort that you put into solving it;
- help you organize and draft a report that justifies the effort;
- show you how to read your report as your readers will so that you can revise it into one that they will read with the understanding and respect it deserves.

Other handbooks touch on these matters, but this one is different. Most current guides acknowledge that researchers rarely move in a straight line from finding a topic to stating a thesis to filling in note cards to drafting and revision. Experienced researchers loop back and forth, move forward a step or two before going back in order to move ahead again, change directions, all the while anticipating stages not yet begun. But so far as we know, no other guide tries to explain how each part of the process influences all the others—how developing a project prepares the researcher for drafting, how drafting can reveal problems in an argument, how writing an introduction can prompt you to do more research.

In particular, the book tries to be explicit about matters that other guides treat as a mysterious creative process beyond analysis and explanation, including

- how to turn a vague interest into a problem readers think is worth posing and solving;
- how to build an argument that motivates readers to take your claim seriously;
- how to anticipate the reservations of thoughtful but critical readers and then respond appropriately;
- how to create an introduction and conclusion answering that toughest of questions from readers, *So what?*;
- how to read your own writing as readers will, and thereby know when and how to revise it.

Central in every chapter is the advice to side with your readers, to imagine how they will judge what you have written.

The book addresses the formal elements common to most genres of research-based writing not just because writers need to understand their superficial shape but also because they help writers *think*. These genres—the research paper, the research report, the white paper, and many others—are not empty patterns or forms: they also embody and enable specific ways of working and arguing; they help us all to develop and refine our projects, test our work, and even discover new lines of thought. How we write thus affects how we argue and research, and vice versa. In this sense, to learn the genres of one's field is to learn the field itself.

The book is informed by another conviction as well: that the skills of research and research-based writing are not just for the elite but can be learned by everyone. Some aspects of advanced research can be learned only in the context of a specific community of researchers, but even if you don't yet belong to one, you can still create something like it on your own. Our "Postscript for Teachers" suggests ways you (and your teachers) can do that.

WHAT THIS EDITION DOES NOT ADDRESS

Like the previous editions of *The Craft of Research*, this fourth edition treats research generally. It does not discuss how to incorporate narratives, "thick descriptions," or audiovisual forms of evidence into your arguments. They are important topics, but too large for us to do justice to them here. Nor does this edition cover research techniques that are specific to particular fields. Likewise, while it discusses the principles that should guide online research, it does not attempt to describe the vast array of specialized search tools and databases now available online and through the library. Our bibliography suggests a number of sources for guidance in those areas.

WHAT'S NEW IN THIS EDITION

In preparing this fourth edition, we have kept in mind the positive reception of earlier editions and the wide audience they attracted, an audience that ranges from first-year students in composition classes, to graduate students and other advanced researchers, and even to professionals working in fields such as business, medicine, and law. Indeed, this audience is an international one: the book has been translated into Russian, Spanish, Portuguese, Korean, Japanese, and Chinese.

What we have been most mindful of is that *The Craft of Research* is the result of an extraordinary collaboration among three gifted teachers and scholars in whose footsteps we are proud to follow. While seeking to help the book speak to new generations of researchers, we have also striven to honor and retain the perspective, content, and voice that have made *The Craft of Research* a recognized classic. Those who are familiar with earlier editions will discover that this edition is faithful to the book's vision and overall structure. At the same time, each chapter has been thoroughly updated to reflect the contemporary landscape of research.

Here, concretely, is what we've done:

- We revised chapters 5 and 6 to incorporate recent developments in library and Internet research and in engaging source materials. Especially, we emphasized new research techniques made possible by online databases and search engines and the value of online sources, balanced by the need to assess these sources' reliability.
- We again revised the chapter on warrants (chapter 11), a matter that has been difficult to explain in previous editions.
- We moved the first two sections of chapter 13 into chapter 12, which is now titled "Planning and Drafting," and switched the order of chapters 13 and 14, now titled "Organizing Your Argument" and "Incorporating Sources," respectively.
- Throughout, as we thought necessary, we clarified concepts and provided fresh examples.
- We differentiated the related but distinct activities of research, argument, and writing.
- Wherever possible, we standardized terms (e.g., using "paper" rather than "report") to reflect the range of academic and professional genres that are the products of research.

In doing all that, we have tried—as Booth, Colomb, and Williams did in prior editions—to preserve the amiable voice, the sense of directness, and the stance of colleagues working together that so many have found crucial to the book's success.

Our Debts

From JB and WF: We wish to thank our editor, David Morrow, and his colleagues at the University of Chicago Press for their insight and guidance and, above all, for the trust they placed in us to revise a text that has no equal in the field. It was a labor of love.

We join Booth, Colomb, and Williams in again thanking the many without whose help the previous editions could never have been realized, especially Jane Andrew, Steve Biegel, and Donald Freeman. These many include Jane Block, Don Brenneis, Sara Bryant, Diane Carothers, Sam Cha, Tina Chrzastowski, John Cox, James Donato, Kristine Fowler, Joe Harmon, Clara Lopez, Bill McClellan, Mark Monmonier, Nancy O'Brien, Kim Steele, David Stern, Ellen Sutton, and Leslie Troutman.

Joe Bizup thanks his wife, Annmarie Caracansi, and daughters, Grace and Charlotte; and Bill FitzGerald likewise thanks his wife, Emilia Lievano, and daughter, Magdalena. We are both grateful for our respective families' love, patience, and support.

We allow Booth, Colomb, and Williams to once again offer their personal acknowledgments in their own words.

From WCB (composed for the second edition): I am amazed as I think back on my more than fifty years of teaching and research by how many students and colleagues could be cited here as having diminished my ignorance. Since that list would be too long, I'll thank mainly my chief critic, my wife, Phyllis, for her many useful suggestions and careful editing. She and my daughters, Katherine Stevens and Alison Booth, and their children, Robin, Emily, and

Aaron, along with all those colleagues, have helped me combat my occasional despair about the future of responsible inquiry.

From GGC: I, too, have been blessed with students and colleagues who have taught me much—first among them the hundreds of grad students who shared with me their learning to be teachers. They, above all, have shown me the possibilities in collaborative inquiry. What I lean on most, though, are home and family: Sandra, Robin, Kikki, Karen, and Lauren. Through turbulent times and calm, they gave point and purpose to it all. Before them was another loving family, whose center, Mary, still sets an example to which I can only aspire.

From JMW: The family has tripled in size since the first edition, and I am ever more grateful for their love and support: Ol, Michele, and Eleanor; Chris and Ingrid; Dave, Patty, Matilde, and Owen; Megan, Phil, Lily, and Calvin; Joe, Christine, Nicholas, and Katherine. And at beginning and end, Joan, whose patience, love, and good sense flow still more bountifully than I deserve.

IN MEMORIAM

Wayne C. Booth
(1921–2005)

Gregory G. Colomb
(1951–2011)

Joseph M. Williams
(1933–2008)

PART I

Research, Researchers, and Readers

PROLOGUE

Becoming a Researcher

WHO NEEDS RESEARCH?

When you think of a researcher, what do you imagine? Someone in a lab coat peering into a microscope? A solitary figure taking notes in a library? That's what most people imagine. But you might have also pictured MSNBC's Rachel Maddow, HBO's John Oliver, or anyone who prepares extensively before writing or speaking. Like just about every successful person, they are not only experts in doing research, but in using the research of others. In fact, that's part of what makes them successful. In an aptly named "age of information," they have learned not only how to find information, but how to evaluate it, then how to report it clearly and accurately. (Often, they challenge *mis*information.) More than ever, those skills are essential for success in any profession.

You may not yet be a professional, but learning to do research now will help you today and prepare you for what's to come. First, it will help you understand what you read as nothing else will. You can accurately judge the research of others only after you've done your own and can understand the messy reality behind what is so smoothly and confidently presented in your textbooks or by experts on TV. The Internet and cable TV flood us with "facts" about the government, the economy, the environment, and the products we buy. Some of these facts are sound, though many are not. That's why, as you learn to do research, you'll also learn to value reliable research reported clearly and accurately.

You'll discover both how new knowledge depends on what questions you ask and how the way you think about and communicate your research shapes those questions and your answers. Most important, you'll come to understand how the knowledge we all rely on depends on the quality of the research that supports it and the accuracy of its reporting. Although some might think it idealistic, another reason for doing research is the sheer pleasure of solving a puzzle, of discovering something that no one else knows.

But learning to do research is not like learning to ride a bike, the sort of thing you learn once and never forget. Each of us has started projects that forced us to rethink how we do our work. Whenever we've addressed a new research community, we've had to learn its ways to help us understand what its members think is important. But even then, we could still rely on principles that all researchers follow, principles that we describe in this book. We think you will find them useful as your projects and readers become more demanding, both in school and after.

We must be candid, though: doing research carefully and reporting it clearly are hard work, consisting of many tasks, often competing for your attention at the same time. And no matter how carefully you plan, research follows a crooked path, taking unexpected turns, sometimes up blind alleys, even looping back on itself. As complex as that process is, we will work through it step-by-step so that you can see how its parts work together. When you can manage its parts, you can manage the often intimidating whole and look forward to doing more research with greater confidence.

STARTING A RESEARCH PROJECT

If you are beginning your first project, the task may seem overwhelming: *How do I focus on a topic? Where do I find information on it? What do I do when I find it?* Even if you've done a "research paper" in a writing class, the idea of another may be even more intimidating if this time it's *the real thing.* If so, you're not alone. Even experienced researchers feel anxious when they tackle a new kind of project for a new audience. So whatever anxiety you feel, most researchers have felt it too. The difference is that experienced researchers know what lies ahead—hard work, but also pleasure; some frustration, but more satisfaction; periods of confusion, but confidence that, in the end, it will all come together and that the result is worth the effort. Most of all, experienced researchers know how to get from start to finish not easily, perhaps, but as efficiently as the complexity of their task allows. That's the aim of this book.

WORKING WITH A PLAN

You will struggle with your project if you don't know what readers look for in a paper or how to help them find it. Experienced researchers know that they most often produce a sound paper when they have a plan, no matter how rough, even if only in their heads. In fact, they create two kinds of plans: the first helps them prepare and conduct their research; the second helps them draft their paper.

They usually begin with a question and a plan to guide their search for an answer. They may not know exactly what they'll find, but they know generally what it will look like, even if it surprises them. They also know that once they have an answer, they don't just start writing, any more than an experienced carpenter just starts sawing. They draw up a second plan, a rough blueprint for a first draft—maybe no more than a sketch of an outline. Shrewd researchers, though, don't let that plan box them in: they change it if they run into a problem or discover something that leads them in a new direction. But before they start a first draft, they begin with *some* plan, even when they know they'll almost certainly change it.

That plan for a draft helps researchers write, but it also helps their readers read. In fact, researchers of all kinds use standard forms to anticipate what readers look for:

- A newspaper reporter writes her story in traditional "pyramid" form, putting the most important information first, not just to make her job of drafting easier, but also so that her readers can find the gist of the news quickly, then decide whether to read on.
- An accountant follows a standard form for her audit report not just to organize her own writing, but so that investors can find the information they need to decide whether the company is another Enron or the next Apple.

- A Food and Drug Administration scientist follows the predictable form for a scientific report—introduction, methods and materials, results, discussion, conclusion—not just to order his own thoughts coherently, but to help readers find the specific issues they have to consider before they accept his findings.

Within these forms, or *genres*, writers are free to emphasize different ideas, to put a personal stamp on their work. But they know that a plan helps them write efficiently and, no less important, helps their readers read productively.

This book will help you create and execute a plan for doing your research and another for reporting it in ways that not only encourage your best thinking but help your readers see its value.

HOW TO USE THIS BOOK

The best way to deal with the complexity of research (and its anxieties) is to read this book twice. First skim it to understand what lies ahead (flip past what seems tedious or confusing). But then as you begin your work, carefully read the chapters relevant to your immediate task. If you are new to research, reread from the beginning. If you are in an intermediate course but not yet at home in your field, skim part I, then concentrate on the rest. If you are an experienced researcher, you will find chapter 4 and parts III and IV most useful.

In part I, we address what those undertaking their first project must think about deliberately: why readers expect us to write up our research in particular ways (chapter 1), and why you should think of your project not as solitary labor but as a conversation with those whose work you read and with those who will in turn read your work (chapter 2).

In part II, we discuss how to frame and develop your project. We explain

- how to find a topic in an interest, then how to focus and question it (chapter 3);
- how to transform those questions into a research problem (chapter 4);

- how to find sources to guide your search for answers (chapter 5);
- how to engage sources in ways that encourage your own best thinking (chapter 6).

In part III, we discuss how to assemble a sound case in support of your claim. That includes

- an overview of a research argument (chapter 7);
- how to evaluate your claim for its significance (chapter 8);
- how to judge what count as good reasons and sound evidence (chapter 9);
- how to acknowledge and respond to questions, objections, and alternative views (chapter 10);
- how to make the logic of your argument clear (chapter 11).

In part IV, we lay out the steps in producing your paper:

- how to plan and execute a first draft (chapter 12);
- how to test and revise it (chapter 13);
- how to incorporate sources (chapter 14);
- how to present complex quantitative evidence clearly and pointedly (chapter 15);
- how to write an introduction and conclusion that convince readers your argument is worth their time (chapter 16);
- how to edit your style to make it clear, direct, and readable (chapter 17).

Between some of the chapters you will find "Quick Tips," brief sections that complement the chapters with practical advice.

In an afterword, "The Ethics of Research," we reflect on a matter that goes beyond professional competence. Doing and reporting research is a social activity with ethical implications. We often read about the dishonest research of historians, scientists, stock analysts, and others. And we see plagiarism among writers at all levels of achievement, from secondary-school students to leaders of their professions. Such events highlight the importance of doing and using your research *ethically.*

In a concluding essay, we address those who teach research. At the end of the book is a bibliography of sources for beginning researchers and for advanced researchers in particular fields.

Research is hard work, but like any challenging job done well, both its process and its results can bring great satisfaction. No small part of that satisfaction comes from knowing that your work sustains the fabric of a community of people who share your interests, especially when you discover something that you believe can improve your readers' lives by changing what and how they think.

1 Thinking in Print

THE USES OF RESEARCH, PUBLIC AND PRIVATE

In this chapter, we define research, then discuss how you benefit from learning to do it well, why we value it, and why we hope you will too.

Whenever we read about a scientific breakthrough or a crisis in world affairs, we benefit from the research of those who report it, who in turn benefited from the research of countless others. When we walk into a library, we are surrounded by more than twenty-five centuries of research. When we go on the Internet, we can read millions of reports written by researchers who have posed questions beyond number, gathered untold amounts of information from the research of others to answer them, then shared their answers with the rest of us so that we can carry on their work by asking new questions and, we hope, answering them.

Teachers at all levels devote their lives to research. Governments spend billions on it, businesses even more. Research goes on in laboratories and libraries, in jungles and ocean depths, in caves and in outer space, in offices and, in the information age, even in our own homes. Research is in fact the world's biggest industry. Those who cannot do it well or evaluate that of others will find themselves sidelined in a world increasingly dependent on sound ideas based on good information produced by trustworthy inquiry and then presented clearly and accurately.

Without trustworthy *published* research, we all would be locked in the opinions of the moment, prisoners of what we alone experience or dupes to whatever we're told. Of course, we want to believe that our opinions are sound. Yet mistaken ideas, even dangerous ones, flourish because too many people accept too many opinions based on too little evidence. And as recent events have shown, those who act on unreliable evidence can lead us—indeed have led us—into disaster.

That's why in this book we will urge you to be amiably skeptical of the research you read, to question it even as you realize how much you depend on it.

1.1 WHAT IS RESEARCH?

In the broadest terms, we do research whenever we gather information to answer a question that solves a problem:

> PROBLEM: Where do I find a new head gasket for my '65 Mustang?
> RESEARCH: Look in the yellow pages for an auto-parts store, then call to see if it has one in stock.
>
> PROBLEM: To settle a bet, I need to know when Michael Jordan was born.
> RESEARCH: You Google "Michael Jordan birthday."
>
> PROBLEM: I'm just curious about a new species of fish.
> RESEARCH: You search the Internet for articles in newspapers and academic journals.

We all do that kind of research every day, and though we rarely write it up, we rely on those who wrote up theirs: Jordan's biographers, the fish discoverers, the publishers of the yellow pages and the catalogs of the auto-parts suppliers—they all wrote up their research because they knew that one day someone would have a question that they could answer.

If you're preparing to do a research project not because you want to but because it's been assigned, you might think that it is just make-work and treat it as an empty exercise. We hope you won't. Done well, your project prepares you to join the oldest and most esteemed of human conversations, one conducted for millennia among philosophers, engineers, biologists, social scientists, historians, literary critics, linguists, theologians, not to mention CEOs, lawyers, marketers, investment managers—the list is endless.

Right now, if you are a beginner, you may feel that the conversation is one-sided, that you have to listen more than you can speak because you have little to contribute. If you are a student, you may feel that you have only one reader: your teacher. All that may be true, for the moment. But at some point, you will join a conversation that, at its best, can help you and your community free us from ignorance, prejudice, and the half-baked ideas that so many charlatans try to impose on us. It is no exaggeration to say that, maybe not today or tomorrow but one day, the research you do and the arguments you make using it can improve if not the whole world, then at least your corner of it.

1.2 WHY WRITE IT UP?

For some of you, though, the invitation to join this conversation may still seem easy to decline. If you accept it, you'll have to find a good question, search for sound data, formulate and support a good answer, and then write it all up. Even if you turn out a first-rate paper, it may be read not by an eager world but only by your teacher. *And, besides,* you may think, *my teacher knows all about my topic. What do I gain from writing up my research, other than proving I can do it?*

One answer is that we write not just to share our work, but to improve it before we do.

1.2.1 Write to Remember

Experienced researchers first write just to remember what they've read. A few talented people can hold in mind masses of information, but most of us get lost when we think about what Smith found in light of Wong's position, and compare both to the odd data in Brunelli, especially as they are supported by Boskowitz—*but what was it that Smith said?* When you don't take notes on what you read, you're likely to forget or, worse, misremember it.

1.2.2 Write to Understand

A second reason for writing is to see larger patterns in what you read. When you arrange and rearrange the results of your research in new ways, you discover new implications, connections, and complications. Even if you could hold it all in mind, you would need help to line up arguments that pull in different directions, plot out complicated relationships, sort out disagreements among experts. *I want to use these claims from Wong, but her argument is undercut by Smith's data. When I put them side by side, I see that Smith ignores this last part of Wong's argument. Aha! If I introduce it with this part from Brunelli, I can focus on Wong more clearly.* That's why careful researchers never put off writing until they've gathered all the data they need: they write from the start of their projects to help them assemble their information in new ways.

1.2.3 Write to Test Your Thinking

A third reason to write is to get your thoughts out of your head and onto paper, where you'll see what you really *can* think. Just about all of us, students and professionals alike, believe our ideas are more compelling in the dark of our minds than they turn out to be in the cold light of print. You can't know how good your ideas are until you separate them from the swift and muddy flow of thought and fix them in an organized form that you—and your readers—can study.

In short, we write to remember more accurately, understand better, and evaluate what we think more objectively. (And as you will discover, the more you write, the better you read.)

1.3 WHY A FORMAL PAPER?

But even when they agree that writing is an important part of learning, thinking, and understanding, some still wonder why they can't write up their research in their own way, why they have to satisfy demands imposed by a community that they have not joined (or even want to) and conform to conventions they did nothing to create. *Why should I adopt language and forms that are not mine? Aren't you just trying to turn me into an academic like yourself? If I write as you expect me to, I risk losing my identity.*

Such concerns are legitimate (most teachers wish students would raise them more often). But it would be a feeble education that did not change you at all, and the deeper your education, the more it will change the "you" that you are or want to be. That's why it is so important to choose carefully what you study and with whom. But it would be a mistake to think that learning to report sound research must threaten your true identity. It will change the way you think, but only by giving you more ways of thinking. You will be different by being freer to choose whom you want to be and what you want to do with your life.

But the most important reason for learning to write in ways readers expect is that when you write for others, you demand more of yourself than when you write for yourself alone. By the time you fix your ideas in writing, they are so familiar to you that you need help to see them not for what you want them to be but for what they really are. You will understand your own work better when you try to anticipate your readers' inevitable and critical questions: *How have you evaluated your evidence? Why do you think it's relevant? What ideas have you considered but rejected?*

All researchers, including us, can recall moments when in writing to meet their readers' expectations, they found a flaw or blunder in their thinking or even discovered a new insight that escaped them in a first draft written for themselves. You can do that only once you imagine and then meet the needs and expectations of informed and careful readers. When you do that, you create what we call a *rhetorical community* of shared values.

You might think, *OK, I'll write for readers, but why not in my own way?* The traditional forms that readers expect are more than just empty vessels into which you must pour your ideas. They also help writers think and communicate in ways they might not otherwise, and they embody the shared values of a research community. Whatever community you join, you'll be expected to show that you understand its practices by presenting your research in the standard forms, or *genres*, that a community uses to represent *what* it knows and *how* it knows. The various genres of research-based writing—the research paper, the scholarly article, the research report, the conference paper, the legal brief, and a great many others—have evolved to meet the needs of the communities that use them. Relatively stable, they allow both newcomers and longtime members of a community to come together through shared practices and expectations. Once you know the genres that belong to and define your particular research community, you'll be better able to answer your community's predictable questions and understand what its members care about and why. As you learn to write the genres of a field or profession, you become a member of that research community.

But as different as research communities are, what counts as good work is the same, whether it's in the academic world or the world of government, commerce, or technology. If you learn to do research well now, you gain an immense advantage in the kind of research you will do later, no matter where you do it.

1.4 WRITING IS THINKING

Writing up your research is, finally, thinking with and for your readers. When you write for others, you disentangle your ideas from your memories and wishes, so that you—and others—can explore, expand, combine, and understand them more fully. Thinking for others is more careful, more sustained, more insightful—in short, more thoughtful—than just about any other kind of thinking.

You can, of course, take the easy way: do just enough to satisfy your teacher. This book will help you do that, but you'll shortchange yourself if that's all you do. If instead you find a topic that *you* care about, ask a question that *you* want to answer, then pursue that answer as best you can, your project can have the fascination of a mystery whose solution richly rewards your efforts. Nothing contributes more to successful research than your commitment to

> Some of the world's most important research has been done by those who persevered in the face of indifference or even hostility, because they never lost faith in their vision. The geneticist Barbara McClintock struggled for years unappreciated because her research community considered her work uninteresting. But she believed in it and pressed on. When her colleagues finally realized that she had already answered questions that they were just starting to ask, she won science's highest honor, the Nobel Prize.

it, and nothing teaches you more about how to think than making a successful (or even unsuccessful) argument using it.

We wish we could tell you how to balance your belief in the worth of your project with the need to accommodate the demands of teachers and colleagues, but we cannot. If you believe in what you're doing and cannot find anyone else who shares your beliefs, all you can do is put your head down and press on. With our admiration.

2 Connecting with Your Reader

CREATING A ROLE FOR YOURSELF AND YOUR READERS

Research counts for little if few read it. Yet even experienced researchers sometimes forget to keep their readers in mind as they plan and draft. In this chapter, we show you how to think about readers even before you begin your project.

Most of the important things we do, we do with others. Some students think research is different. They imagine the lone scholar in a hushed library. But no place is more filled with imagined voices than a library or lab. The view of research you see walking by these sites is only part of the story. When you read a book or a scientific paper, you silently converse with its writers—and through them with everyone else they have read. In fact, every time you go to a written source for information, you join a conversation between writers and readers that began more than five thousand years ago. And when you report your own research, you add your voice and can hope that other voices will respond to you, so that you can in turn respond to them. So it goes and, we hope, will continue for a long time to come.

2.1 CONVERSING WITH YOUR READERS

Conversations are social activities in which we are expected to play our parts. Face-to-face, we can judge how well we and others do that by sensing how a conversation is going. Do we treat each other as equals, speaking and listening civilly, answering each other's questions directly? Or does one of us seem to be playing the role of expert, assigning others the role of audience? We can judge how well a conversation is going as we have it, and we can adjust our roles and behavior to repair mistakes and misunderstandings as they occur. But writing is an *imagined* conversation. Once we decide what role to play and what role to assign our readers, those roles are fixed. If as we read we think, *Well, Abrams acknowledges*

Stanik's evidence, but he's dogmatic in criticizing it and ignores obvious counterexamples, Abrams can't change what we read next to recover from our judgment.

Of course, judgments go both ways: just as readers judge writers, so writers also judge readers, but they do so before they write. Consider these two sentences:

> Interruption of REM sleep has been shown not only to inhibit memory consolidation, especially for declarative memories, but also to significantly impair cognitive processes dependent on working memory function.

> If you don't get enough sleep, not only will you struggle to retain facts and concepts, but your working memory function will also be impaired, making it difficult for you to hold information in mind and consequently to understand, think, and learn.

Both writers make judgments about their readers' needs and goals. The first addresses herself to knowledgeable colleagues interested in learning about the psychology of sleep and memory. She therefore focuses on abstract concepts and freely uses technical terms. The second presents himself as an expert patiently explaining a complicated matter to readers who know little about it, and so he largely avoids technical vocabulary. He also assumes that his readers want practical advice, and so he addresses them directly as "you" and shows them what his information means to them.

The two sentences are very different: the first reads like an excerpt from an advanced textbook; the second, like it comes from a guide on good study habits. But both would be effective if their writers judged their readers correctly.

But suppose the writers switched passages. Readers ignorant of cognitive psychology looking for practical advice would think that the writer of the first was indifferent to their needs; readers knowledgeable about sleep and memory would think that the writer of the second was talking down to them. When writers misjudge their readers in this way, they risk losing them.

In fact, writers can't avoid creating *some* role for themselves and their readers, planned or not. So those roles are worth thinking about from the beginning, before you write a word. If you ignore or miscast your readers, you'll leave so many traces of that mistake in your early drafts that you won't easily fix them in the final one.

In writing this book, we tried to imagine you—what you're like, what you know about research, whether you even care about it. We imagined a *persona* for you, a role we hoped you would adopt: someone who is interested in learning how to do and report research and who shares our belief in its importance (or at least is open to being persuaded). Then we imagined a persona of our own: writers committed to the value of research, interested in sharing how it works, talking not *at* you like a lecturer or *down* to you like a pedant, but *with* the "you" we hoped you want to become. We tried to speak as easily to those of you starting your first project as to those of you doing advanced work. We hoped that new researchers would not be frustrated when we discussed issues they haven't yet faced and that more experienced readers would be patient as we covered familiar ground. Only you can judge how well we've succeeded.

2.2 UNDERSTANDING YOUR ROLE

Since few people read formal research papers for entertainment, you have to create a relationship that encourages them to see why it's in their interest to read yours. That's not easy. Too many beginning researchers offer readers a relationship that caricatures a bad classroom: *Teacher, I know less than you. So my role is to show you how many facts I can dig up. Yours is to say whether I've found enough to give me a good grade.* Do that and you turn your project into a pointless drill that demeans both you and your teacher. Worse, you cast yourself in a role exactly opposite to that of a true researcher.

In true research, you must switch the roles of student and teacher. When you do research, you learn something that others don't know. So when you report it, you must think of your reader as someone who doesn't know it *but needs to* and yourself as someone who will *give her reason to want to know it.* You must imagine a relationship that goes beyond *Here are some facts I've dug up about fourteenth-century Tibetan weaving. Are they enough of the right ones?*

There are three better reasons for offering those facts; the third is most common in academic research.

2.2.1 I've Found Some New and Interesting Information

You take the first step toward true research when you say to your reader, *Here are some facts about fourteenth-century Tibetan weaving that you do not know and may find interesting.* This offer assumes, of course, that your reader wants to know. But even if not, you must still cast yourself in the role of someone who has found something your reader will find interesting and your reader as someone who wants to know, *whether she really will or not.* Down the road, you'll be expected to find (or create) a community of readers who not only share an interest in your topic (or can be convinced to), but also have questions about it that you can answer. But even if you don't have that audience right now, you must write as if you do. You must present yourself as interested in, even enthusiastic about, wanting to share something new, because the interest you show in your work roughly predicts the interest your reader will take in it.

2.2.2 I've Found a Solution to an Important Practical Problem

You take a step toward more significant research when you can say to readers not just *Here are some facts that should interest you,* but *These facts will help you do something to solve a problem you care about.* That is the kind of research that people do every day in business, government, and the professions. They confront practical problems whose solutions require research into the facts of the matter, first to understand the problem, then to figure out how to solve it—problems ranging from insomnia to falling profits to terrorism.

To help new researchers learn that role, teachers sometimes invent "real world" scenarios: an environmental science professor might assign you to write a report for the director of the state Environmental Protection Agency on how to clean up a local lake. In this scenario you are playing the role not of a student delivering data to a teacher, but of a professional giving practical advice to someone who needs it. To make your report credible, however, you must use the right terminology, cite the right sources, find and present the right evidence, all in the right format. But most important, you have to design your report around a specific *intention* that defines your role: to advise a decision maker on what to *do* to solve a problem. That kind of research is typical in the world at large but is less common in academic research than the next one.

2.2.3 I've Found an Answer to an Important Question

Although academic researchers sometimes advise EPA directors on what to do, their more common role is that of scholars who help their research community simply understand something better. Others might use their findings to solve a practical problem—a discovery about the distribution of prime numbers, for example, helped cryptologists design an unbreakable code. But that research itself was aimed at solving not the *practical* problem of keeping secrets, but the *conceptual* problem of not entirely understanding prime numbers. Some researchers call this kind of research "pure" as opposed to "applied."

Teachers occasionally invent "real world" scenarios involving conceptual problems: a political science professor asks you to play the role of a senator's intern researching the voting habits of out-of-state college students. But more typically they expect you to imagine yourself as what you are learning to be: a researcher addressing a community of other researchers interested in issues that they want to understand better. Your report on fourteenth-century Tibetan weaving, for example, could possibly help rug designers sell more rugs, but its main aim is to help scholars better understand something about Tibetan art, such as *How did fourteenth-century Tibetan rugs influence the art of modern China?*

2.3 IMAGINING YOUR READERS' ROLE

You establish your side of the relationship with your readers when you adopt one of those three roles—*I have information for you*; *I can help you fix a problem; I can help you understand something better.* You must, however, cast your readers in a complementary role by offering them a social contract: *I'll play my part if you play yours.* But that means you have to understand their role. If you cast them in a role they won't accept, you're likely to lose them entirely. In this case, the old advice to "consider your audience" means that you must report your research in a way that motivates your readers to play the role you have imagined for them.

For example, suppose you're an expert on blimps and zeppelins. You've been asked to share your research with three different groups with three different reasons for wanting to hear about it. How they receive you will depend on how accurately you imagine the role each intends to play and how well you match your role to theirs. For that, you must understand what they want and what they are in return willing *and able* to do for you.

2.3.1 Entertain Me

Imagine the first group that invited you to speak is the local Zeppelin Club. Its members are not experts, but they know a lot about zeppelins. They read about them, visit historic sites, and collect zeppelin memorabilia. You decide to share some new facts you've found in a letter from your Great-Uncle Otto describing his transatlantic zeppelin flight in 1936, along with some photographs and a menu he saved. His letter comments on the grilled oysters he had for dinner and tells a funny story about why he happened to take the trip in the first place.

In planning your talk, you judge that what's at stake is just a diverting hour of zeppelin trivia. You meet your side of the bargain when you share whatever you think might interest them—hunches, speculation, even unsubstantiated rumors. You won't show PowerPoint slides, present data, or cite scholarly sources to substantiate your claims. Your audience will play its role by listening with interest, asking questions, maybe sharing their own anecdotes. You don't expect them to challenge the authenticity of the letter from Great-Uncle Otto or question how the photos are relevant to the social history of zeppelins, much less of lighter-than-air travel in general. Your job is to give an engaging talk; theirs is to be amiably engaged.

Some beginning researchers imagine their readers belong to a Zeppelin Club, already fascinated by their topic and eager to hear anything new about it. While that sometimes works for experts with the right audience (see the box on page 24), it rarely works for students learning to do and report serious research. Your teachers expect you to report not just *what* you find, but what you can *do* with it.

2.3.2 Help Me Solve My Practical Problem

Imagine that your next meeting is with True-to-Life Films. They plan to make a movie about a zeppelin flight in 1936 and want you to help them get the historical details right, including a scene in the dining cabin. They want to know how the cabin was furnished, what people ate, what the menus looked like, and so on. They don't care whether your facts are new, only whether they are right, so that they can make the scene authentic. You show them your photos and the menu and describe the oysters Great-Uncle Otto ate, but you don't bother with why he took the trip. To succeed in this role, you must help them solve a practical problem whose solution you base not on *all* the data you can find, no matter how new, but on just those *particular* facts that are relevant to the problem of authenticity and whose sources you can show are reliable. Your audience will listen intently and critically, because they want to get the details right.

That's the kind of task you're likely to face if your teacher invents a "real world" assignment—write to an EPA official who needs to *do* something about a polluted lake. Academic researchers sometimes address practical problems like these, but for them another kind of problem is far more common. So pose a practical problem *only if* your teacher creates one; otherwise, check with her first. (We'll discuss practical problems in more detail in chapter 4.)

2.3.3 Help Me Understand Something Better

Now imagine that your audience is the faculty of Zeppo University's Department of Lighter-than-Air Studies. They study all aspects of blimps and zeppelins, do research on their economics and aerodynamics, and participate in a worldwide conversation about their history and social significance. They compete with other lighter-than-air scholars to produce new lighter-than-air knowledge and theories that they publish in lighter-than-air journals and books read by everyone in their lighter-than-air field.

These scholars have invited you to talk about your specialty: the social history of zeppelin travel in the 1930s. They don't want you just to amuse them with new facts (though they'll be happy if you do) or to help them *do* something (though they'd be pleased if you got them consulting work with True-to-Life Films). They want you to use whatever new facts you have to help them better *understand* the social history of zeppelin travel or, better still, of lighter-than-air culture in general.

Because these lighter-than-air scholars are intensely committed to finding the Truth about zeppelins, you know they expect you to be objective, rigorously logical, and able to examine every issue from all sides. You also know that if you don't nail down your facts, they'll hammer you during the question period and if you don't have good answers, slice you up afterward over the wine and cheese, not just to be contentious or even nasty (though some will be), but to get as close as they can to the Truth about zeppelins in the 1930s. If you offer new data, like Great-Uncle Otto's photos, letter, and menu, they'll be glad to see them, but they'll want to know why they matter and might even question their authenticity.

Above all, they will care about your documents *only if* you can show how they serve as *evidence* that helps you answer a question important to understanding something about zeppelins that is *more important* than your uncle's trip. They will receive you especially well if you can convince them that they do not understand the social history of zeppelins as well as they thought and that your new data will improve their flawed understanding. If you can't do that, they'll respond not with *I don't agree*—we all learn to live with that; some of us even thrive on it—but with a response far more devastating: *I don't care.*

So you begin your talk:

> We all have been led to believe by a number of studies on the food service on transatlantic zeppelin flights in the 1930s (especially Schmidt 1986 and Kloepfer 1998) that items were never cooked over an open flame because of the danger of explosions. However, I have recently discovered a menu from the July 12, 1936, crossing of the *Hindenburg* indicating that oysters grilled over charcoal were served. . . . [You then go on to show why that new knowledge matters.]

That is the kind of conversation you join when you report research to a community of scholars. You must imagine them imagining this conversation with you: *Never mind whether your style is graceful (though I will admire your work more if it is); don't bother me with amusing anecdotes about your Great-Uncle Otto (though I like hearing them if they help me understand your ideas better);*

Who Cares about That?

Academic researchers are often scoffed at for studying esoteric topics that matter to no one but themselves. The charge is usually unfair, but some researchers do become fascinated with matters that seem to have little significance. Williams once attended the dissertation defense of a PhD candidate who had discovered reels and reels of film shot by European anthropologists in Africa and Asia in the early twentieth century. This previously unknown footage fascinated the film scholars on the committee. But when Williams asked the candidate, "How do these new films improve our understanding of movies then or now?" she could answer only that "no one has ever seen this footage before." Williams put his question in different ways but never got a better answer. The film scholars, on the other hand, were untroubled (and found Williams's questions naive), because they were already imagining how the footage might change their thinking about early film. And in any event, they all loved old film for its own sake. So sometimes new data alone are enough to interest the right readers. But if that candidate hopes to write anything that interests anyone but a tiny coterie of specialists, she will have to make an offer better than *Here's some new stuff.*

ignore whether what you know will make me rich (though I would be happy if it did). Just tell me something I don't know so that I can better understand our common interest.

Your academic readers will almost always adopt this third role. They will think you've fulfilled your side of the social contract only when you treat them as who they think they are: scholars interested in greater knowledge and better understanding. To be sure, the faculty over in chemistry or philosophy care little about zeppelins, much less their meal service. (*Can you believe the trivia they study over in Helium Hall?*) But then you don't much care about their issues, either. You are concerned with your *particular* community of readers, with *their* interests and expectations, with improving *their* understanding, based on the best evidence you can find. That's the social contract that all researchers must establish with their readers.

QUICK TIP A Checklist for Understanding Your Readers

Think about your readers from the start, knowing that you'll understand them better as you work through your project. Answer these questions early on, then revisit them when you start planning and again when you revise.

1. Who will read my paper?
   - Professionals who expect me to follow every academic convention and use a standard format?
   - Well-informed general readers?
   - General readers who know little about the topic?
2. What do they expect me to do? Should I
   - entertain them?
   - provide new factual knowledge?
   - help them understand something better?
   - help them do something to solve a practical problem in the world?
3. How much can I expect them to know already?
   - What do they know about my topic?
   - Is the problem one that they already recognize?
   - Is it one that they have but haven't yet recognized?
   - Is the problem not theirs, but only mine?
   - Will they take the problem seriously, or must I convince them that it matters?
4. How will readers respond to the solution/answer in my main claim?
   - Will it contradict what they already believe? How?
   - Will they make standard arguments against my solution?
   - Will they want to see the steps that led me to the solution?

PART II

Asking Questions, Finding Answers

PROLOGUE

Planning Your Project—An Overview

If you've skimmed this book once, you're ready to begin your project. If you have a research question and know how to look for its answer, review the next two chapters quickly; then read the remaining ones carefully as they become relevant to your task. You may, however, feel bewildered if you're starting from scratch, without even a topic to guide you. But you can manage if you have a plan and take one step at a time.

If you are starting from scratch, your first task is to find a research question worth investigating that will lead to a research problem worth solving. Here are four steps to that end:

1. Find a topic specific enough to let you master a reasonable amount of information on it in the time you have: not, for example, *the history of scientific writing* but *essays in the* Proceedings of the Royal Society *(1675–1750) as precursors to the modern scientific article*; not *doctors in seventeenth-century drama* but *Molière's mockery of doctors in three early plays.*
2. Question that topic until you find questions that catch your interest. For example, *How did early Royal Society authors demonstrate that their evidence was reliable?* Or, *Why did Molière mock doctors?*
3. Determine the kinds of evidence your readers will expect you to offer in support of your answer. Will they accept reports of facts from secondary sources, or will they expect you to consult primary sources (see 5.1.1)? Will they expect quantitative data, quotations from authorities, or firsthand observations?

4. Determine whether you can find this evidence. There's no point researching a topic unless you have a good chance of finding the right kind of evidence.

Once you think you have enough data to support at least a plausible answer to your question, you'll be ready to assemble an argument that makes your case (see part III), then to plan, draft, and revise it (see part IV).

You'll discover, however, that you can't march through those steps in the neat order we present them. You'll think of a tentative answer to your research question before you have all the evidence you need to support it. And when you think you have an argument worth making, you may discover that you need more and maybe different evidence from new sources. You may even modify your topic. Doing research is not like strolling along an easy, well-marked path to a familiar destination; it's more like zigzagging up and down a rocky hill through overgrown woods, sometimes in a fog, searching for something you won't recognize until you see it. But no matter how indirect your path, you can make progress if at each step of the way you plan for predictable detours (and maybe even avoid some of them).

What Is Your Evidence?

No matter their field, researchers collect information to use as evidence to support their claims. But researchers in different fields call that information by different names. We call it *data*. By *data* we mean not just the numbers that natural and social scientists collect, but anything you find "out there" relevant to answering your research question. The term is used less often by researchers in the humanities, but they, too, gather data in the form of quotations, historical facts, and so on. Data are inert, however, until you use them to support a claim that answers your research question. At that point, your data become *evidence*. If you don't have more data than you can use as evidence, you haven't collected enough. (Incidentally, *data* is plural; a single bit of data is a *datum*.)

Resolve to do lots of writing along the way. Much of it will be routine note-taking, but you should also write reflectively, to understand: make outlines; explain why you disagree with a source; draw diagrams to connect disparate facts; summarize sources, positions, and schools; record even random thoughts. Many researchers find it useful to keep a journal for hunches, new ideas, random thoughts, problems, and so on. You might not include much of this writing-to-discover-and-understand in your final draft. But when you *write as you go, every day,* you encourage your own best critical thinking, understand your sources better, and, when the time comes, draft more productively.

QUICK TIP Creating a Writing Group

A downside of academic research is its isolation. Except for group projects, you'll read and write mostly alone. But it doesn't have to be that way. Look for someone other than your instructor or adviser who will talk with you about your progress, review your drafts, even pester you about how much you've written. That might be a generous friend, but even better is another writer so that you can comment on each other's ideas and drafts.

Best of all is a group of four or five people working on their own projects who meet regularly to read and discuss one another's work. Early on, each meeting should start with a summary of each person's project in this three-part sentence: *I'm working on X because I want to find out Y, so that I (and you) can better understand Z* (more about this in 3.4). As your projects advance, develop an opening "elevator story," a short summary of your project that you could give someone on the way to a meeting. It should include your research question, your best guess at an answer, and the kind of evidence you expect to use to support it. The group can then follow up with questions, responses, and suggestions.

Don't limit your talk to just your story, however. Talk about your readers: Why should they be interested in your question? How might they respond to your argument? Will they trust your evidence? Will they have other evidence in mind? Such questions help you plan an argument that anticipates what your readers expect. Your group can even help you brainstorm when you bog down. Later the group can read one another's outlines and drafts to imagine how their final readers will respond. If your group has a problem with your draft, so will those readers. But for most writers, a writing group is most valuable for the discipline it imposes. It is easier to meet a schedule when you know you must report to others.

Writing groups are common for those writing theses or dissertations. But the rules differ for a class paper. Some teachers think that a group or writing partner provides more help than is appropriate, so be clear what your instructor allows.

3 From Topics to Questions

In this chapter, we discuss how to find a topic among your interests, refine it to a manageable scope, then question it to find the makings of a problem that can guide your research. If you are an experienced researcher or know the topic you want to pursue, skip to chapter 4. But if you are starting your first project, you will find this chapter useful.

If you are new to research, the freedom to pick your own topic can seem daunting. Where do you begin? How do you tell a good topic from a bad one? Inexperienced researchers typically wonder, *Will I find enough information on this topic to write about it?* To their surprise they often compile too much information, much of it not very useful. They do so because their topic lacks focus. Without that focus, any evidence you assemble risks appearing to your readers as little more than a mound of random facts. As you begin a research project, you will want to distinguish a topic from a subject. A subject is a broad area of knowledge (e.g., climate change), while a topic is a specific interest within that area (e.g., the effect of climate change on migratory birds). However, finding a topic is not simply a matter of narrowing your subject. A topic is an approach to a subject, one that asks a *question* whose answer solves a *problem* that your readers care about.

In all research communities, some questions are "in the air," widely debated and researched, such as whether traits like shyness or an attraction to risk are learned or genetically inherited. But other questions may intrigue only the researcher: *Why do cats rub their faces against us? Why does a coffee spill dry up in the shape of a ring?* That's how a lot of research begins—not with a big question that attracts everyone in a field, but with a mental itch about a small question that only a single researcher wants to scratch. If you feel that itch, start scratching. But at some point, you must decide

> ***Question or Problem?***
>
> You may have noticed that we've been using the words *question* and *problem* almost interchangeably. But they are not quite the same. Some questions raise problems; others do not. A question raises a problem if not answering it keeps us from knowing something more important than its answer. For example, if we cannot answer the question *Are there ultimate particles?*, we cannot know something even more important: the nature of physical existence. On the other hand, a question does not raise a problem if not answering it has no apparent consequences. For example, *Was Abraham Lincoln's right thumb longer than his nose?* We cannot think of what we would gain by knowing. At least at the moment.

whether the answer to your question solves a problem significant to some community of researchers or even to a public whose lives your research could change.

Now, that word *problem* is itself a problem. Commonly, a problem means trouble, but among researchers it has a meaning so special that we devote the next chapter to it. But before you can frame your research problem, you have to find a topic that might lead to one. So we'll start there, with finding a topic.

3.1 FROM AN INTEREST TO A TOPIC

Most of us have more than enough interests, but beginners often find it hard to locate among theirs a topic focused enough to support a substantial research project. They may also believe they lack the expertise for the project. However, a research topic is an interest stated specifically enough for you to imagine *becoming* a local expert on it. That doesn't mean you already know a lot about it or that you'll have to know more about it than others, including your teacher. You just want to know a lot more about it than you do now.

If you can work on any topic, we offer only a cliché: start with what most interests you. Nothing contributes to the quality of your work more than your commitment to it. But also ask yourself: *What interests me about this topic? What would interest others?*

3.1.1 Finding a Topic in a Writing Course

Start by listing as many interests as you can that you'd like to explore. Don't limit yourself to what you think might interest a teacher or make you look like a serious student. Let your ideas flow. Prime the pump by asking friends, classmates, even your teacher about topics that interest them. If no good topics come to mind, consult the Quick Tip at the end of this chapter.

Once you have a list of topics, choose the one or two that interest you most and explore their research potential. Do this:

- In the library, look up your topic in a general guide such as *CQ Researcher* and skim the subheadings. In an online database such as Academic Search Premier, you can explore your topic through subject terms. If you have a more narrow focus, you can do the same with specialized guides such as *Women's Studies International.* While some libraries will have copies of general and specialized guides on the shelf, most now subscribe to their online equivalents, but not all of them let you skim subject headings. (We discuss these resources in chapter 5 and list several in the appendix.)
- On the Internet, Google your topic, but don't surf indiscriminately. Look first for websites that are roughly like sources you would find in a library, such as online encyclopedias. Read the entry on your general topic, and then copy the list of references at the end for a closer look. Use *Wikipedia* to find ideas and sources, but always confirm what you find there in a reliable source. Few experienced researchers trust *Wikipedia,* so *under no circumstances cite it as a source of evidence* (unless your topic is *Wikipedia* itself).
- Remember, at this point you are exploring a topic to spur your thinking and to see if that topic is viable. With that in mind, you can also find ideas in blogs, which discuss almost every contentious issue. Since most issues are usually too big for a research paper, look for posts that take a position on narrow aspects of larger issues. If you disagree with a view, investigate it.

3.1.2 Finding a Topic for a First Research Project in a Particular Field

Start by listing topics relevant to your particular class *and* that interest you, then narrow them to one or two promising ones. If the topic is general, such as *religious masks*, you'll have to do some random reading to narrow it. But read with a plan:

- Skim encyclopedia entries in your library or online. Start with standard ones such as the *Encyclopaedia Britannica*. Then consult specialized ones such as the *Encyclopedia of Religion* or the *Stanford Encyclopedia of Philosophy*.
- Skim headings in specialized indexes such as the *Philosopher's Index*, *Psychological Abstracts*, or *Women's Studies Abstracts*. Use subheadings for ideas of how others have narrowed your topic.
- Google your topic, but not indiscriminately. Use Google Scholar, a search engine that focuses on scholarly journals and books. Skim the articles it turns up, especially their lists of sources.

When you know the general outline of your topic and how others have narrowed theirs, try to narrow yours. If you can't, browse through journals and websites until your topic becomes more clearly defined. That takes time, so start early.

3.1.3 Finding a Topic for an Advanced Project

Most advanced students already have interests in topics relevant to their field. Often topics find them as they become immersed in a field. If that is not yet the case, focus on what interests you, but remember that you must eventually show why it should also interest others.

- Find what interests other researchers. Look online for recurring issues and debates in the archives of professional discussion lists relevant to your interests. Search online and in journals like the *Chronicle of Higher Education* for conference announcements, conference programs, calls for papers, anything that reflects what others find interesting.
- Skim the latest issues of journals in your field, not just for articles, but also for conference announcements, calls for papers, and

reviews. Skim recent articles in your library's online databases in your field (e.g., the MLA International Bibliography).

- Investigate the resources that your library is particularly rich in. If, for example, it (or a library nearby) holds a collection of rare papers on an interesting topic, you have found not only a topic but a way into it. Many unexpected finds await discovery in your library's archives.

3.2 FROM A BROAD TOPIC TO A FOCUSED ONE

The most useful way to think about a topic is as a starting place for your research. (The word "topic" comes from *topos,* which is Greek for "place.") From this starting place, you can head off in a particular direction and thus narrow an overly broad topic into a productively focused one. At this point, your biggest risk is settling on a topic so broad that it could be a subheading in a library catalog: *spaceflight*; *Shakespeare's problem plays*; *natural law*. A topic is probably too broad if you can state it in four or five words:

> Free will in Tolstoy
>
> The history of commercial aviation

A topic so broad can intimidate you with the task of finding, much less reading, even a fraction of the sources available. So narrow it down:

Free will in Tolstoy	→	The conflict of free will and inevitability in Tolstoy's description of three battles in *War and Peace*
The history of commercial aviation	→	The contribution of the military in developing the DC-3 in the early years of commercial aviation

We narrowed those topics by adding words and phrases, but of a special kind: *conflict, description, contribution,* and *developing.* Those nouns are derived from verbs expressing actions or relationships: *to conflict, to describe, to contribute,* and *to develop.* Lacking such "action" words, your topic is a static thing.

Note what happens when we restate static topics as full sentences. Topics (1) and (2) change almost not at all:

(1) Free will in Tolstoy$_{topic}$ → There is free will in Tolstoy's novels.$_{claim}$

(2) The history of commercial aviation$_{topic}$ → Commercial aviation has a history.$_{claim}$

In reality, (1) and (2) are not topics at all because they do not lead anywhere. But when (3) and (4) are revised into full sentences, they are closer to claims that a reader might find interesting.

(3) The *conflict* of free will and inevitability in Tolstoy's *description* of three battles in *War and Peace*$_{topic}$ → In *War and Peace*, Tolstoy *describes* three battles in which free will and inevitability *conflict*.$_{claim}$

(4) The *contribution* of the military in *developing* the DC-3 in the early years of commercial aviation$_{topic}$ → In the early years of commercial aviation, the military *contributed* to the way the DC-3 *developed*.$_{claim}$

Such claims may at first seem thin, but you'll make them richer as you work through your project. And that's the point: these topics are actually paths to pursue when devising your project.

Caution: Don't narrow your topic so much that you can't find information on it. Too much information is available on *the history of commercial aviation* but too little (at least for beginning researchers) on *the decision to lengthen the wingtips on the DC-3 prototype for military use as a cargo carrier.*

3.3 FROM A FOCUSED TOPIC TO QUESTIONS

Once they have a focused topic, many new researchers make a beginner's mistake: they immediately start plowing through all the sources they can find on the topic, taking notes on everything they read. With a promising topic such as *the political origins of legends about the Battle of the Alamo*, they mound up endless facts connected with the battle: what led up to it, histories of the Texas Revolution, the floor plan of the mission, even biographies of generals Santa Anna and Sam Houston. They accumulate notes, summaries, descriptions of differences and similarities, ways in which the stories conflict with one another and with what historians think really happened, and so on. Then they dump it all into a paper that concludes, *Thus we see many differences and similarities between . . .*

Many high school teachers would reward such a paper with a good grade, because it shows that the writer can focus on a topic, find information on it, and assemble that information into a report, no small achievement—for a first project. But in *any* college course, such a report falls short if it is seen as just a pastiche of vaguely related facts. If a writer asks no specific *question* worth asking, he can offer no specific *answer* worth supporting. And without an answer to support, he cannot *select* from all the data he could find on a topic just those relevant to his answer. To be sure, those fascinated by Elvis Presley movie posters or the first generation of video games will read *anything* new about them, no matter how trivial. Serious researchers, however, do not document information for its own sake, but to support the answer to a question that they (and they hope their readers) think is worth asking.

So the best way to begin working on your focused topic is not to find all the information you can on it, but to formulate questions that direct you to just that information you need to answer them.

Start with the standard journalistic questions: *who, what, when,* and *where,* but focus on *how* and *why.* To engage your best critical thinking, systematically ask questions about your topic's history, composition, and categories. Then ask any other question you can think of or find in your sources. Record all the questions, but don't stop to answer them even when one or two grab your attention. This inventory of possible questions will help to direct your search activities and enable you to make sense of information you find. (Don't worry about keeping these categories straight; their only purpose is to stimulate questions and organize your answers.) Let's take up the example of masks mentioned earlier.

3.3.1 Ask about the History of Your Topic

- How does it fit into a **larger developmental context**? Why did your topic come into being? *What came before masks? How were masks invented? Why? What might come after masks?*

- What is its own **internal history**? How and why has the topic itself changed through time? *How have Native American masks changed? Why? How have Halloween masks changed? How has the role of masks in society changed? How has the booming market for kachina masks influenced traditional design? Why have masks helped make Halloween the biggest American holiday after Christmas?*

3.3.2 Ask about Its Structure and Composition

- How does your topic fit into the **context of a larger structure or function as part of a larger system**? *How do masks reflect the values of different societies and cultures? What roles do masks play in Hopi dances? In scary movies? In masquerade parties? How are masks used other than for disguise?*
- How do its parts **fit together as a system**? *What parts of a mask are most significant in Hopi ceremonies? Why? Why do some masks cover only the eyes? Why do few masks cover just the bottom half of the face? How do their colors play a role in their function?*

3.3.3 Ask How Your Topic Is Categorized

- How can your topic be **grouped into kinds**? *What are the different kinds of masks? Of Halloween masks? Of African masks? How are they categorized by appearance? By use? By geography or society? What are the different qualities of masks?*
- How does your topic **compare to and contrast with** others like it? *How do Native American ceremonial masks differ from those in Japan? How do Halloween masks compare with Mardi Gras masks?*

3.3.4 Turn Positive Questions into Negative Ones

- *Why have masks* not *become a part of other holidays, like Presidents' Day or Memorial Day? How do Native American masks* not *differ from those in Africa? What parts of masks are typically* not *significant in religious ceremonies?*

3.3.5 Ask *What If?* and Other Speculative Questions

- How would things be different if your topic never existed, disappeared, or were put into a new context? *What if no one ever wore masks except for safety? What if everyone wore masks in public? What if it were customary to wear masks on blind dates? In marriage ceremonies? At funerals? Why are masks common in African religions but not in Western ones? Why don't hunters in camouflage wear masks? How are masks and cosmetic surgery alike?*

3.3.6 Ask Questions Suggested by Your Sources

You won't be able to do this until you've done some reading on your topic. Ask questions that **build on agreement**:

- If a source makes a claim you think is persuasive, ask questions that might extend its reach. *Elias shows that masked balls became popular in eighteenth-century London in response to anxieties about social mobility. Did the same anxieties cause similar developments in Venice?*
- Ask questions that might support the same claim with new evidence. *Elias supports his claim about masked balls with published sources. Is it also supported by letters and diaries?*
- Ask questions analogous to those that sources have asked about similar topics. *Smith analyzes costumes from an economic point of view. What would an economic analysis of masks turn up?*

Now ask questions that reflect **disagreement**:

- *Martinez claims that carnival masks uniquely allow wearers to escape social norms. But could there be a larger pattern of all masks creating a sense of alternative forms of social or spiritual life?*

(We discuss in more detail how to use disagreements with sources in 6.4.)

If you are an experienced researcher, look for questions that other researchers ask but don't answer. Many journal articles end with a paragraph or two about open questions, ideas for more research, and so on (see 4.3.2 for an example). You might not be able to do all the research they suggest, but you might carve out a piece of it. You can also look for Internet discussions on your topic, then "lurk," just reading the exchanges to understand the kinds of questions those on the list debate. Record questions that spark your interest. You can also post questions to the list if they are specific and narrowly focused.

3.3.7 Evaluate Your Questions

After asking all the questions you can think of, evaluate them, because not all questions are equally good. Look for questions whose answers might make you (and, ideally, your readers) think about your topic in a new way. Avoid questions like these:

- Their answers are settled fact that you could just look up. *Do the Inuit use masks in their wedding ceremonies?* Questions that ask *how* and *why* invite deeper thinking than *who, what, when,* or *where,* and deeper thinking leads to more interesting answers.
- Their answers would be merely speculative. *Would church services be as well attended if the congregation all wore masks?* If you can't imagine finding hard data that might settle the question, it's a question you can't settle.
- Their answers are dead ends. *How many black cats slept in the Alamo the night before the battle?* It is hard to see how an answer would help us think about any larger issue worth understanding better, so it's a question that's probably not worth asking.

You might, however, be wrong about that. Some questions that seemed trivial, even silly, have answers more significant than expected. One researcher wondered why a coffee spill dries up in the form of a ring and discovered things about the properties of fluids that others in his field thought important—and that paint manufacturers found valuable. So who knows where a question about cats in the Alamo might take you? You can't know until you get there.

Once you have a few promising questions, try to combine them into larger ones. For example, many questions about the Alamo story ask about the interests of the storytellers and their effects on their stories: *How have politicians used the story? How have the storytellers' motives changed? Whose purposes does each story serve?* These can be combined into a single question:

> *How and why have users of the Alamo story given the event a mythic quality?*

A question like this gives direction to your research (and helps avoid the gathering of endless information). And it begins to imagine readers who will judge whether your question is significant.

3.4 THE MOST SIGNIFICANT QUESTION: *SO WHAT?*

Even if you are an experienced researcher, you might not be able to take the next step until you are well into your project, and if you are a beginner, you may find it frustrating. Even so, once you have a question that holds your interest, you must pose a tougher one about it: *So what?* Beyond your own interest in its answer, why would others think it a question worth asking? You might not be able to answer that *So what?* question early on, but it's one you have to start thinking about, because it forces you to look beyond your own interests to consider how your work might strike others.

Think of it like this: What will be lost if you *don't* answer your question? How will *not* answering it keep us from understanding something else better than we do? Start by asking *So what?* at first of yourself:

> So what if I don't know or understand how butterflies know where to go in the winter, or how fifteenth-century musicians tuned their instruments, or why the Alamo story has become a myth? So what if I can't answer my question? What do we lose?

Your answer might be *Nothing. I just want to know.* Good enough to start, but not to finish, because eventually your readers will ask as well, and they will want an answer beyond *Just curious.* Answering *So what?* vexes all researchers, beginners and experienced alike, because when you have only a question, it's hard to predict whether others will think its answer is significant. But you must work toward that answer throughout your project. You can do that in three steps.

3.4.1 Step 1: Name Your Topic

If you are beginning a project with only a topic and maybe the glimmerings of a good question or two, start by naming your project:

> I am trying to learn about/working on/studying ____________.

Fill in the blank with your topic, using some of those nouns derived from verbs:

> I am studying the *causes* of the *disappearance* of large North American mammals . . .
>
> I am working on Lincoln's *beliefs* about *predestination* and their *influence* on his *reasoning* . . .

3.4.2 Step 2: Add an Indirect Question

Add an indirect question that indicates what you do not know or understand about your topic:

1. I am studying/working on ____________
   2. **because I want to find out who/what/when/where/whether/why/how ____________.**

1. I am studying the causes of the disappearance of large North American mammals
   2. **because I want to find out whether they were hunted to extinction . . .**

1. I am working on Lincoln's beliefs about predestination and its influence on his reasoning
   2. **because I want to find out how his belief in destiny influenced his understanding of the causes of the Civil War . . .**

When you add that *because I want to find out how/why/whether* clause, you state why *you* are pursuing your topic: to answer a question important to you.

If you are a new researcher and get this far, congratulate yourself, because you have moved beyond the aimless collection of data. But now, if you can, take one step more. It's one that advanced researchers know they must take, because they know their work will be judged not by its significance to them but by its significance to others in their field. They must have an answer to *So what?*

3.4.3 Step 3: Answer *So What?* by Motivating Your Question

This step tells you whether your question might interest not just you but others. To do that, add a second indirect question that explains why you asked your first question. Introduce this second implied question with *in order to help my reader understand how, why, or whether*:

1. I am studying the causes of the disappearance of large North American mammals
    2. because I want to find out whether the earliest peoples hunted them to extinction,
        3. **in order to help my reader understand whether native peoples lived in harmony with nature or helped destroy it.**

1. I am working on Lincoln's beliefs about predestination and their influence on his reasoning
    2. because I want to find out how his belief in destiny and God's will influenced his understanding of the causes of the Civil War,
        3. **in order to help my reader understand how his religious beliefs may have influenced his military decisions.**

It is the indirect question in step 3 that you hope will seize your readers' interest. If it touches on issues important to your field, even indirectly, then your readers should care about its answer.

Some advanced researchers begin with questions that others in their field already care about: *Why did the giant sloth and woolly mammoth disappear from North America?* Or: *Is risk taking genetically based?* But many researchers, including at times the five of us, find that they can't flesh out the last step in that three-part sentence until they finish a first draft. So you make no mistake *beginning* your research without a good answer to that third question—*Why does this matter?*—but you face a problem when you *finish* your research without having thought through those three steps at all. And if you are doing advanced research, you *must* take that step, because answering that last question is your ticket into the conversation of your community of researchers.

Regularly test your progress by asking a roommate, relative, or friend to force you to flesh out those three steps. Even if you can't take them all confidently, you'll know where you are and where you still have to go. To summarize: Your aim is to explain

1. what you are writing about—*I am working on the topic of...*
2. what you don't know about it—*because I want to find out...*
3. why you want your reader to know and care about it—*in order to help my reader understand better...*

In the following chapters, we return to those three steps and their implied questions, because they are crucial not just for finding questions but for framing the research problem that you want your readers to value.

QUICK TIP **Finding Topics**

If you are a beginner, start with our suggestions about exploring the Internet and skimming bibliographical guides (see 3.1). If you still draw a blank, try these steps.

FOR GENERAL INTEREST TOPICS

- What special interest do you have—sailing, chess, finches, old comic books? The less common, the better. Investigate something about it you don't know: its origins, its technology, how it is practiced in another culture, and so on.
- Where would you like to travel? Surf the Internet, finding out all you can about your destination. What particular aspect surprises you or makes you want to know more?
- Wander through a museum with exhibitions that appeal to you—artworks, dinosaurs, old cars. If you can't browse in person, browse a "virtual museum" on the Internet. Stop when something catches your interest. What more do you want to know about it?
- Wander through a shopping mall or store, asking yourself, *How do they make that?* Or, *I wonder who thought up that product?*
- Leaf through a Sunday newspaper, especially its features sections. Skim reviews of books or movies, in newspapers or on the Internet.
- Browse a large magazine rack. Look for trade magazines or those that cater to specialized interests. Investigate whatever catches your interest.
- Tune into talk radio or interview programs on TV until you hear a claim that you disagree with. Or find something to disagree with on the websites connected with well-known talk shows. See whether you can make a case to refute it.
- Use an Internet search engine to find websites related to your topic. These include blogs maintained by individuals and organizations. You'll get hundreds of hits, but look only at the ones that surprise you.

- Is there a common belief that you suspect is simplistic or just wrong? A common practice that you find pointless or irritating? Do research to make a case against it.
- What courses will you take in the future? What research would help you prepare for them?

FOR TOPICS FOCUSED ON A PARTICULAR FIELD

If you have experience in your field, review 3.1.2–3.

- Browse through a textbook of a course that is one level beyond yours or a course that you know you will have to take. Look especially hard at the study questions.
- Attend a lecture for an advanced class in your field, and listen for something you disagree with, don't understand, or want to know more about.
- Ask your instructor about the most contested issues in your field.
- Find an Internet discussion list in your field. Browse its archives, looking for matters of controversy or uncertainty.
- Surf the websites of departments at major universities, including class sites. Also check websites of museums, national associations, and government agencies, if they seem relevant.

4 From Questions to a Problem

In this chapter, we explain how to turn a question into a problem that readers think is worth solving. If you are an advanced researcher, you know how essential this step is. If you are new to research, we hope to convince you of its importance, because what you learn here will be essential to all your future projects.

In the last chapter, we suggested that you can identify the significance of your research question by fleshing out this three-step formula:

1. **Topic:** I am studying ________
 2. **Question:** because I want to find out what/why/how ________,
  3. **Significance:** in order to help my reader understand ________.

These steps describe not only the development of your project but your own development as a researcher.

- When you move from step 1 to 2, you are no longer a mere data collector but a researcher interested in understanding something better.
- When you then move from step 2 to 3, you focus on why that understanding is *significant.*

That significance might at first be just for yourself, but you join a community of researchers when you can state that significance *from your readers' point of view.* In so doing, you create a stronger relationship with readers because you promise something in return for their interest in your report—a deeper understanding of something that matters to *them.* At that point, you have posed a *problem* that they recognize needs a solution.

4.1 UNDERSTANDING RESEARCH PROBLEMS

Too many researchers at all levels write as if their task is to answer a question that interests themselves alone. That's wrong:

to make your research matter, you must address a problem that others in your community—your readers—also want to solve. To understand why, you have to understand what research problems look like. And to do that, you have to understand two other kinds of problems, what we'll call practical problems and conceptual problems.

4.1.1 Practical Problems: What Should We Do?

Everyday research usually begins not with dreaming up a topic to think about but with a practical problem that if you ignore it means trouble. When its solution is not obvious, you have to find out how to solve it. To do that, you must pose and solve a problem of another kind, a *research* problem defined by what you *do not know or understand* about your practical problem.

It's a familiar task that typically looks like this:

PRACTICAL PROBLEM: The chain on my bicycle broke.
RESEARCH PROBLEM: Can I find a bike shop that will replace it?

RESEARCH SOLUTION: Here it is: Cycle Source, 1401 East 55th Street.
PRACTICAL SOLUTION: Walk over to get my bike fixed.

Problems like that are in essence no different from more complicated ones.

- The National Rifle Association is lobbying me to oppose gun control. *How many votes do I lose if I refuse?* Do a survey. *Most of my constituents support gun control.* I can reject the request.
- Costs are up at the Omaha plant. *What changed?* Hire a consulting firm to figure it out. *Increase in turnover.* If we improve training and morale, our workers will stick with us.

Put in general terms, a *practical* problem is caused by some condition in the world (from spam to losing money in Omaha to terrorism) that troubles us because it costs us time, money, respect, security, opportunity, even our lives. We solve a practical problem by *doing* something (or by encouraging others to do something) to eliminate or at least mitigate the condition creating these tangible costs.

But to know what to do, someone first has to *understand* something better. That politician being lobbied by the NRA, for example, needs to know how his constituents feel about gun control so he can decide where he stands; the managers of the Omaha plant need to know the cause of their increasing costs so they can address it.

4.1.2 Conceptual Problems: What Should We Think?

That need for knowledge or understanding raises a conceptual problem. In research, a *conceptual* problem arises when we do not understand something about the world as well as we would like. We solve a conceptual problem not by doing something to change the world but by answering a question that helps us understand it better.

We usually answer these questions through research, which is why conceptual problems are also called research problems: the word *conceptual* describes their condition and costs or consequences; the word *research* refers to how we solve them. Graphically, the relationship between practical and conceptual or research problems looks like this:

The term *problem* thus has a special meaning in the world of research, one that sometimes confuses beginners. In our everyday world, a problem is something we try to avoid. But in academic research, a problem is something we seek out, even invent if we have to. Indeed, a researcher without a good conceptual or research problem to work on faces a bad practical problem because without one a researcher is out of work.

Inexperienced researchers sometimes struggle with these notions because experienced researchers often talk about their work in shorthand. When asked what they are working on, they often answer with what sounds like one of those general topics we warned you about: *adult measles, mating calls of Wyoming elk, zeppelins in the 1930s.* As a result, beginners sometimes think that having a topic to read about is the same as having a problem to solve.

When they do, they create a big practical problem for themselves, because with only a topic to guide their work, they gather data aimlessly and endlessly. Without a specific question to answer, they have no way of knowing when they have enough. When they write, they struggle to decide what to include, usually throwing in everything just to be on the safe side. So it's not surprising that they feel frustrated when a reader says, *I don't see the point here; this is just a data dump.*

To avoid that judgment, you need a problem that focuses you on finding just those data that will help you solve it. It might take a while to figure out what that problem is, but from the outset you have to think about it. That begins with understanding how conceptual problems work.

4.2 UNDERSTANDING THE COMMON STRUCTURE OF PROBLEMS

Practical problems and conceptual problems have the same two-part structure:

- a situation or *condition*, and
- undesirable *consequences* caused by that condition, *costs* that you (or, better, your readers) don't want to pay

What distinguishes them is the nature of those conditions and costs.

4.2.1 The Nature of Practical Problems

Consider a flat tire. Ordinarily, it would be a practical problem, because it is (1) a condition in the world (the flat) that imposes (2) a tangible cost that you don't want to pay, like missing a dinner date. But suppose you were bullied into the date and would rather be anywhere else. In that case, the benefit of the flat is more than its cost, so the flat is not a problem but a solution to the bigger problem of an evening spent with someone you don't like. Low cost, big benefit, no problem.

On the other hand, suppose the police set up a sting in which they lure criminals out of hiding by announcing that they have won the lottery. Ordinarily, winning the lottery is not a problem, but here it is, because it has a tangible cost: arrest.

A practical problem has two parts: a condition, which can be anything that imposes intolerable costs, and those costs. To state a practical problem so that others understand it clearly, you must describe both of its parts.

1. Its **condition**:

   I missed the bus.

   The ozone layer is thinning

2. The **costs** of that condition that you (or your reader) don't like:

   I'll be late for work and lose my job.

   Many will die from skin cancer.

But a caution: When you write, readers judge the significance of your problem not by the cost *you* pay, but by the cost *they* pay if you don't solve it. So what *you* think is a problem they might not. To make your problem their problem, you must frame it from *their* point of view, so that they see its costs to *them*. To do that, imagine that when you pose the condition part of your problem, your reader responds, *So what?*

The ozone layer is thinning.

So what?

You answer with the cost of the problem:

> A thinner ozone layer exposes us to more ultraviolet light.

Suppose he again asks, *So what?*, and you respond with the cost of more ultraviolet light:

> Too much ultraviolet light can cause skin cancer.

If, however improbably, he again asks, *So what?*, you have failed to convince him that *he* has a problem. We acknowledge a problem only when we stop asking *So what?* and say, instead, *What do we do about it?*

Practical problems like cancer are easy to grasp because they are concrete: when someone has cancer, we don't ask, *So what?* In academic research, however, your problems will usually be conceptual ones, which are harder to grasp because both their conditions and costs are abstract.

4.2.2 The Nature of Conceptual Problems

Practical and conceptual problems have the same two-part structure, but they have different kinds of conditions and costs.

- The condition of a practical problem can be *any* state of affairs that has a tangible cost for you or, better, for your readers.
- The condition of a conceptual problem, however, is *always* some version of not knowing or not understanding something.

You can identify the condition of a conceptual problem by completing that three-step sentence (see 3.4): The first step is *I am studying/working on the topic of* ________. In the second step, the indirect question states the condition of a conceptual problem, what you do not know or understand:

> I am studying stories of the Alamo, because I want to understand **why voters responded to them in ways that served the interests of Texas politicians.**

That's why we emphasize the value of questions: they force you to state what you don't know or understand but want to.

The two kinds of problems also have two different kinds of costs.

- The **cost** of a practical problem is always some tangible thing or situation we don't like.

A conceptual problem does not have such a tangible cost. In fact, we'll emphasize this difference by calling the cost of a conceptual problem its *consequence.*

- The **consequence** of a conceptual problem is a particular kind of ignorance: it is a lack of understanding that keeps us from understanding something else even more significant. Put another way, because we haven't answered one question, we can't answer another that is more important.

Researchers often choose projects simply because they are curious. In fact, that's how most of us first become interested in the subjects we study. But to make your research matter to others, you have to say more than *Here is something I find interesting.* You have to show them how solving your problem helps them solve theirs. You do that by explaining your problem's consequence.

You express a problem's consequence in the indirect question in step 3 of our formula:

> I am studying stories of the Alamo, because I want to understand why voters responded to them in ways that served the interests of local Texas politicians, in order to help readers understand the bigger and more important question **of how regional self-images influence national politics.**

All of this may sound confusing, but it's simpler than it seems. The condition and the consequence of a conceptual problem are questions that relate to each other in two ways:

- The answer to the first question (Q1) helps you answer the second (Q2).
- The answer to the second question (Q2) is more important than the answer to the first (Q1).

Q1 *helps you answer* **Q2**

Here it is again: The first part of a conceptual or research problem is something you don't know but want to. You can phrase that gap in knowledge or understanding as a direct question: *How have romantic movies changed in the last fifty years?* Or as an indirect question: *I want to find out how romantic movies have changed in the last fifty years.*

Now imagine someone asking, *So what if you can't answer that question?* You answer by stating *something else more important* that you can't know until you answer the first question. For example:

> If we can't answer the question of how romantic movies have changed in the last fifty years,*condition/first question* **then we can't answer a more important question: How have our cultural depictions of romantic love changed?***consequence/larger, more important second question*

If you think that it's important to answer that second question, you've stated a consequence that makes your problem worth pursuing, and if your readers agree, you're in business.

But what if you imagine a reader again asking, *So what if I don't know whether we depict romantic love differently than we did?* You have to pose a yet larger question that you hope your readers will think is significant:

> If we can't answer the question of how our depictions of romantic love have changed,*second question* **then we can't answer an even more important one: How does our culture shape the expectations of young men and women about marriage and families?***consequence/larger, more important question*

If you imagine that reader again asking, *So what?*, you might think, *Wrong audience.* But if that's the audience you're stuck with, you just have to try again: *Well, if we don't answer that question, we can't . . .*

Those outside an academic field often think that its specialists ask ridiculously trivial questions: *How did hopscotch originate?*

But they fail to realize that researchers want to answer a question like that so that they can answer a second, more important one. For those who care about the way folk games influence the social development of children, the conceptual consequences of not knowing justifies the research. *If we can discover how children's folk games originate, we can better understand how games socialize children, and, before you ask, once we know that, we can better understand . . .*

4.2.3 Distinguishing "Pure" and "Applied" Research

We call research *pure* when it addresses a conceptual problem that does not bear directly on any practical situation in the world, when it only improves the understanding of a community of researchers. We call research *applied* when it addresses a conceptual problem that does have practical consequences. You can tell whether research is pure or applied by looking at the last of the three steps defining your project. Does it refer to knowing or doing?

1. **Topic:** I am studying the electromagnetic radiation in a section of the universe
   2. **Question:** because I want to find out how many galaxies are in the sky,
      3. **Significance:** in order to help readers *understand* whether the universe will expand forever or eventually collapse into a point.

That is pure research, because step 3 refers only to understanding.

In applied research, the second step still refers to *knowing* or *understanding*, but that third step refers to *doing*:

1. **Topic:** I am studying how readings from the Hubble telescope differ from readings for the same stars measured by earthbound telescopes
   2. **Question:** because I want to find out how much the atmosphere distorts measurements of electromagnetic radiation,
      3. **Practical Significance:** so that astronomers can use data from earthbound telescopes *to measure* more accurately the density of electromagnetic radiation.

That problem calls for applied research because only when astronomers *know* how to account for atmospheric distortion can they *do* what they want to—measure light more accurately.

4.2.4 Connecting Research to Practical Consequences

Some inexperienced researchers are uneasy with pure research because the consequence of a conceptual problem—merely not knowing something—is so abstract. Since they are not yet part of a community that cares deeply about understanding its part of the world, they feel that their findings aren't good for much. So they try to cobble a practical cost onto a conceptual question to make it seem more significant:

1. **Topic:** I am studying differences among nineteenth-century versions of the Alamo story
    2. **Research Question:** because I want to find out how politicians used stories of such events to shape public opinion,
        3. **Potential Practical Significance:** in order to protect ourselves from unscrupulous politicians.

Most readers would think that the link between steps 2 and 3 is a bit of a stretch.

To formulate a good applied research project, you have to show that the answer to the indirect question in step 2 *plausibly* helps answer the indirect question in step 3. Ask this question:

(a) If my readers want to achieve the goal of ________ [state your objective from step 3],
(b) would they think that they could do it if they found out ________? [state your question from step 2]

Try that test on this applied astronomy problem:

(a) If my readers want to use data from earthbound telescopes to measure more accurately the density of electromagnetic radiation,
(b) would they think that they could if they knew how much the atmosphere distorts measurements?

The answer would seem to be *Yes.*

Now try the test on the Alamo problem:

> (a) If my readers want to protect themselves from unscrupulous politicians,
> (b) would they think they could if they knew how nineteenth-century politicians used stories about the Alamo to shape public opinion?

The answer would probably be *No*. We may see a connection, but it's a stretch.

If you think that the solution to your conceptual problem *might* apply to a practical one, formulate your project as pure research, then *add* your application as a *fourth* step:

1. **Topic:** I am studying how nineteenth-century versions of the Alamo story differ
    2. **Conceptual Question:** because I want to find out how politicians used stories of great events to shape public opinion,
        3. **Conceptual Significance:** in order to help readers understand how politicians use popular culture to advance their political goals,
            4. **Potential Practical Application:** so that readers *might* better protect themselves from unscrupulous politicians.

When you state your problem in your introduction, however, present it as a purely conceptual research problem whose significance is in its conceptual consequences. Then wait until your conclusion to suggest its practical application. (For more on this, see chapter 16.)

Most research projects in the humanities and many in the natural and social sciences have no direct application to daily life. But as the term *pure* suggests, many researchers value such research more than they do applied research. They believe that the pursuit of knowledge "for its own sake" reflects humanity's highest calling: to know more, not for the sake of money or power, but for the transcendental good of greater understanding and a richer life of the mind.

As you may have guessed, we are deeply committed to pure research, but also to applied—so long as the research is done well and is not corrupted by malign motives. For example, the potential for profit might compromise the integrity of both pure and applied research in the biological sciences, because it can influence not only what problems some researchers choose to address but also their solutions: *Tell us what to look for, and we'll provide it!* Such situations raise ethical questions that we touch on in our afterword, "The Ethics of Research."

4.3 FINDING A GOOD RESEARCH PROBLEM

What distinguishes great researchers from the rest of us is the brilliance, knack, or just dumb luck of stumbling over a problem whose solution makes all of us see the world in a new way. It's easy to recognize a good problem when we bump into it, or it bumps into us. But researchers often begin a project without being clear about what their real problem is. Sometimes they hope just to define a puzzle more clearly. Indeed, those who find a new problem or clarify an old one often make a bigger contribution to their field than those who solve a problem already defined. Some researchers have even won fame for *disproving* a plausible hypothesis that they had set out to prove.

So don't be discouraged if you can't formulate your problem fully at the outset of your project. Few of us can. But thinking about it early will save you hours of work along the way (and perhaps panic toward the end). It also gets you into a frame of mind crucial to advanced work. Here are some things you can do to identify and refine a good problem.

4.3.1 Ask for Help

Do what experienced researchers do: talk to colleagues, teachers, classmates, relatives, friends, neighbors—anyone who might be interested. Why would anyone want an answer to your question? What would they do with it? What new questions might an answer raise?

If you are free to work on any problem, look for a small one that is part of a bigger one. Though you won't solve the big one, your small piece of it will inherit some of its larger significance.

(You will also educate yourself about the problems of your field, no small benefit.) If you are a student, ask your teacher what she is working on and whether you can work on part of it. Don't let her suggestions define the limits of your research. Nothing discourages a teacher more than a student who does *exactly* what is suggested *and no more.* Teachers want you to use their suggestions to *start* your thinking, not *end* it. Nothing makes a teacher happier than when you use her suggestions to find something she never expected.

4.3.2 Look for Problems as You Read

You can also find research problems in your sources. Where in them do you see contradictions, inconsistencies, incomplete explanations? Tentatively assume that other readers would or should feel the same. Many research projects begin with an imaginary conversation with the author of a source: *Wait a minute, he's ignoring...* But before you set out to correct a gap or misunderstanding, be sure it's real, not just your own misreading. Countless research papers have refuted a point that no one ever made. Before you correct a source, reread it carefully. (In 6.3 we list several common "moves" that writers make to find a problem in a source, variations on *Source thinks X, but I think Y.*)

Once you think you've found a real puzzle or error, do more than just point to it. If a source says X and you think Y, you may have a research problem, but only if you can show that those who think X misunderstand some larger issue as well.

Finally, read the last few pages of your sources closely. That's where many researchers suggest more questions that need answers. The author of the following paragraph had just finished explaining how the life of nineteenth-century Russian peasants influenced their performance as soldiers:

> And just as the soldier's peacetime experience influenced his battlefield performance, so must the experience of the officer corps have influenced theirs. Indeed, a few commentators after the Russo-Japanese War blamed the Russian defeat on habits acquired by officers in the

> course of their economic chores. In any event, to appreciate the service habits of Tsarist officers in peace and war, *we need a structural—if you will, an anthropological—analysis of the officer corps like that offered here for enlisted personnel.* [our emphasis]

That last sentence offers a new problem waiting for you to tackle.

4.3.3 Look at Your Own Conclusion

Critical reading can also help you discover a good research problem in your own drafts. We often do our best thinking in the last few pages that we write, because there we formulate claims we did not anticipate when we started. If in an early draft you arrive at an unanticipated claim, ask yourself what question it might answer. Paradoxical as it might seem, you may have answered a question that you have not yet asked, and thereby solved a problem that you have not yet posed. Your task is to figure out what that problem might be.

4.4 LEARNING TO WORK WITH PROBLEMS

Experienced researchers dream of finding new problems to solve. A still bigger dream is to solve a problem that no one even knew they had. But that new problem isn't worth much until others think (or can be persuaded) that it needs solving. So the first question an experienced researcher should ask about a problem is not *Can I solve it?* but *Will readers think it should be solved?*

No one expects you to do all that the first time out. But you should begin to develop mental habits that will prepare you for that moment. Research is more than just accumulating and reporting facts. Try to formulate a question that *you* think is worth answering, so that down the road, you'll know how to find a problem that *others* think is worth solving. Until you can do that, you risk the worst response a researcher can get: not *I don't agree,* but *I don't care.*

By now, all this talk about airy academic research may seem disconnected from what some call the "real world." But in business and government, in law and medicine, in politics and international diplomacy, no skill is valued more highly than the ability to recognize a problem, then to articulate it in a way that convinces others both to care about it and to believe it can be solved, especially by you. If you can do that in a class on Byzantine pottery, you can do it in an office on Main Street, Wall Street, or Queen's Road in Hong Kong.

QUICK TIP **Manage the Unavoidable Problem of Inexperience**

We all feel anxious when we start work in a new field whose values, concerns, and ways of thinking and arguing we don't entirely understand. In fact, we authors still experience that newcomer's anxiety again when we begin new kinds of projects on new topics. You can't avoid experiencing that feeling at times, but there are ways to manage it:

- *Know that uncertainty and anxiety are natural and inevitable.* Those feelings don't signal incompetence, only inexperience.
- *Get control over your topic by writing about it along the way.* Don't just retype or photocopy sources: write summaries, critiques, questions, responses to your sources. Keep a journal in which you reflect on your progress. This kind of writing not only helps you understand what you read but stimulates your thinking about it. The more you write early on, no matter how sketchily, the easier it will be to face that intimidating first draft.
- *Break the task into manageable steps and know that they are mutually supportive.* Once you formulate a good question, you'll draft and revise more effectively. The more you anticipate how you will write and revise a first draft, the more effectively you will produce it.
- *If you are a student, count on your teachers to understand your struggles.* They want you to succeed, and you can expect their help. (If they don't help, look for others who will.)
- *Set realistic goals.* You do something significant when you wind up your project feeling that it has changed just what *you* think and that your readers think you did it well, even if they don't agree with your claims.
- *Most important, recognize the struggle for what it is—a learning experience.* To overcome the problems that all beginners face, do what successful researchers do, especially when discouraged: review your plan and what you've written, then press on, confident that it will turn out OK. Perhaps only "OK—considering," but probably a lot better than that.

5 From Problems to Sources

If you are a new researcher and expect to find most of your sources in your library or on the Internet, this chapter will help you develop a plan for your research. If you are more experienced, you might skip to the next chapter.

If you have not yet formulated a research question, you may have to spend time reading generally on your topic to find one. But if you have a question and at least one promising answer (the philosopher C. S. Peirce called it a *hypothesis on probation*), you can start looking for data to test it.

To do that efficiently, you need to have a plan. If you plunge into any and all sources on your topic, you risk losing yourself in an endless trail of books and articles. To be sure, aimless browsing can be fun, even productive. We indulge in it a lot. Many important discoveries have begun in a chance encounter with an unexpected idea. But if you have a deadline, you need more than luck to find good sources in time: you have to search systematically for those sources that will help you advance your research project or, just as usefully, challenge you to improve it. In this chapter, we discuss different ways you can use sources in your research, how you can find useful sources, and how you can winnow your sources to a manageable number. In the next chapter, we focus on how to use sources in your writing.

5.1 THREE KINDS OF SOURCES AND THEIR USES

Sources are conventionally categorized into three kinds: primary, secondary, and tertiary. Their boundaries are fuzzy, but knowing these categories can help you plan your research.

5.1.1 Primary Sources

Primary sources are "original" materials that provide you with the "raw data" or evidence you will use to develop, test, and ultimately justify your hypothesis or claim. What kinds of materials count as primary sources vary significantly by field. In history, primary sources are artifacts or documents that come directly from the period or event you are studying: letters, diaries, objects, maps, even clothing. In literature or philosophy, your main primary source is usually the text you are analyzing, and your data are the words on the page. In arts criticism, your primary source would be the work of art you are interpreting. In social sciences, such as sociology or political science, census or survey data would also count as primary sources. In the natural sciences, reports of original research are sometimes characterized as primary sources (although scientists themselves rarely use that term).

5.1.2 Secondary Sources

Secondary sources are books, articles, or reports that are based on primary sources and are intended for scholarly or professional audiences. The body of secondary sources in a field is sometimes called that field's "literature." The best secondary sources are books from reputable university presses and articles or reports that have been "peer-reviewed," meaning that they were vetted by experts in the field before they were published. Researchers read secondary sources to keep up with developments in their fields and, in this way, to stimulate their own thinking. The standard way of framing new research problems is to challenge or build on the conclusions or methods of others, as presented in secondary sources they have written. You can also borrow evidence from secondary sources to use in your own arguments, but you should do so only if you do not have access to the primary sources from which that evidence was originally taken. Otherwise you risk appearing careless or lazy.

5.1.3 Tertiary Sources

These are books and articles that synthesize and report on secondary sources for general readers, such as textbooks, articles in encyclopedias (including *Wikipedia*), and articles in mass-circulation publications like *Psychology Today*. In the early stages of research, you can use tertiary sources to get a feel for a topic. But if you are making a scholarly argument, you should rely on secondary sources, because these make up the "conversation" in which you are seeking to participate. If you cite tertiary sources in a scholarly argument, you will mark yourself as either a novice or an outsider, and many readers won't take you—or your argument—seriously.

This response may seem unfair, but it's not. Tertiary sources aren't necessarily wrong—many are in fact written by distinguished scholars—but they are limited. Because they are intended for broad audiences who are unfamiliar with the topics that they address, they can sometimes oversimplify the research on which they are based, and they are susceptible to becoming outdated. But if you keep these limitations in mind, tertiary sources can be valuable resources: they can inform you about topics that are new to you, and if they have bibliographies, they can sometimes lead you to valuable secondary sources.

5.1.4 Differentiating Primary, Secondary, and Tertiary Sources

Researchers haven't always divided their sources into these three categories. The distinction between primary and secondary sources originated with historians in the nineteenth century and then spread to other fields. The category of tertiary sources was added later. Although this scheme is now the standard way that students are taught to classify sources, it fits some disciplines better than others: it works very well for history, in which primary sources are materials directly connected to a historical event or moment, and for criticism, in which primary sources are the original works of art, music, or literature that you are interpreting. But it works less well for, say, philosophy, chemistry, or nursing.

It is also important to understand that the classifications of primary, secondary, and tertiary are not absolute but relative to a researcher's project. In most instances, an article in a scholarly journal would generally be considered a secondary source. But it would become a primary source if your research problem concerned its author or the field itself: if, for example, you are writing the author's biography or trying to figure out whether patriotic historians have distorted stories of the Alamo. Likewise, an encyclopedia article would usually be considered a tertiary source, but it would become a primary source if you were studying the way encyclopedias deal with gender issues. T. S. Eliot's essay "Hamlet and His Problems" would be a primary source if you were studying Eliot but a secondary source if you were studying Shakespeare. Change your focus and you change the classification of your sources.

If this is confusing, it need not be. Remember that these classifications are just a means to an end. The important thing, ultimately, is not what you *call* your sources but how well you *use* them to address your research problems, develop new ideas, and make interesting arguments. In the next chapter, we will talk more about how you can use sources in your writing.

5.2 NAVIGATING THE TWENTY-FIRST-CENTURY LIBRARY

Walk into a university library today and you might wonder, "Where are the *books*?" (Answer: they are still there, though many have been moved to off-site storage.) The card catalog has long since been replaced by electronic search engines, and print materials—books, journals, photographs, films, video and audio recordings—are increasingly being digitized. Today you don't even need to enter the library to use many of its resources. But whether you visit in person or through a website, the library is an indispensable tool for research.

Given the volume of data available on the Internet, you might think that libraries are no longer necessary—except, perhaps, for highly specialized research. We believe the opposite is true. Because *so much* information is now at our fingertips, libraries are more essential than ever when conducting research. Libraries not only let us access information but also ensure that our sources are reliable. Even if your public or academic library is comparatively small, it can serve as a *portal* to a much broader range of resources—research guides, reference works, and online databases—that extends the library's reach. Of course, to benefit from these resources, you must learn to navigate the twenty-first-century library.

5.2.1 Planning Your Library Search

Before you can use sources, you must first find and evaluate them. Some materials that will eventually serve as sources will be physically located in your library, but others are likely to be located elsewhere, whether online or at another library. To take advantage of what libraries have to offer, then, you must *plan* your search. Fortunately, this is where libraries—and librarians—are most useful.

Knowing where to begin your search can be overwhelming at first. It is tempting to simply search a few terms and see what comes up. We do this too, but we also know that the library offers more systematic and productive methods for discovering useful and credible sources. Use the library to learn more about your topic and about promising avenues for exploring your research question.

Ask a Librarian. Perhaps the best advice we can offer is to rely on the research expertise of librarians. Both general reference librarians and (in larger libraries) subject area specialists can help you refine your search parameters and direct you to the right tools for your specific research question. They can help you use the catalog to locate materials held by your library or by other libraries (and obtainable through interlibrary loan). These same librarians typically design research guides that identify reference works and online databases for specific fields.

And don't be shy. Librarians love to assist researchers of all levels and at all stages of the research process. They can help you formulate your research question and plan, develop search terms, and inventory your results to ensure you haven't overlooked something of value. The only embarrassing question is the one you *failed to ask* but should have. Of course, it pays to meet busy librarians halfway by preparing in advance. If you have a well-developed research question ready to share, your librarian will be able to give you better advice. You might describe your project using the three-step rubric from chapter 3:

1. I am working on educational policy in the 1980s
   2. to find out how school boards in the Midwest dealt with desegregation,
      3. because I want to understand regional differences in race relations.

Consult Reference Works. If you already know a lot about your topic, you probably also know how to find sources on it. But if you are new to a topic, resist the temptation to go straight to primary or secondary sources that strike you as relevant. This approach is unreliable and unpredictable and probably won't save you any time. A more successful strategy is to allow reference works to shape your search efforts. Compiled by experts, both general reference works such as the *Encyclopaedia Britannica* and more specialized works such as the *Encyclopedia of Philosophy* will give you the lay of the land, so that later it will be easier to see how your sources fit within the bigger picture. In addition, reference works often include citations or bibliographies that can lead you to sources you might otherwise overlook.

Especially valuable at early stages of research are bibliographic works, many of which provide abstracts summarizing significant articles or books on a topic. Look, especially, for annotated bibliographies or annual literature reviews that sum up recent books or articles; these offer the most promising leads for your research.

Explore Online Databases. What sets libraries apart from the Internet are their subscriptions to indexes and databases. After books, these are arguably a library's most valuable assets, since they give researchers access to materials they could not obtain otherwise. Each library's subscriptions will differ, with major research libraries offering the most comprehensive access to specialized indexes and databases. However, every academic library and many public libraries offer a powerful set of online tools that greatly extend their actual collections. You will certainly want to make use of these general and specialized resources in your research. At least become familiar with the major databases to which your library subscribes, such as Academic Search Premier, MLA International Bibliography, or PubMed. Many academic databases either provide abstracts or direct you to articles that include abstracts. Looking at these can help you decide if an article itself is worth reading carefully. Some databases allow you to access full-text articles and even books. But be aware: If your library does not subscribe to a particular journal included in a database, you might be asked to pay a fee to access a full-text article. Before doing so, *always* speak with a librarian about other means of access.

5.2.2 Finding Specific Sources

Having identified a range of search strategies and resources, you are now in a position to look for specific sources in and beyond the library. Of course, this process is not strictly linear. A single source can lead to others and return you to catalogs and databases you have already visited, only this time with new search terms. Novice researchers often rely too heavily on only a few terms or on terms that prove to be too broad—or narrow—to call up relevant sources. Successful researchers know they have to be flexible: searches typically involve trial and error to discover those terms that will yield the most relevant sources.

Search Your Library Catalog. In your research, you will probably need to use your library's catalog in two complementary ways: keyword searching and browsing. When you have examined some sources to identify a list of *keywords* associated with your topic, you are ready to use these terms to search the catalog. In most libraries, you must choose the category (books, articles, journals, etc.) you wish to use for your search.

If your sources include books, you can use Library of Congress subject headings, found either on the back of their title page or on their "details" page in the online catalog, to search for related materials. On the back of this book's title page are the terms

1. Research—Methodology. 2. Technical writing.

If you search an online catalog for those terms, you will find all the books on those subjects in that library. A book may be cross-listed under multiple subject headings. In that case, take a quick look at the titles listed under those headings as well. You may find useful sources you would have missed otherwise. You can also *browse* the catalog for books with similar *call numbers*. Once you identify a book that seems on target, use its call number to find others shelved along with it. Look for the browse link in your book's catalog entry. This list will be less focused than a keyword list, but it may also contain unexpected gems. So don't restrict yourself to books nearest your target. Invest the time to browse widely.

The problem with any online search is that it may produce an overwhelming number of titles. The University of Chicago library has more than three hundred books on Napoleon and thousands with the word *environment* in their titles. If your search turns up too many sources, narrow it down. Today's online catalogs let you limit searches in many ways: by date of publication, language, subject, resource type (books, articles, databases, etc.), and possibly others depending on the catalog. If you can't decide how to narrow your search, start with the date of publication. Restrict it to those sources published in the last fifteen years; if that still turns up too many, cut to the last ten years.

After you search the Library of Congress or a large university catalog, you may discover that your own library holds only a fraction of what you found, but that it can borrow most of what you need. For books too new to be in a library catalog but crucial to your research, find an online bookseller. Those books might turn up on your library's new acquisitions shelf, and you can always recommend books to your library for acquisition. But if you need those books quickly, you'll probably have to buy them.

On the other hand, if you find nothing, your topic may be too narrow or too far off the beaten track to yield quick results. But you could also be on to an important question that nobody else has thought about, at least not for a while. For example, "friendship" was once an important topic for philosophers, but it was then ignored by major encyclopedias for centuries. Recently, though, it has reemerged as a topic of serious research. Chances are you'll make something of a neglected topic only through your own hard thinking. In the long run, that research might make you famous, but it probably won't work for a paper due in a few weeks.

Prowl the Stacks. Doing research online is faster than on foot, but if you never go into the stacks of your library (assuming you're allowed to), you may miss crucial sources that you'll find only there. More important, you'll miss the benefits of serendipity—a chance encounter with a valuable source that occurs only when a title happens to catch your eye. (All of us have found important sources in this way.)

If you can get into the stacks, find the shelf with books on your topic, then scan the titles on that shelf, then on the ones above, below, and on either side, especially for books with new bindings published by university presses. Then turn around and skim titles behind you; you never know. When you spot a promising title, skim its table of contents and index for keywords related to your question and answer. Then skim its bibliography for titles that look relevant. You can do all that faster with a book in your hand than you can online. Be suspicious of a book with no index or bibliography. (See 5.4 for more on systematic skimming.)

You can check tables of contents for most journals online, but browsing among shelved journals can be more productive. Once you identify promising journals online or in bibliographies, find them on the shelf. Skim the bound volumes for the last ten years (most have an annual table of contents in front). Then take a quick look at journals shelved nearby. You'll be surprised how often you find a relevant article that you would have missed online.

Follow Bibliographic Trails. Most sources will give you trailheads for bibliographical searches. When you find a book that seems useful, skim its bibliography or works cited. Its index will list the authors cited most often (generally, the more citations, the more important an author is). Journal articles usually begin with a review of previous research, all cited. By following this bibliographic trail, you can navigate the most difficult research territory, because one source always leads to others, which lead to others, which lead to . . .

Use Citation Indexing. Many online catalogs and databases let you look up *other* sources that cite one that you already know. This technique, called citation indexing, is like following a bibliographic trail, forward or backward. Instead of searching for sources that a given source cites, *backward* citation, you can search for sources that cite a given source, or *forward* citation. A source's credibility can thus be gauged both by the sources it cites and by the sources that cite it. The more a given source is later cited, the greater its reputation and its impact factor.

To do this kind of research, researchers used to have to consult printed citation indexes, a process that could take hours or even days. But today's online catalogs and databases make it easy. By following bibliographic trails and using citation indexing in tandem, you can build up a rich network of sources to support your own research.

5.3 LOCATING SOURCES ON THE INTERNET

You probably already know how to search the publicly available Internet: type a few words into the text box of a public search engine like Google, and pages of links—delivered as URLs, or uniform resource locators—arrive on your screen. We use this technique all the time, to find movie times, restaurant reviews, stock prices, news items, and so on. Its ubiquity in our everyday lives is reflected in our language. We've turned the name of a company into a verb: in everyday parlance, to "Google" something is to search for it.

Your practical experience with such everyday research might lead you to regard the Internet as comprehensive and reliable. (You use it to price a smartphone or pair of jeans, so why not for your academic or professional research?) But that would be a mistake.

Again, remember that your library's catalogs and databases will allow you to access a great deal of information that you cannot get through a search engine. When using the Internet for research, maintain a healthy skepticism: most of what we retrieve using Google or some other search engine is perfectly reliable, but not everything is. In contrast to your library's catalogs and databases, the Internet is essentially unmonitored. There is no one to vouch for the credibility of materials posted to, and sent from, countless websites. And finally, keep in mind that companies offering free search engines make their money by acquiring data about you through your online behavior and by selling advertising, and that webmasters routinely modify their sites to make them appear higher in search results. These practices are not necessarily nefarious, but you should remember that search engine companies and websites themselves have an interest in where you go and what you see online.

But if you keep these limitations in mind, using the Internet can be a valuable component of your research plan. Here are some ways in which we use the Internet in our own research:

- To get our bearings with respect to a new topic—regarding everything we learn at this stage as provisional
- To explore potential keywords to use in a more systematic search
- To remind ourselves of dates or facts—again remembering to check these against more reliable sources
- To locate the authors of sources whom we might wish to contact: profiles of many scholars and researchers are available on college and university websites
- To get a "ballpark" sense of what we are likely to find through a search of specialized databases by a quick search using Google Scholar

Publicly available general tertiary sources such as *Wikipedia* and specialized ones such as the Victorian Web are often quite reliable. But you should still view them skeptically. In general, don't use the Internet to find secondary sources, as these depend for their credibility on the checks inherent in the academic publishing system, especially that of peer review. You can, however, use the Internet freely as a primary source. For example, if you study how soap opera story lines respond to their fans' reactions, fan blogs would be fine primary sources. (We discuss evaluating sources in the next section.)

Respecting Authors' Rights. Sites such as Project Gutenberg and Google Books can provide reliable online copies of older texts no longer in copyright. But postings of more recent texts (in the United States, those published in 1923 or later) may violate the author's copyright. Careful readers dislike seeing unauthorized copies cited not only because that breaks the law but also because such texts are often inaccurately reproduced. So unless a recent text is posted with the author's clear permission (as in a database), use its print rather than its e-version.

5.4 EVALUATING SOURCES FOR RELEVANCE AND RELIABILITY

When you start looking for sources, you'll find more than you can use, so you must quickly evaluate their usefulness. To do so use two criteria: relevance and reliability.

5.4.1 Evaluating Sources for Relevance

If your source is a book, do this:

- Skim its index for your keywords, then skim the pages on which those words occur.
- Skim the first and last paragraphs in chapters that use a lot of your keywords.
- Skim prologues, introductions, summary chapters, and so on.
- Skim the last chapter, especially the first and last two or three pages.
- If the source is a collection of articles, skim the editor's introduction.
- Check the bibliography for titles relevant to your topic.

If your source is an e-book, you should still follow these steps, but you can also search the whole text for your keywords.

If your source is an article, do this:

- Read the abstract, if it has one.
- Skim the introduction and conclusion; or if they are not marked off by headings, skim the first six or seven paragraphs and the last four or five.
- Skim for section headings, and read the first and last paragraphs of those sections.
- Check the bibliography for titles relevant to your topic.

If your source is online, do this:

- If it looks like a printed article, follow the steps for a journal article, and also search on your keywords.
- Skim sections labeled "introduction," "overview," "summary," or the like. If there are none, look for a link labeled "About the Site" or something similar.
- If the site has a link labeled "Site Map" or "Index," check it for your keywords and skim the referenced pages.
- If the site has a "search" resource, type in your keywords.

This kind of speedy reading can guide your own writing and revision. If you do not structure your paper so your readers can skim it quickly and see the outlines of your argument, your paper has a problem, an issue we discuss in chapters 12 and 13.

5.4.2 Evaluating Sources for Reliability

You can't judge a source until you read it, but there are signs of its reliability:

1. **Is the source published or posted online by a reputable press?** Most university presses are reliable, especially if you recognize the name of the university. Some commercial presses, which are presses not associated with a university, are reliable in some fields, such as Norton in literature, Ablex in sciences, or West in law. Be skeptical of a commercial book that makes sensational claims, even if its author has a PhD after his name. Be especially careful about sources on hotly contested social issues such as stem-cell

research, gun control, and global warming. Many books and articles are published by individuals or organizations driven by ideology. Libraries often include them for the sake of coverage, but don't assume they are reliable.

2. **Was the book or article peer-reviewed?** Most reputable presses and journals ask experts to review a book or article before it is published; this is called peer review. Essay collections published by university presses are often but not always peer-reviewed; sometimes they are reviewed only by the named editor or editors. Few commercial magazines use peer review. If a publication hasn't been peer-reviewed, be suspicious.
3. **Is the author a reputable scholar?** This is hard to answer if you are new to a field. Most publications cite an author's academic credentials; you can find more with a search engine. Most established scholars are reliable, but be cautious if the topic is a contested social issue such as gun control or abortion. Even reputable scholars can have axes to grind, especially if their research is financially supported by a special interest group. Go online to check out anyone an author thanks for support, including foundations that supported her work.
4. **If the source is available only online, is it sponsored by a reputable organization?** A website is only as reliable as its sponsor. You can usually trust one that is sponsored and maintained by a reputable organization. But if the site has not been updated recently, it may have been abandoned and may no longer be endorsed by its sponsor. Some sites supported by individuals are reliable; most are not. Do a web search for the name of the sponsor to find out more about it.
5. **Is the source current?** You must use up-to-date sources, but what counts as current depends on the field. In computer science, a journal article can be out-of-date in months; in the social sciences, ten years pushes the limit. Publications have a longer shelf life in the humanities: literary or art criticism, for example, can remain relevant for decades and even centuries. In general, a source that sets out a major position or theory that other researchers accept will stay current longer than those that respond

to or develop it. Assume that most textbooks are *not* current. If you are unsure whether a source will be considered current, take your lead from the practice of established researchers in the field. Look at the dates of articles in the works cited lists of a few recent books or articles in the field: a good rule of thumb is that you can cite works as old as the older ones in that list (but to be safe, perhaps not as old as the oldest). Try to find a standard edition of primary works such as novels, plays, letters, and so on: it is usually not the most recent. Be sure that you consult the most recent edition of a secondary or tertiary source: researchers often change their views, even rejecting ones they espoused in earlier editions.

6. **If the source is a book, does it have notes and a bibliography?** If not, be suspicious, because you have no way to follow up on anything that the source claims.
7. **If the source is a website, does it include bibliographical data?** You cannot judge the reliability of a site that does not indicate who sponsors and maintains it, who wrote what's posted there, and when it was posted or last updated.
8. **If the source is a website, does it approach its topic judiciously?** Your readers are unlikely to trust a site that engages in heated advocacy, attacks those who disagree, makes wild claims, uses abusive language, or makes errors of spelling, punctuation, and grammar.

The following criteria are particularly important for advanced students:

9. **If the source is a book, has it been well reviewed?** Many fields have indexes to published reviews that tell you how others evaluate a source (see our "Appendix: Bibliographic Resources").
10. **Has the source been frequently cited by others?** You can roughly estimate how influential a source is by how often others cite it. Citation indexing makes this easy to do (see 5.2.2). If you find that a source is cited repeatedly by other scholars, you can infer that experts in the field regard it as reliable and significant. Such sources are said to have a high "impact factor." You should keep an

Whom Can You Trust?

The highly respected *Journal of the American Medical Association* appointed a committee to review articles published by reputable journals for reliability. Even though those papers had been approved by experts in the field, the reviewers reported that "statistical and methodological errors were common" ("When Peer Review Produces Unsound Science," *New York Times*, June 11, 2002, p. D6). In the face of such revelations, some just dismiss what scientists publish: if the reviewers of scientific articles can't guarantee reliable data, what is a mere layperson to do? You do what we all do—the best you can: read critically, and when you report data, do so as accurately as you can. We'll return to this question in chapter 8.

Error is bad, but dishonesty is worse. One of Booth's students got a summer job with a drug company and was assigned to go through stacks of doctors' answers to questionnaires and shred certain ones until nine out of ten of those left endorsed the company's product. These bogus data were then used to "prove" that the product worked. The student quit in disgust and was, no doubt, replaced by someone less ethical.

eye out for such sources and use them to orient yourself in your field of research.

These indicators do not guarantee reliability. Reviewers sometimes recommend that a reputable press publish something weakly argued or with thin data because other aspects of its argument are too important to miss—we have each done so. So don't assume that you can read uncritically just because a report is written by a reputable researcher and published by a reputable press.

5.5 LOOKING BEYOND PREDICTABLE SOURCES

For a class paper, you'll probably use the sources typical in your field. But if you are doing an advanced project, an MA thesis, or a PhD dissertation, search beyond them. If, for example, your project were on the economic effects of agricultural changes in late

> ***When They Beat You to the Punch***
> Don't panic if you find a source that seems to pose and solve precisely your problem: "Transforming the Alamo Legend: History in the Service of Politics." At that moment you might think, *I'm dead. Nothing new to say.* (It happened to Williams when he was writing his doctoral dissertation and to Colomb just before his first book came out.) You may be right, but probably not. If the source does in fact settle your exact question, you have to formulate a new one. But the question your source asked is probably not as close to yours as you first feared. And you may find that you can do the source one better: if the author failed to get things entirely right, you have an unwitting ally in formulating your problem.

sixteenth-century England, you might read Elizabethan plays involving country characters, look at wood prints of agricultural life, find commentary by religious figures on rural social behavior. Conversely, if you were working on visual representations of daily life in London, you might research the economic history of the time and place. When you look beyond the standard *kinds* of references relevant to your question, you enrich not only your analysis but your range of intellectual reference and your ability to synthesize diverse kinds of data, a crucial competence of an inquiring mind. Don't ignore a work on your topic that is not mentioned in the bibliographies of your most relevant sources—you will get credit for originality if you turn up a good source that others have ignored.

5.6 USING PEOPLE TO FURTHER YOUR RESEARCH

One of the paradoxes of twenty-first-century research is that even as new technologies allow us to access an unprecedented wealth of materials with unprecedented ease, research has also become more personal. So as you undertake your project, don't forget about the human element.

Most obviously, people can be sources of primary data, collected through observation, surveys, or interviews. Be creative when using people for primary research: don't ignore people in local business, government, or civic organizations. For example, if you were researching school desegregation in your town, you might go beyond the documents to ask the local school district whether anyone there has memories to share. We can't explain the complexities of interviewing (there are many guides to that process), but remember that the more you plan by determining *exactly* what you want to know, the more efficiently you will get what you need. You don't need to script an interview around a set list of questions—in fact, that can be a bad idea if it makes the interviewee freeze up. But prepare so that you don't question your source aimlessly. You can always reread a book for what you missed, but you can't keep going back to people because you didn't prepare well enough to get what you needed the first time. And always remember that when conducting primary research that involves people, you must adhere to rigorous ethical standards (see the Quick Tip at the end of this chapter).

People can also lead you to good secondary sources or serve as such sources themselves. We noted earlier that the body of secondary sources on a topic constitutes the scholarly "conversation" about it. That was a metaphor. But you can and should have real conversations about your research as well. Above we encouraged you to discuss your research with one kind of expert: your reference librarian. Your librarian is an expert on the processes of library research. You can also benefit from talking directly with experts on your topic. Ask them about the important open questions in the field. Ask them what they think of your project or provisional thesis. Ask them to suggest secondary sources for you to read. This kind of personal guidance can be invaluable to a novice researcher, and many experts will be happy to talk with you (or at least engage in a little e-mail correspondence).

All of us have made these kinds of queries with great success in our own research, and all of us have responded to them in turn, by helping those who have contacted us. One of us once invited an eminent scholar to talk about his research process to a group of first-year college students. He began his talk by saying, "I don't really have a research process; I just ask my smart friends what I should read." This scholar was being at least a bit tongue in cheek, but we could all do worse than to rely on such smart friends, at least to get us started.

QUICK TIP **The Ethics of Using People as Sources of Data**

In recent years we have become increasingly aware that research using people may inadvertently harm them—not just physically but by embarrassing them, violating their privacy, and so on. So every college or university now has a committee that reviews all research directly or indirectly involving people, whether done by students or professional researchers. These committees go by different names—Human Subjects Committee, Institutional Review Board, Ethics Research Board, and so on—but they all aim to ensure that researchers follow the maxim that should govern research as it does medicine: *Do no harm.* Consult with that committee if you use people as sources of data—whether by interviewing, surveying, perhaps even just observing them. Jumping through these hoops may feel like bureaucratic make-work, but if you don't, you could harm those who help you and may even damage your institution.

6 Engaging Sources

To make your research reliable, you must use your sources fairly and accurately. In this chapter, we explain how to engage your sources productively and how to take notes so that readers can trust you when you rely on or critique a source.

In this chapter, we show you how to get the most out of your sources, especially your secondary sources. We've chosen that focus for a simple reason: it's a topic on which we can offer useful, general advice. The ways that researchers find or create their data, and the kinds of data readers expect as evidence, vary wildly from field to field. Historians and literary critics typically comb primary sources for passages they can use as evidence. Other researchers, however, don't use primary sources at all: depending on their fields, they might analyze soil samples in a lab, or conduct a survey, or build a computer model. But every field has its body of secondary sources, sometimes called its *literature*, that document the field's conversation. And researchers in all fields engage these sources in similar ways.

How you use your secondary sources depends on where you stand in your search for a project. Experienced researchers read secondary sources regularly to keep up with work in their fields, and so they usually begin their projects with a question or problem in mind. But if you are new to a subject or you still have only a topic, you may have to read a lot of sources to find a problem to pursue, and then even more to figure out how to solve it. In this chapter, we show you how to read secondary sources as experienced researchers do: not just for data you can use in your own argument but more importantly for questions, problems, and arguments that spur your own thinking.

6.1 RECORDING COMPLETE BIBLIOGRAPHICAL INFORMATION

First things first: once you decide a source is worth reading, record *all* of its bibliographical information. Do this before you do anything else: it only takes a moment, and we promise that no habit will serve you better for the rest of your career.

You need the bibliographic information for your sources not only so that you can recall what you have read, but also so that you can credit your sources when you write. In your own notes, you can record bibliographic data in whatever format you like—so long as your records are complete; when you cite sources in your writing, you should follow the citation style of your field (see 14.5).

For printed books, record

- author(s)
- title (including subtitle)
- editor(s) and translator(s) (if any)
- edition
- volume
- place published (only the first city if more than one is listed)
- publisher
- date published
- page numbers of articles or chapters consulted
- library call number (if any)
- ISBN

For electronic books, record everything you would record for a printed book plus

- URL (if any)
- name of database (if any)
- date of access
- electronic format of the book

For journal articles, record

- author(s)
- title (including subtitle) of article

- title of journal
- volume and issue number
- date
- page numbers of article
- library call number (if any)

For online sources, record as much of the above as applies. Also record

- URL
- name of database (if any)
- date of access
- Webmaster (if identified)

If you access a printed text online, record bibliographical data from the original printing as well as your source of online access.

If you scan or photocopy a passage from a book, also scan or photocopy its title page and the bibliographic information on the reverse side. Then add the library call number if you know it. You won't need to include the call number when you cite the source, but knowing it will allow you to find the source again easily if you need it.

You may think this advice is overly cautious, but it isn't. Nothing is more frustrating than having the perfect quotation or bit of data in your notes and being unable to use it in your writing, because you didn't completely document your source and can't find it again.

> Williams once had to withhold a publication on Elizabethan social history for more than a year because he failed to document a source fully. Years earlier he had come across some data—a list of renters in London in 1638—he thought he would someday find useful. But he had failed to record complete information on his source, so when that day came, he could not use its data. He searched the library at the University of Chicago for hours, until one night he sat up in bed, realizing that the source was in a different library!

6.2 ENGAGING SOURCES ACTIVELY

Experienced researchers don't read passively; they engage their sources actively, entering into conversation with them. If you can, read important sources twice. First, read generously. Pay attention to what sparks your interest. Reread passages that puzzle or confuse you. Don't look for disagreements right away, but read in ways that help the source make sense. Otherwise, you'll be tempted to emphasize its weaknesses if it presents an argument that rivals yours. Resist that temptation, at least at first.

Then, if your source seems important or seems to challenge your own position, read it a second time slowly and more critically. When you read a passage, think not only about what it says but about how you would respond. Record those responses in your notes or—if you own the source or are working from a copy—in the margins of the source itself. Test your understanding by summarizing: if you can't sum up a passage in your mind, you don't understand it well enough to disagree.

Don't accept a claim just because an authority asserts it. For decades, researchers cited the "fact" that the Inuit people of the Arctic had many terms for types of snow. But another researcher found that they have just three (or so she claims). And understand that experts frequently disagree. If Expert A says one thing, B will assert the opposite, and C will claim to be an expert but is not. When some students hear experts disagree, they become cynical and dismiss expert knowledge as just opinion. But don't mistake informed and thoughtful debate over legitimately contested issues for mere opinion. In fact, it's the mark of an active field.

If you are an advanced researcher, check the accuracy of everything important to your argument. Researchers whose work has been used by others will tell you, as often as not, that it was reported inaccurately, summarized carelessly, or criticized ignorantly. Writers regularly write to the *New York Review of Books* and the "Book Review" of the *New York Times*, pointing out how reviewers distorted their ideas or made factual errors criticizing them.

Check—and Check Again

Researchers rarely misrepresent sources deliberately, but they are occasionally careless or intellectually lazy. Colomb heard a prominent researcher confess after her talk that she had never read the work she had just discussed. One of Booth's books was "refuted" by a critic who apparently read only the title of a section, "Novels Must Be Realistic." Failing to read beyond it, he didn't know that Booth himself was attacking the claim in the title, along with other misconceptions about fiction. One reviewer of a book by Williams misquoted him and then, thinking he was disagreeing with him, argued for the point Williams made in the first place!

6.3 READING FOR A PROBLEM

Once you have a research problem, use it to guide your search for evidence, models, and arguments to respond to. But if you don't yet have one, you won't know which data, models, or arguments might be relevant. So read sources not randomly but deliberately to find a problem. Look for claims that seem puzzling, inaccurate, or simplistic—anything you can disagree with. You're more likely to find a research problem when you disagree with a source, but you can also find one in sources you agree with.

6.3.1 Look for Creative Agreement

If you believe what a source claims, try to extend that claim: What new cases might it cover? What new insights can it provide? Is there confirming evidence the source hasn't considered? Here are some ways to find a problem through creative agreement.

1. **Offer additional support.** You can offer new evidence to support a source's claim.

    Smith uses anecdotes to show that the Alamo story had mythic status beyond Texas, but editorials in big-city newspapers offer better evidence.

- Source supports a claim with old evidence, but you offer new evidence.
- Source supports a claim with weak evidence, but you offer stronger evidence.

2. **Confirm unsupported claims.** You can prove something that a source only assumes or speculates about.

   Smith recommends visualization to improve sports performance, but MRI studies of the mental activities of athletes offer evidence that shows why that is good advice.

   - Source speculates _______ might be true, but you offer evidence to show that it is.
   - Source assumes _______ is true, but you can prove it.

3. **Apply a claim more widely.** You can extend a position.

   Smith argues that medical students learn physiological processes better when they are explained with many metaphors rather than with just one. The same seems true for engineering and law students.

   - Source correctly applies _______ to one situation, but you apply it to new ones.
   - Source claims that _______ is true in a specific situation, but you show it's true in general.

6.3.2 Look for Creative Disagreement

If you read actively, you'll inevitably find yourself disagreeing with your sources. Don't brush those disagreements aside, because they often point to new research problems. Look for these types (the list is not exhaustive, and some kinds overlap):

1. **Contradictions of kind.** A source says something is one kind of thing, but it's another.

   Smith says that graffiti is merely vandalism, but it is better understood as a form of public art.

   - Source claims that _________ is a kind of _________, but it's not.
   - Source claims that _________ always has _________ as one of its features or qualities, but it doesn't.

- Source claims that _________ is normal/good/significant/useful/moral/interesting, but it's not.

You can reverse those claims and the ones that follow to state the opposite:

- Though a source says _________ is *not* a kind of _________, you can show that it is.

2. **Part-whole contradictions.** You can show that a source mistakes how the parts of something are related.

   Smith has argued that coding is irrelevant to a liberal education, but in fact, it is essential.

   - Source claims that _________ is a part of _________, but it's not.
   - Source claims that one part of _________ relates to another in a certain way, but it doesn't.
   - Source claims that every _________ has _________ as one of its parts, but it doesn't.

3. **Developmental or historical contradictions.** You can show that a source mistakes the origin or development of a topic.

   Smith argues that the world population will rise, but it won't.

   - Source claims that _________ is changing, but it's not.
   - Source claims that _________ originated in _________, but it didn't.
   - Source claims that _________ develops in a certain way, but it doesn't.

4. **External cause-effect contradictions.** You can show that a source mistakes a causal relationship.

   Smith claims that legalizing marijuana will increase its use among teenagers, but evidence shows that it doesn't.

   - Source claims that _________ causes _________, but it doesn't/they are both caused by _________.
   - Source claims that _________ is sufficient to cause _________, but it's not.

- Source claims that _________ causes only _________, but it also causes _________.

5. **Contradictions of perspective.** Most contradictions don't change a conceptual framework, but when you contradict a "standard" view of things, you urge others to think in a new way.

   Smith assumes that advertising has only an economic function, but it also serves as a laboratory for new art forms.

   - Source discusses _________ from the point of view of _________, but a new context or point of view reveals a new truth [the new or old context can be social, political, philosophical, historical, economic, ethical, gender specific, etc.].
   - Source analyzes _________ using theory/value system _________, but you can analyze it from a new point of view and see it in a new way.

6.4 READING FOR ARGUMENTS

6.4.1 Read for Arguments to Respond To

No argument is complete until it acknowledges and responds to its readers' predictable questions and disagreements. You can find some of those competing views in secondary sources. What alternatives to your claims do they offer? What evidence do they cite that you must acknowledge? Some new researchers think that they weaken their case if they mention any views opposing their own. The opposite is true. When you acknowledge the views of others, you show that you not only know those views, but have carefully considered and can confidently respond to them (for more on this, see chapter 10).

Experienced researchers also use those competing views to improve their own. You can't really understand what you think until you understand why a rational person might think differently. So as you look for sources, don't look just for those that support your claims. Be alert for sources that contradict them, because they are sources that your readers are likely to know.

6.4.2 Read for Models of Reasoning and Analysis

You can use secondary sources in another way as well: as models of reasoning and analysis. If you have never made an argument like the one you plan to, you might follow the pattern of other arguments that you find in your secondary sources. You can't use specific ideas (that would be plagiarism), but you do not plagiarize a source when you borrow its ways of arguing or of analyzing data. (Don't worry that using a source as a model will make your research seem unoriginal. Research arguments are often unoriginal in their methods and ways of reasoning. Readers will look for originality in your problem, claim, and evidence.)

Suppose you want to argue that the Alamo legend thrived because it served the political interests of those who created it and satisfied the emotional needs of those who repeated it. You will need reasons and evidence unique to your claim, but you can raise the *kinds* of issues that readers see in similar arguments about other legends, real or fictional. If, for example, a source shows how the King Arthur legend helped to shape English society and politics, you might make a similar argument about the Alamo and the Republic of Texas. You are not obliged to cite your model, but to gain credibility, you might note that it makes an argument similar to yours:

> Just as the Arthurian legends helped to forge a definitively English social and political identity (Weiman 1998), so the legend of the Alamo . . .

6.5 READING FOR DATA AND SUPPORT

6.5.1 Read for Data to Use as Evidence

New researchers regularly mine secondary sources for data, but if you can, check the primary source. If an important quotation is available in its original form and context, it is risky and intellectually lazy not to look it up. You don't have to agree with a source to use its data; in fact, its argument does not even have to be relevant to your question, so long as its data are. However, use statistical data only if you can judge for yourself whether they were collected and analyzed appropriately. (You serve yourself well if you take a course or two in statistics and probability, an area where most Americans are shamefully ignorant.)

6.5.2 Read for Claims to Use as Support

Researchers often use the results they find in secondary sources to bolster their own arguments. If you find a useful claim, you can cite it to support your own, especially if it has been well supported and widely accepted. But many claims show nothing more than that another researcher agrees with you. To use such claims as evidence, you have to report not only the conclusion of the source but its reasoning and supporting evidence as well.

6.6 TAKING NOTES

Once you find a source that you think you can use, you must read it purposefully and carefully. But that will do you little good if you can't locate it again or remember it well enough to use. So again, before you do anything else, record the source's full bibliographic information. Then take notes in a way that will help you not only to remember and use what you have read but also to further your own thinking.

You can take notes on index cards or in a notebook, or you can use your computer or handheld device. You can even take notes online, using any number of web-based solutions, from word processors to elaborate reference-management systems. Each of these approaches has its advantages and disadvantages. You need to understand them and pick the approach that will work best for you.

6.6.1 Taking Notes on Paper

Years ago, the standard way to take notes on sources was to create a file of index cards:

Sharman, Swearing, p. 133	HISTORY/ECONOMICS (GENDER?)
Says swearing became economic issue in 18th c. Cites Gentleman's Magazine, July 1751 (no page reference): woman sentenced to ten days' hard labor because couldn't pay one-shilling fine for profanity.	
"... one rigid economist practically entertained the notion of adding to the national resources by preaching a crusade against the opulent class of swearers."	
[*Way to think about swearing today as econmic issue? Comedians more popular if they use bad language? Movies more realistic? A gender issue here? Were 18th-c. men fined as often as women?*]	
GT3080/S6	

At the top left is the author, short title, and page number. At the top right are keywords that let the researcher sort and re-sort notes into different categories and orders. The body of the card summarizes the source, records a direct quotation, and includes a comment or thought about further research that is clearly distinguished from the quotation. At bottom left is the call number of the source.

Although few researchers use this method extensively today, we can still learn important principles from it:

- Record complete bibliographic information for each source so that you can cite it properly and find it again easily.
- Separate notes on different topics: don't jumble together your notes on different topics, even if they come from the same source.
- Make sure your notes are accurate, because you need to be able to rely on them later. (If you want to quote more than a few lines, consider photocopying, scanning, or cutting-and-pasting the passage, or simply saving the whole document.)
- Perhaps most important: clearly distinguish (1) what you quote from a source, (2) what you paraphrase or summarize from a source, and (3) your own thoughts. If you are writing on paper, use headings or brackets or different colors of ink to differentiate these different kinds of note. If you are using a computer or taking notes online, use different fonts or different colors of type.

We stress that you must *unambiguously* distinguish your own words from those of your sources because it is so easy to confuse the two.

Compared to computer files, paper notes can be cumbersome to store, back up, index, and access, and they are susceptible to transcription errors: when hand-copying quotations, it is surprisingly easy to alter their wording, even when you think you are being careful. Still, paper notes have their uses. For example, a notebook or pack of index cards is cheap and portable, and paper can sometimes go where technology cannot—some archives still require patrons to take notes with paper and pencil. The main reason some researchers still rely on paper notes is that they help with thinking. Since you can't write out everything, using paper forces you to think about what's most important. Likewise, if your notes are on cards or sheets of paper, you can group them, shuffle them, or lay them out on a desk, a table, or even the floor. And the very act of *writing out* your notes can help you not only remember what's in them but also see connections and develop your own ideas.

Still, few researchers today rely on paper notes alone. Most use their computers.

6.6.2 Taking Notes on a Computer

When you take notes using a computer, you have several options:

- Most simply, you can use a word processor. Create a separate file (or at least a separate page) for each source, and be sure to unambiguously distinguish your own words from those of your source. Word processors are easy to use, but they also limit your ability to index, organize, sort, and search your notes. So for long or complex projects especially, you may want to consider other options.
- You can use a dedicated note-taking application to create and organize your notes for a project. Such applications can help you to index, sort, and access your notes, but since they sometimes use proprietary formats, they can make it difficult for you to share your notes or use them with other programs.

- You can use a full reference-management system. Such systems do much more than help you organize and access your notes. They can often pull information directly from online library catalogs and databases, and they can format and update your citations and bibliographies when you write. Some will even store full electronic copies of your sources within the reference management system, helping you build and maintain your personal library of sources. But like note-taking programs, these systems sometimes use proprietary formats, and you have to learn to use them.

All three types of application are also available in web-based versions, meaning that the application and your notes reside not on your own computer but in the "cloud." This protects your data from inadvertent loss or corruption (you don't have to worry about your hard drive crashing) and can help you share information and collaborate with other researchers.

But whatever technology you use, you have to consider some basic questions:

- How will you stay organized? For example, if you plan to create a separate word-processing document for each source, you then need a system for naming and storing your files. Without such a system, it is very easy to "lose" your notes on your hard drive.
- How will you use your notes? You may decide to store your notes differently for small projects and large ones, for discrete projects and ongoing ones, for individual projects and collaborative ones.
- What applications are available through your school or library? Many schools offer note-taking or reference-management systems to faculty and students, sometimes integrating these tools with their catalogs. If your school offers such resources, consider using them.
- Most important: what approach best suits your own ways of writing, thinking, and working? As you grow as a writer and researcher, you will develop ways of working that are particular to you. Others may find them cumbersome or confusing or even incomprehensible. No matter. Remember that your goal is not to

create an elaborate set of notes but to research and write capably and intelligently. If a piece of software doesn't help you do that, it isn't useful—to you.

6.6.3 Decide Whether to Quote, Paraphrase, or Summarize

If you can photocopy, scan, or download your source, or you know that you can access it online when you write, you can focus less on preserving its exact words than on your own engagement with it. That's a great advantage. Summarize the source, which will also help you understand it, and note passages you may want to quote or paraphrase when you write. Note also your own responses to the source. Where did you find yourself agreeing with it? Disagreeing? Wanting to say, *Yes, but . . . ?*

If you can't preserve your source and you don't know whether you will be able to access it later, you have a tougher choice. It takes too long to transcribe the exact words of every passage that's interesting or potentially useful, but it's a nuisance when you realize later that you want to quote something you only summarized. So when taking notes, you must choose as you go whether to quote, paraphrase, or summarize. In general, researchers in the humanities quote most often; social and natural scientists usually paraphrase and summarize. But every choice depends on how you plan to use your source:

- Summarize when you need only the point of a passage, section, or even whole article or book. Summary is useful for context or views that are related but not specifically relevant. A summary of a source never serves as good evidence.
- Paraphrase when the specific words of a passage are less important than its meaning. Paraphrasing doesn't mean changing just a word or two. You must replace most of the words and phrasing of the original with your own. A paraphrase is never as good evidence as a direct quotation.
- Record exact quotations for these purposes:
  —The quoted words are evidence that backs up your reasons. If, for example, you claimed that different regions responded to the Battle

of the Alamo differently, you would quote exact words from different newspapers. You would paraphrase them if you needed only their general sentiments.

—The words are from an authority you plan to rely on or challenge.

—The words are strikingly original or so compelling that the quotation can frame the rest of your discussion.

—The source makes a claim that you disagree with, and to be fair you want to state that claim exactly.

Never abbreviate a quotation thinking you can accurately reconstruct it later. You can't. And if you misquote, you'll undermine your credibility.

6.6.4 Get the Context Right

You can't record *everything*, but you have to record *enough* to ensure that you accurately capture the source's meaning. As you use material from your sources, record not just what they say but how they use the information.

1. **When you quote, paraphrase, or summarize, be careful about context.** You cannot entirely avoid quoting out of context, because you cannot quote all of an original. So when you draft a paraphrase or summary or copy a quotation, do so within the context that matters most—that of your own grasp of the original. When you record a part of an argument, note the line of reasoning that the author was pursuing:

   NOT: Bartolli (p. 123): The war was caused by Z.

   NOT: Bartolli (p. 123): The war was caused by X, Y, and Z.

   BUT: Bartolli: The war was caused by X, Y, and Z (p. 123). But the most important cause was Z (p. 123), for three reasons: reason 1 (pp. 124–26); reason 2 (p. 126); reason 3 (pp. 127–28).

Sometimes you will care only about the conclusion, but readers usually want to see how a conclusion emerges from the argument supporting it. So when you take notes, record not only conclusions but also the arguments that support them.

2. **When you record a claim, note its role in the original.** Is it a main point? A minor point? A qualification or concession? By noting these distinctions you avoid this kind of mistake:

> ORIGINAL BY JONES: "Researchers recognize that lung cancer has a number of causes, including genetic predisposition and exposure to environmental factors such as asbestos, radon, and fine particulates. But no one who has studied the data doubts that lung cancer's leading cause is smoking."
>
> MISLEADING REPORT ABOUT JONES: Smoking is just one cause of lung cancer among many. Jones, for example, claims that "lung cancer has a number of causes, including genetic predisposition and exposure to environmental factors such as asbestos, radon, and fine particulates."

Jones did not make that point at all. He *conceded* a point to set up the point he wanted to make. Anyone who deliberately misreports in this way violates basic standards of truth. But you can make such a mistake inadvertently if you note only a source's words and not their role in an argument.

To avoid such mistakes, distinguish statements that are central to an argument from qualifications or concessions that the author acknowledges but downplays. Unless you are reading "against the grain" of the writer's intention—to expose hidden tendencies, for example—do not report minor aspects of a source as though they were major or, worse, as if they were the source's whole point.

3. **Record the scope and confidence of a claim.** These are not the same:

> Chemicals in french fries cause cancer.
>
> Chemicals in french fries may be a factor in causing cancer.
>
> Some chemicals in french fries correlate with a higher incidence of some cancers.

4. **Don't mistake a summary of another writer's views for those of an author summarizing them.** Some writers do not clearly indicate

when they summarize another's argument, so it is easy to quote them as saying what they set out to disprove rather than what they in fact believe.

5. **Note why sources agree and disagree.** Two social scientists might claim that a social problem is caused by personal factors, not by environmental forces, but one might cite evidence from genetic inheritance while the other points to religious beliefs. How and why sources agree is as important as the fact that they do. In the same way, sources might disagree because they interpret the same evidence differently or take different approaches to the problem.

It is risky to attach yourself to what any one researcher says about an issue. It is not "research" when you uncritically summarize another's work. Even if your source is universally trusted, be careful. If you rely on at least two sources, you'll usually find that they do not agree entirely, and that's where your own research can begin. *Which has the better argument? Which better respects the evidence?* In fact, you have a research problem right there—whom should we believe?

6.7 ANNOTATING YOUR SOURCES

6.7.1 Marginal Annotations

As an alternative to taking notes on paper or a computer, you can directly annotate many sources in print or digital form. Annotation is a technique of marking up a text through comments, questions, and cross-references to other texts. Annotating in the margins is generally more productive than simply highlighting because it brings into relief the relevance of a source to your project.

In annotating, you document the active reading practices discussed in this chapter. You can use annotations to identify a source's claims and keywords or "argue" with a source by questioning (or extending) its reasons, evidence, and warrants (see part III). As your project develops, you can return to an annotated text to see what you were thinking earlier.

The Value of Reading Widely

We have emphasized how important it is to have a good question to focus your research. Don't think, however, that you waste time reading sources that turn out to be irrelevant. In fact, when you read and record more than you use, you build up a base of knowledge crucial to the exercise of good thinking. Good thinking is a skill that you can learn, but you can exercise it only when you have a deep and wide base of knowledge to work on. So read sources not just to answer the question you ask today, but to help you think better about every question you'll ask for the rest of your research career. To that end, everything you read is relevant.

Of course, not every text is equally available for annotation. You can't write in the margins of library books or other texts you do not own. Many texts are accessible only (or most conveniently) in digital form. Fortunately, however, there are digital annotation tools that let you document your reading in digital environments. You can use these tools to annotate a wide range of texts, including images, and to link your readings of various texts to create a searchable database for later retrieval.

6.7.2 Annotated Bibliography

One approach to engaging sources is an annotated bibliography—a list of possible sources featuring both a citation and a brief descriptive summary of each source. (For more on citations, see 14.5.) There are multiple types of annotations based on the motive for creating them. For a research project, an annotated bibliography offers a bird's-eye view of a range of sources and the roles they might play in your paper. Often the assembling of an annotated bibliography is a distinct stage in a research process, one that allows you (and your teacher) to reflect on the sources you have collected. Each annotation is an opportunity to evaluate the credibility of a source, summarize its argument, and explain its relevance to your project.

Compiling an annotated bibliography can serve as a checkpoint to gauge how thoroughly you have conducted your research and how deeply you have engaged the sources you have collected. If you can't summarize your sources or explain their relevance, you are likely not ready to write your paper.

QUICK TIP Manage Moments of Normal Anxiety

As you get deeper into your project, you may experience a moment when everything seems to run together into a hopeless muddle. That usually happens when you accumulate notes faster than you can sort them. Such moments can be stressful, but they can also be a sign that you are on the verge of a new insight or discovery.

You can minimize the panic by taking every opportunity to organize and summarize what you have gathered by *writing as you go* and by returning to the central questions: *What question am I asking? What problem am I posing?* Keep rehearsing that formula, *I am working on X to learn more about Y, so that my readers can better understand Z.* Writing regularly about these questions does more than help you stay focused; it also helps you think.

You can also turn to friends, classmates, teachers—anyone who will serve as a sympathetic but critical audience. Explain how what you have learned bears on your question and helps you resolve your problem. Ask them, *Does this make sense? Am I missing anything important? What else would you like to know?* You will profit from their reactions, but even more from the mere act of explaining your ideas to non-specialists.

PART III

Making an Argument

PROLOGUE
Assembling a Research Argument

You can't wait to plan your argument until after you've gathered every last bit of data and found every last relevant source. In the first place, you'll never get them all. In the second, you'll end up researching mechanically or aimlessly, accumulating more and more stuff with no sense of what you'll do with it or following trails of bread crumbs who knows where. Of course, you have to do some research to get a handle on your project. But as soon as you have a sense of your problem and its likely solution, you should begin planning your argument. Your plan will change as your research progresses—if it doesn't, you probably aren't doing your best thinking—but making a plan early and modifying it as you go will help you grasp your material better and research more purposefully: only when you try to make a *research argument* that answers your readers' predictable questions can you see what research you have yet to do.

A research argument is not like the heated exchanges we hear every day. Those arguments usually involve a dispute: children argue over a toy, roommates over what music to play, drivers over who had the right-of-way. Such arguments can be polite or nasty, but most involve conflict, with winners and losers. To be sure, researchers sometimes wrangle over each other's reasoning and evidence and occasionally erupt into charges of carelessness, incompetence, and even fraud. But that kind of argument is not what made them researchers in the first place.

In the next five chapters, we examine a kind of argument that

Getting to Know You

You've been told endlessly to think about your audience, but nothing is harder than imagining questions from someone you don't know. Experienced researchers have the advantage of knowing many of their readers personally. They talk with them about research projects, trying out ideas before writing them up. If you are a beginning researcher or a student, you may not yet know your readers in this personal way. But you can do some homework to understand how they write, argue, and think:

- Read journals that publish research like yours. Notice the kinds of questions the articles acknowledge and respond to.
- Rehearse your argument with a more experienced researcher or a teacher. After you have a plan but before you draft, talk over your ideas, asking whether any seem doubtful or confusing.
- Ask a few people you trust to read your drafts and indicate where they have questions or see alternatives. Find people as much like your intended readers as possible.

You can even try to get to know some actual readers. For example, a group of physicists once wanted biologists to notice their research but were unhappy when the first manuscript they sent to a biology journal was rejected. So they started attending biology conferences, reading biology journals, even hanging around the biology department's faculty lounge. After they figured out how biologists think, they rewrote their arguments and published papers that influenced the field. You may not be able to travel to conferences or hang out in a faculty lounge, but you can still get to know faculty and students on your campus working in your field. The better you know them, the better you will be able to imagine questions they might ask you.

is less like a prickly dispute with winners and losers and more like a lively conversation with amiable and sometimes skeptical colleagues. It is a conversation in which you and your imagined readers *cooperatively* explore an issue that you both think is important to resolve, a conversation that aims not at coercing each other into agreement, but at cooperatively finding the best answer to an important but challenging question.

In that conversation, though, you do more than politely trade opinions. We are all entitled to our opinions, and no law requires us to explain or defend them. But in a research argument, we are expected to show readers why our claims are important and then to support our claims with good reasons and evidence, as if our readers were asking us, quite reasonably, *Why should I believe that?*

In fact, although we more easily notice the heated disputes, we have these collaborative arguments every day, each time we trade good reasons for deciding what to do—when discussing with a friend what cell phone to buy, what books to read, even whether to get pizza or Chinese food. Like those friendly discussions, a research argument doesn't force a claim on readers. Instead, you start where your readers do, with their predictable questions about why they should accept your claim, questions they ask not to sabotage your argument but to test it, to help both of you find and understand a truth worth sharing. Of course, when you *write* an argument, no one is there to ask you those questions in person. So you must imagine them on your readers' behalf. It's those imagined questions and your answers that make your argument part of an ongoing conversation. In chapter 7 we survey the elements that constitute a research argument. In chapters 8–11 we explain each element in detail. In part IV, we show you how to put that argument into writing.

7 Making Good Arguments

AN OVERVIEW

In this chapter, we explain what a research argument is and the five questions whose answers constitute one.

In part II, we argued that real research involves more than just amassing information on a topic; we argued that it means developing solutions to problems you and your readers care about. Likewise, sharing the results of your research involves more than just giving your readers a "data dump" that says, *Here are some facts about my topic*; it means explaining your problem and justifying your solution in a *research argument*.

7.1 ARGUMENT AS A CONVERSATION WITH READERS

In a research argument, you make a *claim*, back it with *reasons* supported by *evidence*, *acknowledge* and *respond* to other views, and sometimes explain your *principles* of reasoning. There's nothing arcane about these things: you do them in every conversation that inquires thoughtfully into an unsettled issue:

ABBY: I hear last semester was a little rocky. How do you think this term will go? [*Abby poses a problem that interests her, put in the form of a question.*]

BRETT: Better, I hope. [*Brett makes a claim that answers the question.*]

ABBY: Why is that? [*Abby asks for a reason to believe Brett's claim.*]

BRETT: I'll finally be taking courses in my major. [*Brett offers a reason.*]

ABBY: Why will that make a difference? [*Abby doesn't see how Brett's reason is relevant to his claim that he will do better.*]

BRETT: When I take courses I'm interested in, I work harder. [*Brett offers a general principle that relates his reason to his claim.*]

ABBY: What courses? [*Abby asks for evidence to back up Brett's reason.*]

BRETT: History of architecture, introduction to design. [*Brett offers specific instances on which he based his reason.*]

ABBY: But what about that calculus course you have to take again? [*Abby offers a point that contradicts Brett's reason.*]

BRETT: I know I had to drop it last time, but I found a really good tutor. [*Brett acknowledges Abby's objection and responds to it.*]

ABBY: But won't you be taking five courses? [*Abby raises another reservation.*]

BRETT: I know. It won't be easy. [*Brett concedes a point he cannot refute.*]

ABBY: Will you pull up your GPA? [*Abby asks about the limits of Brett's claim.*]

BRETT: I should. I'm hoping for a 3.0, as long as I don't have to get a part-time job. [*Brett limits the scope of his claim and adds a condition.*]

If you can imagine yourself in that conversation, you'll find nothing strange about assembling a research argument. That's because the five elements of any argument are just answers to the kinds of questions Abby asks Brett—and that you must ask yourself on your reader's behalf:

1. **Claim:** What do you want me to believe? What's your point?
2. **Reasons:** Why do you say that? Why should I agree?
3. **Evidence:** How do you know? Can you back it up?
4. **Acknowledgment and Response:** But what about . . . ?
5. **Warrant:** How does that follow? What's your logic? Can you explain your reasoning?

In fact, you can think of your research as the process of figuring out answers to these questions.

7.2 SUPPORTING YOUR CLAIM

At the core of every research argument is the answer to your research question, the solution to your problem—your main claim. You have to back up that claim with two kinds of support: reasons and evidence.

7.2.1 Support Claims with Reasons

The first kind of support, a reason, is a statement that leads readers to accept your claim. We often join a reason to a claim with *because*:

Clarifying Some Terms

So far, we've used two terms to name the statement that sums up the results of your research. In the context of questions, we called it your *answer.* In the context of problems, we called it your *solution.* Now in the context of an argument, we'll call it your *claim.*

- A *claim* is an assertion (which can be a single sentence or more) that demands support: *Climate change is threatening coastal cities; Toni Morrison's most important novel is* Beloved. Your *main claim* is the assertion your whole research argument supports. Some call this assertion your *thesis.*
- A *reason* is an assertion that supports a claim: *[Because] climate change is causing ocean levels to rise; [Because] in* Beloved, *Morrison's major themes find their fullest development.*
- *Evidence* is data deployed to support a reason. Unlike a claim or a reason, evidence is not always framed as an assertion: a data table documenting rising ocean levels over the past decade or quotations from *Beloved* illustrating Morrison's major themes would be forms of evidence.

These terms can be confusing, because a reason is also a subclaim that can be supported by more reasons and because both reasons and evidence are kinds of support. But if you stick with us, you'll see why these distinctions are important.

> Elementary schools should make teaching foreign languages a priority$_{\textit{claim}}$ because we acquire languages best and most easily when we are young.$_{\textit{reason}}$

You often need more than one reason to support a claim, and in a complex argument, your reasons themselves will usually require further support:

> Elementary schools should make teaching foreign languages a priority$_{\textit{claim 1}}$ because we acquire languages best and most easily when we are young.$_{\textit{reason 1 supporting claim 1/claim 2}}$ In fact, those who begin second

languages as adults rarely attain the level of fluency of those who learn them as children.*reason 2 supporting reason 1 and claim 2/claim 3* Teaching foreign languages at the elementary-school level also contributes to children's ethical development,*reason 3 supporting claim 1/claim 4* because it fosters an awareness of cultures and societies beyond their own.*reason 4 supporting reason 3 and claim 4/claim 5.*

7.2.2 Base Reasons on Evidence

The second kind of support is the evidence on which you base your reasons. We've said that reasons can be supported by still more reasons, but these chains don't go on forever. Eventually you have to show some data. That's your evidence. This distinction between reasons and evidence can seem just a matter of semantics, and in some contexts the words do seem interchangeable:

You have to base your claim on good reasons.

You have to base your claim on good evidence.

But they are not synonyms, and distinguishing them is crucial in making sound arguments. Compare these two sentences:

What evidence do you base your reason on?

What reason do you base your evidence on?

That second sentence seems odd: we don't base evidence on reasons; we base reasons on evidence.

There are other differences:

- We use our minds to think up reasons.
- We have to search for evidence "out there" in the world, then make it available for everyone to see.

It makes no sense to ask, *Where do I go to see your reasons?* It does make sense to ask, *Where do I go to see your evidence?*

In casual conversation, we usually support a claim with just a reason:

We should leave.*claim* It looks like rain.*reason*

Few ask, *What's your evidence that it looks like rain?* But when you address serious issues, readers expect you to base each reason on its own foundation of evidence, because careful readers don't accept reasons at face value. They ask for the evidence, the data, the facts on which you base those reasons:

> Elementary schools should make teaching foreign languages a priority *claim 1* because we acquire languages best and most easily when we are young. *reason 1 supporting claim 1/claim 2* In fact, those who begin second languages as adults rarely attain the level of fluency of those who learn them as children. *reason 2 supporting reason 1/claim 3* In a study of over one hundred second-language learners, Jones (2013) identified an inverse correlation between second-language proficiency and . . . (see table 1). *evidence supporting reason 2*

With reasons and evidence, we have the core of a research argument:

CLAIM *because of* → REASON *based on* → EVIDENCE

But in most cases, this core alone isn't enough: you also have to flesh out your research argument by *acknowledging and responding* to other points of view and, sometimes, by offering *warrants* that show how a reason is *relevant* to a claim.

7.3 ACKNOWLEDGING AND RESPONDING TO ANTICIPATED QUESTIONS AND OBJECTIONS

Careful readers will question *every* part of your argument, so you must anticipate as many of their questions as you can, and then acknowledge and respond to the most important ones. For example, when readers consider the claim that schools should make foreign-language instruction a priority, they may wonder if doing that might detract from the teaching of other subjects. If you think readers might ask that question, you would be wise to acknowledge and respond to it:

> Elementary schools should make foreign languages a priority *claim 1* because we acquire languages best and most easily when we are

> young.*reason 1 supporting claim 1/claim 2* . . . Of course, if schools increase the attention they give to foreign languages, quality of instruction in other subjects might decline.*acknowledgment* But little evidence exists to support that fear and much dispels it. . . .*response*

The challenge all researchers face, however, is not just responding to readers' questions, alternatives, and objections, but imagining them in the first place. (We'll address that issue in chapter 10.)

Since no research argument is complete without acknowledgments and responses, we add them to our diagram to show how they relate to all the other parts of an argument:

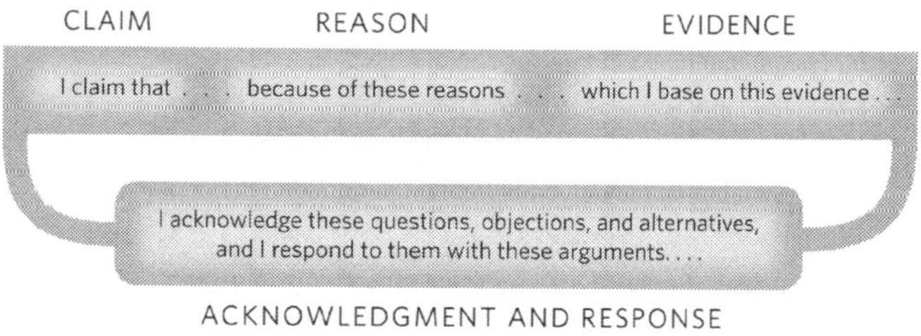
CLAIM
REASON
EVIDENCE
I claim that . . .
because of these reasons . . .
which I base on this evidence . . .
I acknowledge these questions, objections, and alternatives, and I respond to them with these arguments. . . .
ACKNOWLEDGMENT AND RESPONSE

7.4 CONNECTING CLAIMS AND REASONS WITH WARRANTS

Even when your readers agree that a reason is true, they may still object that it's not *relevant* to your claim. Consider this argument:

> We are facing significantly higher health care costs in Europe and North America*claim* because climate change is moving the line of extended hard freezes steadily northward.*reason*

Readers might accept the *truth* of that reason but question its *relevance* to the claim, asking: *What do higher health costs have to do with hard freezes? I don't see the connection.* To answer, you must offer a *general* principle that justifies relating your *particular* reason to your *particular* claim:

> When an area has fewer hard freezes, it must pay more to combat new diseases carried by subtropical insects no longer killed by those freezes.

Like all warrants, this one says that if a general circumstance exists (an area has fewer hard freezes), then we can infer a general consequence (that area will have higher costs to combat new diseases). The logic behind all warrants is that if a generalization is true or reasonable, then so must be specific instances of it.

But for that logic to work, readers must agree with four things. Two are easy to understand:

1. The warrant is true or reasonable: fewer hard freezes in fact mean higher medical costs.
2. The reason is true or reasonable: hard freezes in fact are moving north.

The next two are more difficult:

3. The specific circumstance in the reason qualifies as a *plausible instance* of the general circumstance in the warrant.
4. The specific consequence in the claim qualifies as a *plausible instance* of the general consequence in the warrant.

We can illustrate that logic like this:

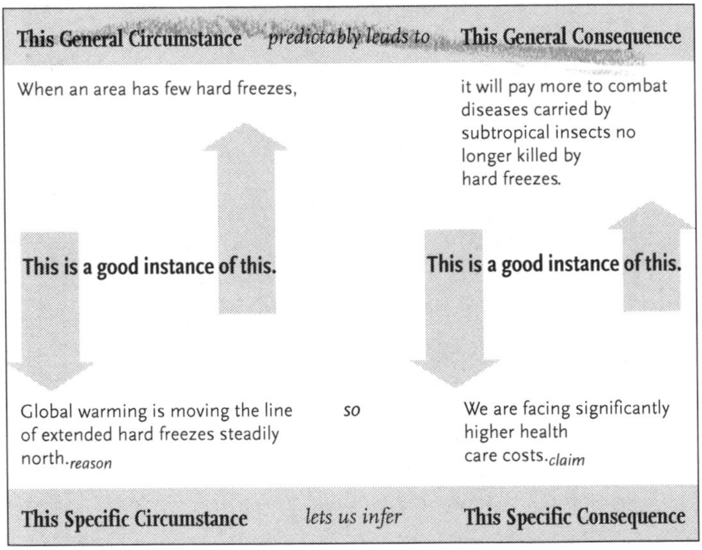

This General Circumstance
predictably leads to
This General Consequence
When an area has few hard freezes,
it will pay more to combat diseases carried by subtropical insects no longer killed by hard freezes.
This is a good instance of this.
This is a good instance of this.
Global warming is moving the line of extended hard freezes steadily north.reason
so
We are facing significantly higher health care costs.claim
This Specific Circumstance
lets us infer
This Specific Consequence

As we'll see, it's not easy to decide when you even need a warrant. Experienced researchers usually state them on only two occasions: when they think readers in their fields might ask how a reason is relevant to a claim or when they are explaining their fields' ways of reasoning to general readers. If you think your readers might not see the connection between a claim and reason, you must add a warrant to justify it:

> **When an area has fewer hard freezes, it can expect higher medical costs to cope with diseases carried by subtropical insects that do not survive freezes.***warrant* Europe and North America must thus expect higher health care costs *main claim* because climate change is moving the line of extended hard freezes steadily north. *reason* In the last one hundred years, the line of hard freezes lasting more than two weeks has moved north at the rate of roughly . . . *evidence*

We can add warrants to our diagram to show that they connect a claim and its supporting reason:

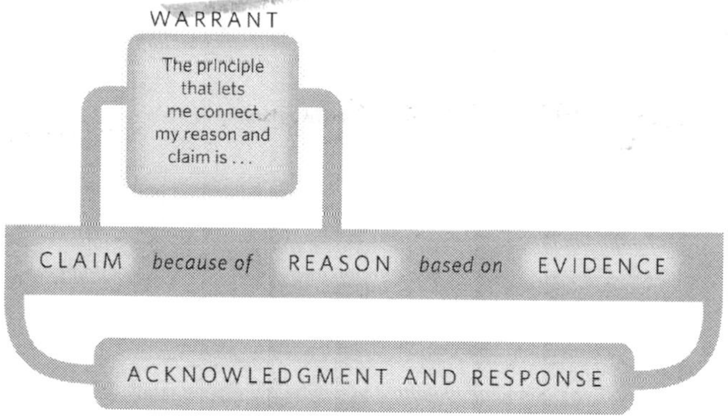

(We know this matter of warrants is not easy to grasp; we explain it again in more detail in chapter 11.)

7.5 BUILDING A COMPLEX ARGUMENT OUT OF SIMPLE ONES

Those five elements constitute a "basic" argument, but research arguments are more complex.

- We almost always support a claim with two or more reasons, each of which must be supported by its own additional reasons and evidence and perhaps justified by its own warrant.
- Since readers think of many alternatives and objections to any complex argument, careful researchers typically have to respond to a number of them.

Moreover, each reason, warrant, or response to an objection (all of which are statements or assertions) may itself have to be treated

Cognitive Overload: Some Reassuring Words

It's at about this point that many students new to research begin to feel overwhelmed. If so, your anxieties have less to do with your intelligence than with inexperience. One of us was explaining to teachers of legal writing how being a novice makes many first-year law students feel like incompetent writers. At the end of the talk, one woman reported that she had been a professor of anthropology whose published work was praised for the clarity of her writing. Then she switched careers and went to law school. She said that during her first six months, she wrote so incoherently that she feared she was suffering from a degenerative brain disease. Of course, she was not: she was going through the painful transition most of us experience when we try to write about matters we do not entirely understand for an audience we understand even less. She was relieved to find that the better she understood the law, the better she wrote about it.

If you feel overwhelmed, you can take comfort in that story, as did one reader who e-mailed us this:

> In *Craft of Research* you write about a woman who switched from anthropology to law and suddenly found herself unable to write clearly. After being an assistant professor of graphic design for five years, I recently switched to anthropology and suddenly found that writing anthropology papers is like pulling teeth. I thought to myself that I might have a degenerative brain disorder! I laughed out loud when I read about the anthropologist who switched to law. It made me feel a bit better.

as a subclaim and supported by its own argument. Only the evidence "stands alone," but even then you may have to explain where you got it, why you think it's reliable, and how it supports your reason—and that may require yet another argument.

And finally, most arguments also include background, definitions, explanations of issues that readers might not understand, and so on. If, for example, you were making an argument about the relationship between inflation and money supply to readers not familiar with economic theory, you would have to explain how economists understand those concepts. Serious arguments are complex constructions. (Chapters 8–11 explain them in detail.)

7.6 CREATING AN ETHOS BY THICKENING YOUR ARGUMENT

Readers judge your arguments not just by the reasons and evidence you offer but also by how well you anticipate and address their questions and concerns. By "thickening" your argument in this way, you earn the confidence of your readers, building up what is traditionally called your *ethos*: the character you project in your argument. Do you seem to be the sort of person who considers issues from all sides, who supports claims with evidence that readers accept, and who thoughtfully considers other points of view? Or do you seem to be someone who sees only one point of view and dismisses or even ignores the views of others?

When you acknowledge other views and explain your principles of reasoning in warrants, you give readers good reason to work *with* you in developing and testing new ideas. In the long run, the ethos you project in individual arguments hardens into your reputation, something every researcher must care about, because your reputation is the tacit sixth element in every argument you write. It answers the unspoken question, *Can I trust you?* That answer must be *Yes.*

QUICK TIP **A Common Mistake—Falling Back on What You Know**

If you are an inexperienced researcher, you may be tempted to rely too heavily on what feels familiar. For example, you might embrace a claim too early, perhaps even before you have done much research, because you "know" you can prove it. But falling back on that kind of certainty will just keep you from doing your best thinking. Being a researcher means allowing yourself to be surprised by your discoveries and insights. So when you start a project, begin not with a claim you know you can prove but with a problem you want to explore and solve.

Likewise, when you are new to a field, you may be tempted to rely on ways of arguing that are familiar to you from your education or experience. If, for example, you learned in a literature class how to present and analyze quotations, do not assume that you can do the same in fields that emphasize "objective data," such as biology or experimental psychology. On the other hand, if as a biology or psychology major you learned to gather hard data and perform statistical analyses, do not assume that you can do the same in art history. This does not mean that what you learn in one class is useless in another. All fields share the elements of argument we describe here. But you have to learn what's distinctive in the way a field handles those elements and be flexible enough to adapt, trusting the skills you've learned.

And when you become familiar with your field, you may be tempted to oversimplify in a different way. When some beginning researchers succeed at making one kind of argument, they just keep making it over and over. Their mastery of one kind of complexity blinds them to another: they fail to see that their field, if it is an active one, is marked by competing methodologies, competing solutions, competing goals and objectives. Don't fall into this trap. If you've mastered one type of argument, try others: seek out alternative methods, formulate not only multiple solutions but multiple ways of supporting them, ask whether others would approach your problem differently.

When you are new to a topic or a field, you need ways to manage the complexity of new ideas and new ways of thinking. But guard against uncritically imposing familiar methods on new problems. As you learn more, you'll recognize that things are neither as blindingly complex as you first feared nor as simple as you then hoped.

8 Making Claims

In this chapter, we discuss how to recognize the kind of claim that answers your research question and how to tell if your claim is specific and significant enough to serve as the main point of your argument.

You need a tentative answer to your research question to focus your search for evidence that will test and support its answer. As you test it, you will likely revise it, but as you assemble your argument, you must understand the kind of claim you are making. You must also be sure that your claim is not just sound, but significant enough to need an argument in the first place. Ask yourself three questions:

1. What kind of claim should I make?
2. Is it specific enough?
3. Will my readers think it is significant enough to need an argument supporting it?

When you can answer those three questions, you're ready to assemble your argument.

8.1 DETERMINING THE KIND OF CLAIM YOU SHOULD MAKE

The kind of problem you pose determines the kind of claim you make and the kind of argument you need to support it. As we saw in chapter 4, academic researchers usually pose not *practical* problems but *conceptual* ones, the kind whose solution asks readers not to *act* but to *understand*:

> The Great Recession of 2008-2011 was caused largely by negligent financial regulation that let banks take on too much risk.

8.1.1 Making Conceptual Claims

Beyond distinguishing between practical and conceptual claims, it is useful to recognize that claims address a range of questions: *Does a thing or a situation exist? If so, how should we characterize it? How did it get this way? Is it good or bad? What can or should be done about it?* Depending on the question or questions implicit in a claim, different kinds of evidence will be required to support it. The claims you make on a topic will fall into one (or more) of the following classes:

- Claims of fact or existence:

  Average global temperatures have risen to unprecedented levels within the past decade.

- Claims of definition and classification:

  Birds, not reptiles, are the direct descendants of dinosaurs.

- Claims of cause and consequence:

  Exposure to asbestos is a leading contributor to lung cancer.

- Claims of evaluation or appraisal:

  Shakespeare's greatest comedy is *As You Like It*.

- Claims of action or policy:

  Pennsylvania should increase extraction fees on natural gas drilling to fund education.

The first four classes—fact, definition, cause, and value—concern conceptual claims. For claims of fact or existence, you must provide evidence that a situation is, in fact, as you characterize it. Claims of definition or classification depend on reasoning about similarities or differences that assigns an entity to some broader class or distinguishes it from other entities. Effective claims of evaluation or appraisal depend on criteria of judgment to justify why something is good or bad (or better or worse than something else). Finally, claims of cause or consequence connect sets of facts to show that some situation does (or doesn't) follow from or lead to another.

8.1.2 Making Practical Claims

A practical claim is one that argues for (or against) some action or policy. It is usually built from a chain of conceptual claims: one that demonstrates that a problem exists, another that shows what causes the problem, and still another that explains how doing what you propose will fix it. Readers may also expect you to explain the following:

- Why your solution is feasible; how it can be implemented with reasonable time and effort.
- Why it will cost less to implement than the cost of the problem.
- Why it will not create a bigger problem than the one it solves.
- Why it is cheaper or faster than alternative solutions—a claim often difficult to support.

If you advance a practical claim but don't make those four subarguments, your readers may reject your whole argument.

So as you assemble your argument, be clear about the kinds of claims you are making, whether conceptual or practical. Don't inflate the importance of a conceptual claim by tacking on a practical action, at least not early in your paper. If you want to suggest a practical application of your conceptual claim, do so in your conclusion. There, you can offer it as an action worth considering without having to develop a case for it (we return to this in chapter 16).

8.2 EVALUATING YOUR CLAIM

We can't tell you how to find a good claim, but we can show you how to evaluate the one you have from the point of view of your readers. Above all, they expect your claim to be both specific and significant.

8.2.1 Make Your Claim Specific

Vague claims lead to vague arguments. The more specific your claim, the more it helps you plan your argument and keep your readers on track as they read it. You make a claim more specific through precise language and explicit logic.

Precise Language. Compare these two claims:

> TV inflates estimates of crime rates.
>
> Graphic reports of violence on local TV news lead regular viewers to overestimate by as much as 150 percent both the rate of crime in their neighborhood and the personal danger to themselves and their families.

The first claim is so vague that we have little idea about what's to come. The second has more specific concepts that not only help readers understand the claim more clearly, but also give the writer a richer set of concepts to develop in what follows. Indeed, the precision of the claim signals how the argument is likely to proceed.

We do *not* recommend long, wordy claims for their own sake. But you benefit when you include in early versions of your claim more terms than you might ultimately use. That final claim should be only as specific as your readers need and should include only those concepts that you develop as themes in your argument.

Explicit Logic. You can also be explicit in the logic of your claim. Even with its relatively precise language, this claim offers only a single proposition:

> Regular TV viewers overestimate both the rate of crime in their neighborhood and the personal danger to themselves and their families.

In the natural and social sciences, claims like that are common, even preferred. But in the humanities, such a claim might seem a bit thin. As you draft your working claim, try elaborating its logic in two ways:

- Introduce it with a qualifying clause beginning with *although* or *even though.*
- Conclude it with a reason-clause beginning with *because.*

For example:

> **Although violent crime is actually decreasing,** regular TV viewers over estimate their neighborhood crime rate by 150 percent and therefore

misjudge personal danger to themselves and their families **because local TV evening news regularly opens with graphic reports of mayhem and murder in familiar locations, making many believe that crime happens nightly outside their front door.**

While that claim may seem overwritten, it foreshadows three of the five elements that you need for a full argument: (1) *Although I acknowledge X,* (2) *I claim Y* (3) *because of reason Z.*

You can use an introductory *although* clause to acknowledge three kinds of alternative views:

- Something that your readers believe but your claim challenges:

  Although most people believe they are good judges of their security, regular TV viewers overestimate . . .

- A point of view that conflicts with yours:

  Although many security professionals see fear as the best motivation for safety precautions, regular TV viewers overestimate . . .

- A condition that limits the scope or confidence of your claim:

  Although it is difficult to gauge their real feelings about personal security, regular TV viewers overestimate . . .

If readers might think of those qualifications, acknowledge them first. You not only imply that you understand their views, but commit yourself to responding to them in the course of your argument.

When you add a final *because* clause, you forecast some of the reasons that support your claim:

> Although many believe that school uniforms help lower the incidence of violence in public schools,$_{qualification}$ the evidence is at best weak$_{claim}$ **because researchers have not controlled for other measures that have been instituted at the same time as uniforms**$_{reason\ 1}$ **and because the data reported are statistically suspect.**$_{reason\ 2}$

Again, we don't suggest that your final draft should offer a claim as bloated as these. But the richer your *working* claim, the more satisfying your argument is likely to be.

8.2.2 Make Your Claim Significant

After the specificity of a claim, readers look most closely at its *significance,* a quality they measure by how much it asks them to change what they think. While we can't quantify significance, we can roughly estimate it: *if readers accept a claim, how many other beliefs must they change?* The most significant claims ask a research community to change its deepest beliefs (and it will resist such claims accordingly).

Some research communities consider a claim significant enough if it asks them only to accept new evidence on a topic of common interest:

> I describe here six thirteenth-century Latin grammars of the Welsh language. Found just recently, these grammars are the only examples of their kind. They help us better appreciate the range of grammars written in the medieval period.

(Recall those reels of newly discovered film in 2.3.3.)

Readers value research more highly when it not only offers new data but *uses* those data to settle what seems puzzling, inconsistent, or otherwise problematic:

> There has been a long debate about how fluctuations in consumer confidence affect the stock market, but new statistical tools suggest little relationship between . . .

But readers value most highly when new facts or conjectures *upset* what seems long settled:

> It has long been an article of faith in modern physics that the speed of light is constant everywhere at all times, under all conditions, but new data suggest it might not be.

A claim like that would be contested by legions of physicists because if true, it would mean that physicists would have to change their minds not just about the speed of light but about lots of other things as well.

Early in your career, you won't be expected to know what those in a field think should (or even could) be revised. But you can still gauge the significance of your claim by asking how strongly readers might *contest* it. One way to do that is by considering *opposite* claims:

> Hamlet is not a superficial character.
>
> This report summarizes recent research on the disappearance of bees.

To assess how much either claim is worth contesting, change an affirmative claim into a negative one and vice versa:

> Hamlet *is* a superficial character.
>
> This report does *not* summarize recent research on the disappearance of bees.

If the reverse of a claim seems obviously false (like the first one) or trivial (like the second), then readers are likely to think the original claim is not worth an argument. (Of course, some great thinkers have successfully contradicted apparently self-evident claims, as Copernicus did when he asserted foolishly—or so it seemed at the time—that *the sun does* not *go around the earth.*)

If you are an advanced researcher, you measure the significance of your claim by how much it changes what your community thinks and how it does its research. Few discoveries have been as significant as Crick and Watson's structure of DNA. Not only did it make biologists think about genetics differently, but it opened up new lines of research.

But you don't have to make big claims to make a useful contribution: small findings can open up new lines of thinking. If, for example, you discovered that Abraham Lincoln read some obscure philosopher, historians would comb Lincoln's texts for traces of that influence.

If you are new to research, of course, your claim doesn't have to challenge the experts, just impress your teacher. If you can't predict whether it will, imagine your reader is someone like yourself. What did *you* think before you began your research? How much has your claim changed what *you* now think? What do *you* understand now that you didn't before? That's the best way to prepare for readers who will someday ask you the most devastating question any researcher can face: not *Why should I believe this?* but *Why should I care?*

8.3 QUALIFYING CLAIMS TO ENHANCE YOUR CREDIBILITY

Some new researchers think their claims are most credible when they are stated most forcefully. But nothing damages your ethos more than arrogant certainty. As paradoxical as it seems, you make your argument stronger and more credible by modestly acknowledging its limits. You gain the trust of your readers when you acknowledge and respond to their views, showing that you have not only understood but considered their position (for more, see chapter 10). But you can lose that trust if you then make claims that overreach. Limit your claims to what your argument can actually support by qualifying their scope and certainty.

8.3.1 Acknowledge Limiting Conditions

Every claim has limiting conditions:

> We conclude that the epicenter of the earthquake was fifty miles southwest of Tokyo, **assuming the instrumentation was accurately calibrated.**
>
> We believe that aviation manufacturing will not match its late twentieth-century levels, **unless new global conflicts increase military spending.**

But every claim is subject to countless conditions, so mention only those that readers might plausibly think of. Scientists rarely acknowledge that their claims depend on the accuracy of their instruments, because everyone expects them to ensure that they are. But economists often acknowledge limits on their claims, both because their predictions are subject to changing conditions and because readers want to know which conditions to watch for.

Consider mentioning important limiting conditions even if you feel readers would not think of them. For example, in this next example, the writer not only shows that she was careful but gives a fuller and more accurate statement of the claim:

> Today Franklin D. Roosevelt is revered as one of our most admired historical figures, but toward the end of his second term, he was

> quite unpopular, **at least among certain segments of American society.***claim* Newspapers, for example, attacked him for promoting socialism, a sign that a modern administration is in trouble. In 1938, 70 percent of Midwest newspapers accused him of wanting the government to manage the banking system. . . . Some have argued otherwise, including Nicholson (1983, 1992) and Wiggins (1973), both of whom offer anecdotal reports that Roosevelt was always in high regard,*acknowledgment* but these reports are supported only by the memories of those who had an interest in deifying FDR.*response* **Unless it can be shown that the newspapers critical of Roosevelt were controlled by special interests,***limitation on claim* their attacks demonstrate significant popular dissatisfaction with Roosevelt's presidency.*restatement of claim*

8.3.2 Use Hedges to Limit Certainty

Only rarely can we state in good conscience that we are 100 percent certain that our claims are unqualifiedly true. Careful writers qualify their certainty with words and phrases called *hedges*. For example, if anyone was entitled to be assertive, it was Crick and Watson, the discoverers of the helical structure of DNA. But when they announced their discovery, they hedged the certainty of their claims (hedges are boldfaced; the introduction is condensed):

> We **wish to suggest a** [note: not *state the*] structure for the salt of deoxyribose nucleic acid (D.N.A.). . . . A structure for nucleic acid has already been proposed by Pauling and Corey. . . . **In our opinion,** this structure is unsatisfactory for two reasons: (1) **We believe** that the material which gives the X-ray diagrams is the salt, not the free acid. . . . (2) **Some** of the van der Waals distances **appear** to be too small. (J. D. Watson and F. H. C. Crick, "Molecular Structure of Nucleic Acids")

Without the hedges, Crick and Watson would be more concise but more aggressive. Compare that cautious passage with this more forceful version (much of the aggressive tone comes from the *lack* of qualification):

> We **announce** here **the** structure for the salt of deoxyribose nucleic acid (D.N.A.). . . . A structure for nucleic acid has already been proposed by

> Pauling and Corey. . . . Their structure **is** unsatisfactory for two reasons: (1) The material which gives their X-ray diagrams is the salt, not the free acid. . . . (2) Their van der Waals distances **are** too small.

Of course, if you hedge too much, you will seem timid or uncertain. But in most fields, readers distrust flatfooted certainty expressed in words like *all, no one, every, always, never,* and so on. Some teachers say they object to all hedging, but what most of them really reject are hedges that qualify every trivial claim. And some fields do tend to use fewer hedges than others. It takes a deft touch. Hedge too much and you seem mealy-mouthed; hedge too little and you can seem overconfident. Unfortunately, the line between the two is thin. So watch how those in your field manage uncertainty and do likewise.

9 Assembling Reasons and Evidence

In this chapter, we discuss two kinds of support for a claim: reasons and evidence. We show you how to distinguish between the two, how to use reasons to organize your argument, and how to evaluate the quality of your evidence.

Readers look first for the core of an argument, a claim and its support. They look particularly at its set of reasons to judge its plausibility and their order to judge its logic. If they think those reasons make sense, they will look at the evidence you present, the bedrock of every argument. If they don't believe the evidence, they'll reject the reasons and, with them, your claim.

So as you assemble your argument, you must offer readers a plausible set of reasons, in a clear, logical order, based on evidence they will accept. This chapter shows you how to do that.

9.1 USING REASONS TO PLAN YOUR ARGUMENT

When you order your reasons, you build a logical structure for your argument. To test that structure, you can make a traditional outline or visualize your plan in other ways. You might find it useful to create a chart-like outline known as a "storyboard." To start a storyboard, write your main claim and each reason (and subreasons) at the top of separate index cards or pages. Then below each reason (or subreason), list the evidence that supports it. If you don't have the evidence yet, note the *kind* of evidence you'll need. Finally, arrange the pages or index cards on a table or wall to make their logical relationships visible at a glance.

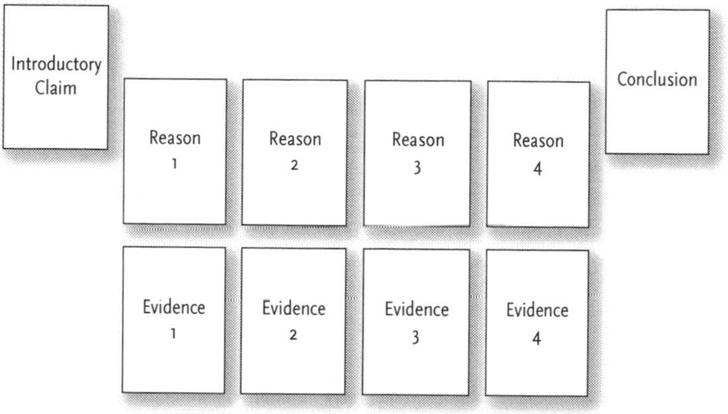

Read just the reasons, not the details, to see if that order makes sense. If it doesn't, try out different orders until it does. At this point, you are outlining only your argument, not your paper. When you turn to a first draft, you will reconsider your reasons in light of your readers' understanding (and yours) and perhaps arrange a new order (for more on ordering parts, see 12.1.3).

9.2 DISTINGUISHING EVIDENCE FROM REASONS

Once you've arranged your reasons in a plausible order, be sure you have sufficient evidence to support each one. Readers will not accept a reason until they see it anchored in what *they* consider to be a bedrock of established fact. The problem is, you don't get to decide that; your readers *do*. To count as evidence, a statement must report something that readers agree not to question, at least for the purposes of the argument. But if they do question it, what you think is hard factual evidence is for them only a reason, and you have not yet reached that bedrock of evidence on which your argument must rest.

Consider this argument:

> American higher education must curb escalating tuition costs,*claim* because the price of college is becoming an impediment to realizing the American dream.*reason* **Today a majority of students leave college with a crushing debt burden.***evidence*

In that last sentence, the writer offers what she believes is a "fact" hard enough to serve as evidence to support her reason.

But a skeptical reader might ask, *That's just a generalization. What hard numbers do you have to back up "a majority of students" or "crushing debt burden"?* Such a reader treats that statement not as an unquestioned fact but as a soft reason still in need of hard evidence. The writer would have to add something like this:

> In 2013, nearly 70 percent of students borrowed money for college with loans averaging $30,000, a debt that prevents many from buying a home, beginning a family, or pursuing a higher degree.*evidence*

Of course a *really* skeptical reader could again ask, *What backs up those numbers? What justifies the claim that this situation is a crisis?* If so, the writer would have to provide still harder data, breaking down those numbers to document the consequences of debt for recent graduates. If she did her own research, she could show her raw data. If she found her data in a secondary source, she could cite it, but she might then be asked to prove that her source is reliable. Really skeptical readers just never give up.

If you can imagine readers plausibly asking, not once but many times, *How do you know that? What facts make it true?*, you have not yet reached what readers want—a bedrock of uncontested evidence. And at a time when so-called experts are quick to tell us

Our Foundational Metaphors for Evidence

When we talk about evidence, we typically use foundational metaphors: good evidence is *solid, hard, the bedrock foundation* on which we *build* arguments, something we can *see for ourselves*. Bad evidence is *flimsy, weak,* or *thin*. Language like that encourages readers to think of evidence as a reality independent of anyone's interpretation and judgment. But data are always constructed and shaped by those who collect and use them as evidence. As you build your argument, keep in mind that your evidence will *count* as evidence only if your readers accept it without question, at least for the moment.

what to do and think based on studies whose data we never see, careful readers have learned to view reports of evidence skeptically. Even when you think you have good evidence, be clear how it was collected and by whom. If it was collected by others, find and cite a source as close to the evidence as you can get.

9.3 DISTINGUISHING EVIDENCE FROM REPORTS OF IT

Now a complication: researchers rarely include in any report *the evidence itself*. Even if you collect your own data, counting rabbits in a field or interviewing the unemployed, your paper can only *refer to* or *represent* those rabbits and unemployed in words, numbers, tables, graphs, pictures, and so on. For example, when a prosecutor says in court, *Jones was a drug dealer, and here is the evidence to prove it,* he can hold up a bag of cocaine, even let jurors hold it in their own hands. (Of course, both he and the jurors must believe the officer who says it's the same bag he took from Jones and the chemist who says that the white stuff really is cocaine.) But when he *writes* a brief on the case, he cannot staple that bag to the page; he can only refer to or describe it.

In the same way, researchers cannot share with their readers "the evidence itself." For example:

> Emotions play a larger role in rationality than many think.*claim* In fact, without the emotional centers of the brain, we could not make rational decisions.*reason 1 supporting claim* Persons whose brains have suffered physical damage to their emotional centers cannot make the simplest decisions.*reason 2 supporting reason 1* For example, consider the case of Mr. Y, who . . .*report of evidence*

That argument doesn't offer as evidence real people with damaged brains; it can only report observations of their behavior, copies of their brain scans, tables of their reaction times, and so on. (In fact, we prefer to read reports of others than to have to test brains and read MRI scans ourselves.)

We know this distinction between evidence and reports of evidence must seem like a fine one, but it emphasizes two important issues. First, data you take from a source have invariably been shaped by that source, not to misrepresent them, but to put them in a form that serves that source's ends. For example, suppose you want to show that the cult of celebrity distorts rational compensation, and you need evidence that athletes and entertainers are paid far more than top doctors, generals, and government officials. You could find government salaries in official reports. But unless you can peek at the tax returns of Oprah and Tiger Woods (and who knows how reliable they would be), you would have to depend on reports of those incomes that may or may not have been systematically collected and compiled from still more distant reports. Unless you can talk to those who counted, organized, and reported the original data, you'll be at three or four removes from the evidence itself before you use it for your own purposes. (And at least one reporter in that chain of reports almost certainly miscopied some of the data.)

Second, when you in turn report those data as your own evidence, you cannot avoid manipulating them once again, at least by putting them in a new context. Even if you collected the data yourself, you tidied them up, making them seem more coherent than what you actually saw, counted, and recorded in your notes. In fact, even before you started collecting any facts at all, you had to decide what to count, how to categorize the numbers, how to order them, whether to present them in the form of a table, bar chart, or graph. Even photographs and video recordings reflect a particular point of view. In short, facts are shaped by those who collect them and again by the intentions of those who use them.

This often squishy quality of reports of reports (of reports of reports) is why people who read lots of research are so demanding about the reliability of evidence. If you collect data yourself, they'll want to know how you did it. If you depend on sources, they'll expect you to use primary sources, and if you didn't, to get as close to primary sources as you can. And they want complete citations and a bibliography so that they could, if they wanted to, look at your sources themselves. In short, they want to know that they can trust the complete chain of reports between what's "out there" and what they are reading.

Trusting Evidence Three Hundred Years Ago and Now

In the early days of experimental science, researchers conducted experiments before what they called "witnesses," reputable scientists who observed the experiments so that they could attest to the accuracy of the reported evidence. Researchers don't rely on witnesses anymore. Instead, each area of study has standardized its methodologies for collecting and reporting evidence to ensure that it is reliable (though some researchers still get away with fraud). When you observe the standard procedures in your field, you encourage readers to accept your evidence at your word, without their needing to see it themselves. So as you read secondary sources, note the kind of evidence they cite, how they cite it, then do likewise. When in sociology, do as sociologists do.

We live in an age where we are all subjected to research reports and opinion surveys that are at best dubious and at worst faked, so you have to assure your readers that they can trust your data. The last link in that chain of credibility is you, so be thoughtful about whose data you use and how you use them.

9.4 EVALUATING YOUR EVIDENCE

Once you know the kind of evidence your readers expect, you must test the reliability of yours: is it *sufficient* and *representative*, reported *accurately* and *precisely*, and taken from an *authoritative* source? These are not exotic criteria unique to academic research. We all apply them in our most ordinary conversations, even with children. In the following, "Parent" faults "Child" on all those criteria:

CHILD: I need new sneakers.$_{claim}$ Look. These are too small.$_{evidence}$

PARENT: Your feet haven't grown that much in a month, and they don't seem to hurt you much [*i.e., your evidence could be relevant, but I reject it because it is not accurate and because even if it were accurate, "too small" is not sufficiently precise*].

CHILD: But they're too grungy for school.$_{reason}$ Look at this dirt and these raggedy laces.$_{evidence}$

PARENT: The dirt will wash off and the laces can be replaced. That's not enough to buy new sneakers [*i.e., you may be factually correct, but dirt and raggedy laces alone are not sufficient evidence that they are unfit for school*].

CHILD: They hurt.$_{reason}$ Look at how I limp.$_{evidence}$

PARENT: You were walking fine a minute ago [*i.e., your evidence is not representative*].

CHILD: Everybody thinks I should get new sneakers.$_{reason}$ Harry said so.$_{evidence}$

PARENT: Harry's opinion doesn't matter in this house [*i.e., Harry may have said that, but his opinions are not authoritative*].

Readers judge reports of evidence by the same criteria a parent uses with a child. They want evidence to be accurate, precise, sufficient, representative, and authoritative. (Readers also expect evidence to be *relevant*, but we'll discuss that in chapter 11.) As you assemble your evidence, screen it for those criteria before you add it to your storyboard.

9.4.1 Report Evidence Accurately

Careful readers are predisposed to be skeptical, so they will seize on the most trivial mistake in your evidence as a sign of your unreliability in everything else. Whether your research argument depends on data collected in a lab, in the field, in the library, or online, record those data completely and clearly, then double-check them before, as, and after you write them up. Getting the easy things right shows respect for your readers and is the best training for dealing with the hard things. You can sometimes use even questionable evidence, *if you acknowledge its dubious quality.* In fact, if you point to evidence that seems to support your claim but then reject it as unreliable, you show yourself to be cautious, self-critical, and thus trustworthy.

9.4.2 Be Appropriately Precise

Your readers want you to state your evidence precisely. They hear warning bells in words that hedge your claim in such a way that they cannot assess its substance:

> The Forest Service has spent **a great deal** of money to prevent forest fires, but there is still **a high probability** of **large, costly** ones.

How much money is *a great deal*? How probable is *a high probability*—30 percent? 80 percent? What counts as *large* and *costly*? Watch for words like *some, most, many, almost, often, usually, frequently, generally*, and so on. Such words can appropriately limit the breadth of a claim (see 8.3), but they can also fudge it if the researcher didn't work hard enough to get the precise numbers.

What counts as precise, however, differs by field. A physicist measures the life of quarks in fractions of a nanosecond, so the tolerable margin of error is vanishingly small. A historian gauging when the Soviet Union was at the point of collapse would estimate it in months. A paleontologist might date a new species give or take tens of thousands of years. According to the standards of their fields, all three are appropriately precise. (Evidence can also be too precise. Only a foolhardy historian would assert that the Soviet Union reached its point of inevitable collapse at 2:13 p.m. on August 18, 1987.)

9.4.3 Provide Sufficient, Representative Evidence

Beginners typically offer too little evidence. They think they prove a claim with one quotation, one number, one personal experience (though sometimes only one bit of evidence is sufficient to *disprove* it). For example:

> Shakespeare must have hated women because those in *Hamlet* and *Macbeth* are evil or weak.

Readers need more than that to accept such a significant claim.

Even if you offer lots of evidence, your readers still expect it to be *representative* of the full range of variation in what's available. The women in one or two Shakespearean plays do not represent all his women, any more than Shakespeare represents all Elizabethan drama. Readers are especially wary when your evidence is a small sample from a large body of data, as in surveys. Whenever you use sampled data, not only must your data *be* representative, but you must *show* that it is.

A charge related to the claim that your evidence is unrepresentative is that it is *anecdotal.* It *might* be representative but, then again, it might not. If your claim depends on one or two examples, however well-chosen to be representative, there is a risk that your evidence will be dismissed as a form of cherry-picking. Of course, anecdotal evidence can be persuasive in ways that statistical representations of data are not. The very persuasiveness of the telling example, the case study, or the exception that proves the rule makes argument by anecdote attractive but also risky because an argument is only as strong as its evidence.

9.4.4 Consider the Weight of Authority

Different fields define and evaluate evidence differently. If you're a beginner, you'll need time to learn the kinds of evidence that readers in your field accept and reject. The most painful way to gain that experience is to be the object of their criticism. Less painful is to seek examples of arguments that failed because their evidence was judged unreliable. Listen to lectures and class discussions for the kinds of arguments that your instructors criticize because they think that the evidence is weak. Failed arguments help you understand what counts as reliable better than do successful ones.

A particular kind of weak evidence comes from sources that readers do not consider authoritative. Early in the twentieth century, New Yorkers accepted the word of a local newspaper: "If you see it in the *Sun,* it's so." In general, readers assign degrees of authority to sources based on their reputation for rigor and objectivity. For example, most people will accept data on the transmission of viruses that a researcher obtains from the U.S. Centers for Disease Control as credible evidence, even allowing for the possibility of error. However, evidence from *Wikipedia* will not be accepted in many circles because *Wikipedia* is not regarded as authoritative. "Consider the source" is the skeptic's rebuttal to evidence dismissed for lack of authority.

10 Acknowledgments and Responses

An argument is not complete if it fails to recognize other points of view. This chapter shows how you can make your argument more convincing by acknowledging and responding to questions, objections, and alternatives your readers might raise.

The core of your argument is a claim backed by reasons based on evidence. You thicken it with more reasons, perhaps supporting each with additional subreasons and evidence. But if you give your readers only claims, reasons, and evidence—no matter how compelling these are to you—they may still find your argument thin or, worse, ignorant or dismissive of their views. To craft a successful argument, you must do more than assemble a sound edifice of claims, reasons, and evidence; you must also position those claims as contributions to an ongoing conversation in which your readers are invested (see chapter 7).

You can do this in your introduction by presenting your main claim as a solution to a problem your readers care about (we'll talk more about introductions in chapter 16). But you can do it throughout your argument as well by anticipating, acknowledging, and responding to questions, objections, and alternatives that your readers are likely to raise along the way. As you plan and draft your paper, your readers won't be there to question you or to offer their own views. So you have to *imagine* their questions and views and take them into account. That's how you establish a cooperative relationship with readers, by imagining yourself conversing with them.

In this chapter, we show you how to imagine and address two kinds of questions that readers may ask about your argument:

- They may question its *intrinsic* soundness by challenging the clarity of your claim, the relevance of your reasons, or the quality of your evidence.
- They may question its *extrinsic* soundness by asking you to consider alternatives—different ways of framing the problem, evidence you've overlooked, or what others have written on your topic.

When you anticipate, acknowledge, and respond to both kinds of questions, you create an argument that readers are more likely to trust and accept.

10.1 QUESTIONING YOUR ARGUMENT AS YOUR READERS WILL

When planning and drafting your argument, you may freeze up if you try from the outset to imagine every possible reaction to it. Therefore, focus first on what you yourself want to say, on the claims, reasons, and evidence that make up your argument's core. Once you have that core, try to imagine readers' responses to it. Doing this may be hard, because you know your own argument too well and may believe in it too much to seriously challenge it. If you can share the core of your argument with a friend, mentor, or colleague you trust, do it. That will help you identify questions, objections, and alternatives that other readers might raise. If you can't, then imagine a group of particularly skeptical hypothetical readers questioning your argument more sharply than you hope your actual readers will.

For this exercise, you might suspend your conception of argument as collaborative inquiry and imagine it not quite as warfare, but as something close to a warm debate. View your argument through the eyes of someone who has a stake in a different outcome, someone who *wants* you to be wrong.

First, examine your problem. Here are some questions with possible answers from an imagined reader:

1. *Why do you think there's a problem at all?* "The costs or consequences of the situation you are responding to don't seem that significant."

2. *Have you properly defined the problem? Is it practical or conceptual?* "Maybe the problem involves not the issue you raise but another one."

Then consider your solution:

3. *Is your solution practical or conceptual? That is, does it ask readers to do something or to understand something? And does it match the problem (practical problems demand practical solutions; conceptual problems conceptual ones)?* "You explain what's wrong, but you don't say how we can change it." "You assert that our current understanding falls short, but you don't offer a new way of looking at the issue."
4. *Have you stated your claim too strongly?* "I can think of exceptions and limitations."

5a. *Why is your practical solution better than others?* "I think that what you propose will cost too much and create new problems."

5b. *Why is your conceptual solution better than others?* "It doesn't seem to fit with all this other well-established knowledge."

If you come up with a question that you can't answer, decide whether you can find the answer before you go on. Don't go easy on yourself with this one: the time to fix a problem with your argument is when you find it.

Note where your argument might seem weak but actually isn't. If, for example, you anticipate that readers will think your solution has costs that it does not, you can defuse that concern by acknowledging and responding to it:

> It might seem that by focusing on the actions of specific banks, we are minimizing the systemic forces that contributed to the financial crisis, but, in fact, our case studies will show . . .

Next, question your support. Imagine a reader challenging your evidence. A reader might question its nature:

1. "I want to see a different *sort* of evidence—hard numbers, not anecdotes (or stories about real people, not cold numbers)."

If you present the right kind of evidence, a reader might still question its quality:

2. "It isn't accurate. The numbers don't add up."
3. "It isn't precise enough. What do you mean by 'many'?"
4. "It isn't current. There's newer research than this."
5. "It isn't representative. You didn't get data on all the groups."
6. "It isn't authoritative. Smith is no expert on this matter."

The toughest objection, however, is usually this one:

7. "You need more evidence. One data point (quotation/number/anecdote) is not sufficient."

Most researchers have difficulty finding enough good evidence to make a solid case, especially those working on short deadlines. But teachers grumble most about students who seem to think that the evidence they find first is all they need.

Readers can be particularly skeptical when they have a stake in a solution that differs from yours. So if you feel your evidence is less than unassailable, you may want to admit its limitations candidly, before readers reject your argument because you overstated it.

Finally, readers may not see how your reasons support your claims, or how your claim follows from your reasons. We devote all of chapter 11 to this problem.

In sum, when assembling your argument, test your claims, reasons, and evidence as your most skeptical readers will—and even in ways they might not. You can then address at least the most important objections that you can imagine them raising. Show readers that you put your argument through your own wringer before they put it through theirs.

10.2 IMAGINING ALTERNATIVES TO YOUR ARGUMENT

When you recognize your own argument's limitations, you build credibility by showing readers that you are making an honest case and dealing with them fairly. But that's just a defensive move. You will seem even more credible if you show not just that you understand the strengths and limitations of your own argument, but that you also understand and have thought about the alternatives to it. To do that, you have to bring those alternative views into your argument by acknowledging and responding to them.

If you know your subject and readers very well, you can try to imagine those alternatives yourself. But usually the best way to identify alternative views is to look to your sources. In chapter 6, we encouraged you to actively *engage* your sources during your research, to use them not just for data but to stimulate your own thinking. Your sources also offer a ready supply of alternative views that you can respond to in your own argument.

You can think of your secondary sources as a written record of the conversation about your topic, question, or problem. Knowing that conversation allows you to contribute to it. When you read your sources, note where they advance claims different from yours, take different approaches, focus on different aspects of the problem, and so on. Note especially where—and why—you and your sources disagree. Also note where one source disagrees with another. All those disagreements can help you identify alternatives to acknowledge in your own argument. If you know how you would respond to a particular source, add that response to your notes as you read.

You can respond not only to your sources' claims but also to their evidence. If you find a source's evidence unreliable or irrelevant, don't simply ignore it. If your readers might take it seriously, you can acknowledge it but explain why you didn't use it.

Finally, your sources also help you imagine your readers and anticipate their reactions to your argument. Often your readers will be like your sources' authors; sometimes they may even include them.

10.3 DECIDING WHAT TO ACKNOWLEDGE

If you can imagine just a few of the questions, alternatives, and objections that your readers might have, you'll face a Goldilocks moment: acknowledge too many and you distract readers from the core of your argument; acknowledge too few and you seem indifferent to or even ignorant of their views. You need to figure out how many acknowledgments will feel "just right."

10.3.1 Choosing What to Respond To

To narrow your list of alternatives or objections, consider these priorities:

- plausible charges of weaknesses that you can rebut
- alternative lines of argument important in your field
- alternative conclusions that readers *want* to be true
- alternative evidence that readers know
- important counterexamples that you have to address

Look for alternatives that let you repeat a part of your argument. For example, if readers might think of exceptions to a definition that in fact are not, acknowledge them and use the response to reinforce your point:

> Some have argued that even food can be addictive, but remember we are concerned here only with substances for which addiction is the norm, not those . . .

Or if readers might think of an alternative solution close to yours, use it to reiterate the virtues of your solution:

> Most researchers argue that rules and other forms of formal writing advice degrade rather than improve performance because writing "is a non-conscious act of making meaning, not a conscious process of following rules." That is true for parts of the process: writers should not consult rules as they draft sentences. But writing involves not just drafting but many conscious processes as well. What we show here is what kinds of formal advice do and do not work for *conscious* aspects of writing. . . .

Finally, acknowledge alternatives that may particularly appeal to your readers, but only if you can respond without seeming to be dismissive. Better to ignore what your readers like than to disparage it.

10.3.2 Acknowledging Flaws in Your Argument

If you discover a flaw in your argument that you cannot fix or explain away, try to redefine your problem or rebuild your argument to avoid it. But if you cannot, you face a tough decision. You could just ignore the flaw and hope your readers don't notice it. But that's dishonest. If they do notice it, they will doubt your competence, and if they think you tried to hide it, they will question your honesty. Our advice may seem naive, but it works: candidly acknowledge the issue and respond that

- the rest of your argument more than balances the flaw.
- while the flaw is serious, more research will show a way around it.
- while the flaw makes it impossible to accept your claim fully, your argument offers important insight into the question and suggests what a better answer would need.

Occasionally researchers turn failure into success by treating a claim they wanted to support but couldn't as a hypothesis that others might find reasonable. Then they show why it isn't:

> It might seem that when jurors hear the facts of a case in a form that focuses on the victim and emphasizes her suffering, they will be more likely to blame the accused. That is, after all, the standard practice of plaintiffs' lawyers. But in fact, we found no correlation between . . .

10.3.3 Acknowledging Questions You Can't Answer

Beginning researchers sometimes think that their goal is to have the last word on a topic, that is, to make an argument that allows for no response but total assent. But that's a mistake. Experienced researchers and teachers understand that no argument is entirely unassailable and that any one version of the truth is often complicated and always contestable. In fact, the most stimulating research is often that which provides not answers to questions we already know, but new sets of questions we haven't yet thought to ask. This is especially true for research addressing conceptual problems, but it can be true for applied research as well.

Knowledgeable readers will think better of your argument and of you if, rather than pretending you have all the answers, you acknowledge your argument's limits, especially those that squeeze you more than you like. Concessions invite readers into the conversation by legitimizing their views, always a gesture that helps sustain a community of researchers. And they will be especially grateful if you can give them new and interesting questions to think about. That's what keeps the conversation going.

10.4 FRAMING YOUR RESPONSES AS SUBORDINATE ARGUMENTS

Acknowledging alternatives and objections gives you an opportunity to respond. But you can't just offer a competing claim. Even a minimal response gives a reason to limit or reject what you have acknowledged:

> Some have argued that food can be addictive,*acknowledgment of objection* but we are concerned here only with substances for which addiction is the norm.*reason why objection is irrelevant*

That initial response may be enough, but only if readers recognize the basis for it, either because it's obvious or because you've made the argument before. Otherwise, explain its basis using additional reasons and evidence:

> Some have argued that food can be addictive,*acknowledgment of objection* but we are concerned here only with substances for which addiction is the norm.*reason why objection is irrelevant* Some who taste chocolate once may be unable to resist it thereafter, but their number is a fraction of those who are immediately addicted to crack cocaine after a single exposure.*subreason* Chernowitz (1998) found that just one exposure resulted in . . . .*report of evidence*

For more substantial responses, you need a full argument, with multiple reasons, evidence, and perhaps even warrants and additional acknowledgments and responses. (At this point, add acknowledgments and responses to the appropriate places in the working plan of your argument. In chapter 12 we'll discuss where to put them in the plan of your first draft.) Again, when responding to alternatives, you face a Goldilocks choice: not too much, not too little. Only experience can teach you how to find this balance. So notice how experts achieve it and do likewise.

10.5 THE VOCABULARY OF ACKNOWLEDGMENT AND RESPONSE

Some writers fail to acknowledge alternatives because they can't think of any. The strategies in this chapter will help you overcome that problem. Others can think of views to acknowledge, but fear that if they do, they weaken their argument. In fact, most readers think that such acknowledgments enhance a writer's credibility. Writers also shy away from acknowledging and responding to objections and alternatives because they don't know how to do those things in writing, on the page or screen. This section shows you how.

When you want to acknowledge and respond to an objection or alternative, you have to decide how much credence to give it: options range from just mentioning an objection and dismissing it to addressing it at length. We present our advice roughly in that order, from most dismissive to most respectful. (Brackets and slashes indicate alternative choices.)

10.5.1 Acknowledging Objections and Alternatives

Acknowledge an objection or alternative in language that shows how much weight you give it. Here are some options.

1. You can downplay an objection or alternative by introducing it with *despite, regardless of,* or *notwithstanding*:

   [**Despite/Regardless of/Notwithstanding**] Congress's claims that it wants to cut taxes,*acknowledgment* the latest budget proposals suggest that . . .*response*

   Use *although, while,* and *even though* in the same way:

   [**Although/While/Even though**] Hong Kong is experiencing economic problems,*acknowledgment* Southeast Asia remains a strong . . .*response*

2. You can signal an acknowledgment indirectly with *seem, appear, may,* or *could,* or with an adverb like *plausibly, justifiably, reasonably, surprisingly,* or even *certainly*:

   In his letters Lincoln expresses what [**seems/appears**] to be depression.*acknowledgment* But those who observed him . . .*response*

This proposal [**may have/plausibly has**] some merit,*acknowledgment* but we . . .*response*

3. You can attribute an objection or alternative to an unnamed source, which gives it a little weight:

   It is easy to [**think/imagine/say/claim/argue**] that taxes should . . .*acknowledgment* But there is [**another/alternative/possible**] [**explanation/line of argument/account/possibility**].*response*

   Some evidence [**might/may/can/could/does**] [**suggest/indicate/point to/lead some to think**] that we should . . . ,*acknowledgment* but . . .*response*

4. You can attribute an objection or alternative to a generic interlocutor, giving it more weight:

   There are [**some/many/a few**] who [**might/may/could/would**] [**say/think/argue/claim/charge/object**] that Cuba is not . . .*acknowledgment* But, in fact, . . .*response*

   Although [**some researchers/critics/scholars**] have argued that . . . ,*acknowledgment* our research shows . . .

   Note that you can weaken your case if you prematurely denigrate those you disagree with:

   Some **naive** researchers have claimed that . . .

   The **occasionally careless** historian H has even claimed that . . .

   Save criticism for the response, and direct it at the work rather than the person.

5. You can acknowledge an objection or alternative in your own voice, using *I* or *we*, a passive verb, or a word or phrase such as *admittedly, granted, to be sure*, and so on, which concedes it some validity:

   I [**understand/know/realize**] that liberals believe in . . . ,*acknowledgment* but . . .*response*

   It is [**true/possible/likely**] that electronic cigarettes are less carcinogenic than conventional cigarettes.*acknowledgment* However, . . .*response*

It [**must/should/can**] be [**admitted/acknowledged/noted/conceded**] that no good evidence proves that . . .*acknowledgment* Nevertheless, . . .

[**Granted/Certainly/Admittedly/True/To be sure/Of course**], Adams has claimed . . .*acknowledgment* However, . . .*response*

We [**would/could/can/might/may**] [**say/argue/claim/think**] that public health programs such as needle exchanges encourage . . . ,*acknowledgment* but these effects are outweighed by . . .*response*

10.5.2 Responding to Objections and Alternatives

Begin your response with a term or phrase that signals disagreement, such as *but, however,* or *on the other hand.* If readers do not already know the basis for that response, support it with at least one reason or even with a complete subordinate argument.

You can respond in ways that range from tactful to blunt.

1. You can regret not that the source is unclear, but that *you* don't entirely understand:

   But [**I do not quite understand how/I find it difficult to see how/It is not clear to me how**] X can claim that, when . . .*response*

2. Or you can note that there are unsettled issues:

   But there are **other issues here** . . ./But there **remains the problem of** . . .*response*

3. You can respond more forcefully, claiming the acknowledged position is irrelevant or unreliable:

   But as insightful as that may be,*acknowledgment* it [**ignores/is irrelevant to/does not bear on**] the issue at hand.*response*

   But the [**evidence/reasoning**] is [**unreliable/shaky/thin**].*response*

   But the argument is [**untenable/weak/confused/simplistic**].*response*

   But the argument [**overlooks/ignores/misses**] key factors.*response*

You have to decide how blunt your response should be. If an alternative seems obviously flawed, say so, but focus on the work rather than the person.

4. When you think another researcher seems to have not thought through an issue carefully, you usually should say so civilly. Here are a few possibilities:

    Smith's evidence is important,*acknowledgment* **but we must look at all the available evidence.***response*

    That explains some of the problem,*acknowledgment* **but it is too complex for a single explanation.***response*

    That principle holds in many cases,*acknowledgment* **but not in all.***response*

QUICK TIP Three Predictable Disagreements

There are three kinds of alternatives that at least some readers are likely to think of.

1. **There are causes in addition to the one you claim.** If your argument is about cause and effect, remember that no effect has a single cause and no cause has a single effect. If you argue that X causes Y, every reader will think of other causes. European honeybee colonies may be collapsing because of pesticide use, but an informed reader could also list other possible factors, including loss of habitat, disease, genetically modified crops, and parasites. So if you focus on one cause out of many, acknowledge the others. And if you feel readers might think that some cause deserves more attention than you give it, acknowledge that view and explain why you deemphasized it.
2. **What about these counterexamples?** No matter how rich your evidence, readers are likely to think of exceptions and counterexamples that they believe undermine your argument. So you must think of them first, acknowledge the more plausible ones, especially if they are vivid, and then explain why you don't consider them as damaging as your reader might. Be particularly wary when you make claims about a phenomenon with a wide range of variation, such as the climate. Readers who do not understand statistical reasoning will focus on an aberrant case, even though it falls within a normal distribution: a cold Fourth of July in Florida does not disprove a claim about global warming, any more than a warm New England Christmas proves it.
3. **I don't define X as you do. To me, X means . . .** To accept your claim, readers must accept your definitions, because definitions are crucial warrants (see the next chapter): if you are researching nicotine addiction, your readers must understand what you mean by that term. Does it mean just a strong craving, a craving that some people can't resist, or a craving that *no one* can? You can find definitions ranging from a few lines in a dictionary to pages in a medical reference work. But regardless of what those sources

say, readers tend to redefine terms they encounter to suit their own views. Cigarette manufacturers long argued that cigarettes are not addictive because some people can quit; their critics argued that cigarettes are addictive because more people can't.

When your argument hinges on the meaning of a term, define it to support your solution and offer a subordinate argument for your definition. Don't treat a dictionary definition as authoritative (never begin, "According to *Webster's*, 'addiction' means . . ."). Be aware of plausible alternative definitions that you may need to acknowledge. If you use a technical term that also has a common meaning (like *social class* or *theory*), acknowledge that common meaning and explain why you have adopted the technical one. Conversely, if you do not use a technical term as expert readers expect you to, acknowledge that and explain why you've opted for another meaning.

11 Warrants

Warrants are general principles that connect reasons to claims. This chapter explains when and how to use them. In general, you should state your warrants only when your readers will not understand your argument without them or when you expect your readers to challenge your reasoning. When you write for experts in a field, you can leave most of your warrants unstated, because your readers will usually know them already and take them for granted.

Consider this argument:

> The Russian Federation faces a falling standard of living,*claim* because its birthrate is only 13.2 per 1,000 and life expectancy for men is only about 63 years.*reason*

Someone responds:

> Well, you're right about Russia's birthrate and life expectancy, but I don't see how that's relevant to your claim that its standard of living will fall. What's the connection?

How would the person making the argument answer? More important, if that argument were in writing, how would she know that she had to answer that question *before it was asked?* Such questions address the fifth and most complex element of an argument: its warrants. A warrant is a principle that connects a reason to a claim. Warrants are important because readers may challenge not just the validity of a reason but its *relevance* as well.

In this chapter, we explain how warrants work, how to test them, and when and when not to state them. The basic principle is this: state your warrants only if your readers will not be able to understand your reasoning without them, or if you anticipate that your reasoning will be challenged.

But as we get started, a word of caution: everyone struggles to understand warrants—including, from time to time, all of us. So if at the end of this chapter you still have questions, you're not alone.

11.1 WARRANTS IN EVERYDAY REASONING

Warrants are hard to grasp, but we understand them easily enough when people offer proverbs to justify their reasoning. That's because proverbs are warrants that we all know. For example, someone says:

> I hear the FBI has been questioning the mayor's staff.$_{reason}$ He must be involved in something crooked.$_{claim}$

Another person might object, *You're right. The FBI has been questioning his staff, but why does that mean he's crooked?* To explain the reasoning that led to that conclusion, the first person might offer the proverb, *Well, where there's smoke, there's fire.* That is, when we see a sign of something wrong, we can infer that something is in fact wrong.

The logic behind that reasoning is this. Most proverbs describe a situation made up of two distinct parts: a circumstance (*Where there's smoke, . . .*) and its consequence (*. . . there's fire*). If the connection between the circumstance and consequence is true or reasonable in general, it must also be true or reasonable in specific instances. In the case of smoke, fire, the FBI, and the mayor, that logic looks like this:

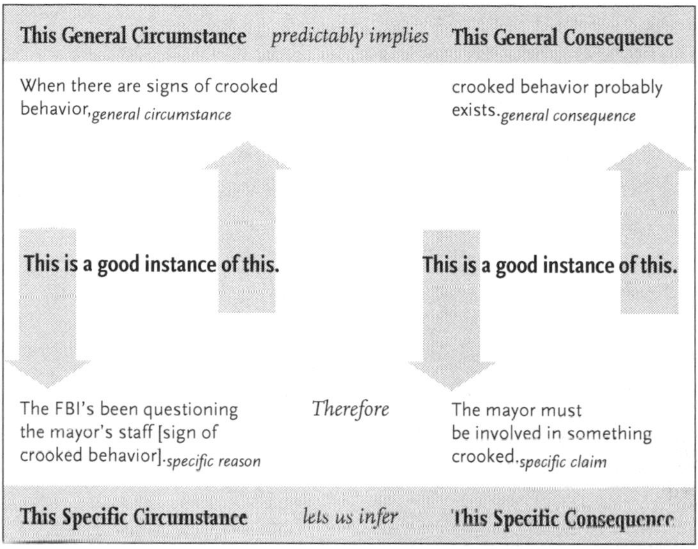
This General Circumstance
predictably implies
This General Consequence
When there are signs of crooked behavior,general circumstance
crooked behavior probably exists.general consequence
This is a good instance of this.
This is a good instance of this.
The FBI's been questioning the mayor's staff [sign of crooked behavior].specific reason
Therefore
The mayor must be involved in something crooked.specific claim
This Specific Circumstance
lets us infer
This Specific Consequence

We use proverbs to justify many kinds of everyday reasoning: cause and effect (*Haste makes waste*); rules of behavior (*Look before you leap*); reliable inference (*One swallow does not a summer make*). But such proverbs are not our only examples of everyday warrants. We use warrants everywhere: in sports (*Defense wins championships*); in cooking (*Serve oysters only in months with an "r"*); in definitions (*A prime number can be divided only by itself and one*); even in research (*When readers find an error in one bit of evidence, they distrust the rest*).

11.2 WARRANTS IN ACADEMIC ARGUMENTS

In academic arguments, warrants work in exactly the same way. But in contrast to proverbs and other everyday warrants, academic warrants can be difficult to manage—especially for researchers new to a field—for three reasons.

First, academic warrants aren't commonplaces we all share. They are specific principles of reasoning that belong to particular communities of researchers, and they are countless. A fact of life is that it just takes time for new researchers to grasp the warrants of their fields.

Second, experienced researchers rarely state their warrants explicitly when they write for specialized readers in their fields because they can safely assume that these readers already know them. (To state the obvious would seem not helpful but condescending.) This practice serves specialized readers well. But it poses a challenge to novices, who have to figure out what makes some reasons relevant to claims and others not, something those experts take for granted. That's why beginners in any field struggle with the *logic* of arguments written for specialists.

Here's an example of an academic warrant at work. Assuming the available evidence supported the reason, biologists would accept this argument:

> A whale is more closely related to a hippopotamus than to a cow,*claim* because it shares more DNA with a hippopotamus.*reason*

No biologist would ask, *What makes DNA relevant to measuring relationship?* So no biologist writing for her colleagues would offer a warrant answering that question. If, however, a non-biologist asked that question, the biologist would answer with a warrant other biologists take for granted:

> When a species shares more DNA with one species than it does with another,*circumstance* we infer that it is more closely related to the first.*consequence*

Of course, the biologist would probably then have to explain that warrant as well. The point is this: whether or not a warrant gets stated explicitly depends not only on the argument but also on the audience. Experts state principles that are obvious to other experts only when they communicate with non-experts—or when challenged.

Third, academic warrants are often stated in ways that compress their circumstances and consequences. In most proverbs, these parts are distinct: *Where there's smoke,circumstance there's fire.consequence* But we can also compress those two parts into one short statement: *Smoke means fire.* That's something we rarely do with proverbs but that experts often do with their specialized warrants:

> Shared DNA is the measure of the relationship between species.

Phrased this way, our biologist's warrant doesn't explicitly distinguish a circumstance from its predictable consequence. But however compressed a warrant might be, we can always infer those two parts. For purposes of clarity, we'll state warrants in their most explicit two-part form: *When X, then Y.*

11.3 UNDERSTANDING THE LOGIC OF WARRANTS

Here again is that argument about Russia's economic future:

> The Russian Federation faces a falling standard of living,*claim* because its birthrate is only 13.2 per 1,000 and life expectancy for men is only about 63 years.*reason*

If someone objects that the reason seems *irrelevant* to the claim, the person making the argument would have to justify the connection with a warrant consisting of two parts: (1) a general circumstance that lets us draw a conclusion about (2) a general consequence.

> When a nation's labor force shrinks,*general circumstance* its economic future is grim.*general consequence*

Both the circumstance and consequence have to be more general than the specific reason and claim. Visually, that logic looks like this:

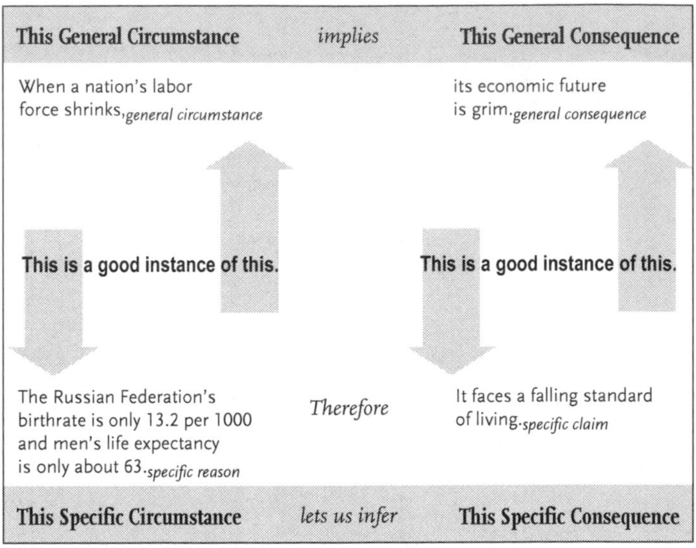
This General Circumstance
implies
This General Consequence
When a nation's labor force shrinks,general circumstance
its economic future is grim.general consequence
This is a good instance of this.
This is a good instance of this.
The Russian Federation's birthrate is only 13.2 per 1000 and men's life expectancy is only about 63.specific reason
Therefore
It faces a falling standard of living.specific claim
This Specific Circumstance
lets us infer
This Specific Consequence

That's the same pattern we saw in the argument about smoke, fire, and the crooked mayor.

11.4 TESTING WARRANTS

Readers challenge warrants in predictable ways. Consider this argument:

> Contrary to popular belief, gun ownership in America was probably not widespread in the first half of the nineteenth century and before,*claim* because guns were rarely mentioned in wills.*reason* A review of 4,465 wills filed in seven states from 1750 to 1850 shows that only 11 percent mention a long gun or handgun.*report of evidence*

Such a claim is likely to be resisted by those who believe that those who founded the United States owned guns. So even if they accept that the reason is true—that guns were in fact rarely mentioned in wills—they may still object: *But I don't see how that counts as a reason to believe that few people owned a gun. It's irrelevant.*

If a writer anticipated that readers would raise that objection, she would offer a warrant to link the specific reason to the specific claim before she stated them:

> In the eighteenth and early nineteenth centuries, valuable objects were listed in wills, **so when someone failed to mention a valuable object in his will, he did not own one.***warrant* Since guns were valuable but were rarely mentioned in wills before 1850,*reason* gun ownership must not have been widespread.*claim*

But if she wants her readers to accept that warrant, she must ask herself five questions before her readers do:

1. Is that warrant reasonable?
2. Is it sufficiently limited?
3. Is it superior to any competing warrants?
4. Is it appropriate to this field?
5. Is it able to cover the reason and claim?

11.4.1 Is Your Warrant Reasonable?

A warrant seems reasonable when readers can accept that its consequence follows from its circumstance. If readers don't accept that, you must first convince them to accept your warrant by treating it as a claim in its own argument, supported by its own reasons and evidence:

> In the eighteenth and early nineteenth centuries, valuable objects were listed in wills, so when a will failed to mention such a valuable object, the person did not own one.*warrant/claim* Watson (1989) confirmed that to be the case.*reason* In a study of 1,356 wills filed in Cumberland County between 1750 and 1825, he found . . .*evidence*

11.4.2 Is Your Warrant Sufficiently Limited?

Most warrants are reasonable only within certain limits. For example, that warrant about gun ownership seems to allow no exceptions:

> In the eighteenth and early nineteenth centuries, valuable objects were listed in wills.

That version is too broad; it might seem more plausible if it were qualified:

> In the eighteenth and early nineteenth centuries, **most** household objects **considered valuable by their owners** were **usually** listed in wills.

But once you start qualifying a warrant with words like *most* and *usually*, you then have to show that its exceptions do not exclude your reason and claim: *What frequency are* most *and* usually? *Were guns always considered valuable*?

11.4.3 Is Your Warrant Superior to Any Competing Warrants?

You may think your warrant is reasonable and sufficiently limited, but others might contradict it. Here are two more competing warrants, both arguably reasonable:

> **When parents believe a medical procedure may harm their children, they have a right to refuse it.** Taylor and Chris believe the measles vaccine causes autism, so they can refuse to have it administered to their daughter.

> **When medical decisions concern matters of public health, the state has a right to regulate them.** When most children in a population are vaccinated against measles, everyone is safer, so the state can compel Taylor and Chris to allow their daughter to be vaccinated.

Which warrant should prevail? That's a matter for yet another argument.

You can sometimes reconcile competing warrants by limiting them:

> **When parents believe a medical procedure may harm their children, they have a right to refuse it, so long as that does not jeopardize the health of others.**

> **When medical decisions concern matters of public health, the state has a right to regulate them, so long as the state encroaches as little as possible on parents' prerogative to make medical decisions for their children**.

Finding the right balance is not easy. Again, it's a matter for argument.

11.4.4 Is Your Warrant Appropriate to This Field?

Your warrant may be reasonable, sufficiently limited, and superior to others, but your readers might still reject it if it is not appropriate to their particular research community. Law students get a painful lesson in the law when they find that many warrants they take for granted have no place in legal arguments. For example, like most of us, they start law school holding this commonsense belief:

> When a person is wronged, the law should correct it.

But law students have to learn that legal warrants may trump such commonsense ideas. For example:

> When one ignores legal obligations, even inadvertently, one must suffer the consequences.

Therefore:

> When elderly home owners forget to pay real estate taxes, others can buy their houses for back taxes and evict them.

Against their most decent instincts, law students must learn to argue that justice is not the outcome they believe to be ethical but the one that the law and the courts support.

11.4.5 Is Your Warrant Able to Cover Your Reason and Claim?

Finally, you must be sure that your reason and claim are good instances of your warrant's general circumstance and general consequence. For example:

AHMED: You should buy a gun,$_{\textit{claim}}$ because you live alone.$_{\textit{reason}}$
BETH: Why does living alone mean I should buy a gun?
AHMED: When you aren't safe,$_{\textit{general circumstance}}$ you should protect yourself.$_{\textit{general consequence}}$
BETH: But living alone doesn't make me unsafe.

Beth objects not that Ahmed's reason is false but that it is not a valid *instance* of his warrant's general *circumstance.* So to her, Ahmed's reason isn't covered by his warrant and is therefore not *relevant.* Beth might also have responded that owning a gun would make her home less safe (rather than more). In that case, she would be objecting that Ahmed's claim isn't a good instance of the warrant's *consequence*, that is, that it doesn't *follow* from his reason: even if she was unsafe, a gun would not allow her to protect herself.

If all this seems complicated, know that you are in good company: the relationship of warrants to claims and reasons has vexed logicians since at least the time of Aristotle. But just knowing the ways that readers typically challenge warrants will help you write better arguments, which is why we've listed those five questions above.

11.5 KNOWING WHEN TO STATE A WARRANT

An argument in any field depends on countless principles of reasoning, but most of these principles are so deeply embedded in our tacit knowledge that we rarely state them. There are three occasions, however, when you may have to:

1. *Your readers are outside your field.* When you write as an expert for non-expert readers, you may need to explain how experts draw conclusions and support their claims, especially if these ways of reasoning are unusual.
2. *You use a principle of reasoning that is new or controversial in your field.* When you rely on unconventional principles of reasoning, you can anticipate that at least some of your readers will be skeptical. So defuse that skepticism by stating your warrant and then justifying it. Refer to others in your field who also use it. If you can't do that, make an argument of your own defending your reasoning.
3. *You make a claim that readers will resist because they just don't want it to be true.* In this case, a good strategy is to start with a warrant that you hope readers will accept *before* you lay out a reason and claim that you fear they will resist. They may not like the

> ***What You Don't Say Says Who You Are***
> You treat readers courteously when you state and support warrants to explain principles of reasoning that they may not recognize. But you make an equally strong (though less friendly) gesture when you keep silent about warrants you should state for readers not in the know. One way or the other, warrants significantly affect how readers perceive the ethos you project through your arguments.

claim any better, but you will at least encourage them to see that it is not unreasonable. For example:

> We should accept that human actions are largely responsible for climate change,*claim* because virtually all climate scientists hold that view.*reason*

Some readers may resist that claim because it threatens other strong convictions they hold. A writer confronting such readers might encourage them at least to consider that claim by giving them a warrant that they should be able to accept:

> **When an overwhelming majority of competent experts arrive at the same conclusion, we can probably trust it.***warrant* We should therefore accept that human actions are largely responsible for climate change,*claim* because virtually all climate scientists hold that view.*reason*

When readers accept that a warrant is reasonable, that a reason is true, and that the reason and claim are good instances of the warrant's general circumstance and consequence, then they are logically obliged at least to consider the claim. If they don't, no rational argument is likely to change their minds.

11.6 USING WARRANTS TO TEST YOUR ARGUMENT

All arguments rely on warrants, even if they aren't stated explicitly. You can test the soundness of an argument by trying to imagine a warrant for it. Here is a flawed argument about how violent video games affect children:

> Children aged 12-16 today are significantly more violent than their counterparts from a generation ago.*reason* Brown (2013) has shown that . . .*evidence* Given these facts, it seems highly likely that violent video games are exerting a destructive influence on today's youth.*claim*

To understand what's wrong here, we can imagine a warrant that would allow us to draw a conclusion about the effect of video games on children:

> **When children are constantly exposed to images of sadistic violence, they are influenced for the worse.***warrant* Children aged 12-16 today are significantly more violent than their counterparts from a generation ago.*reason* Brown (2013) has shown that . . .*evidence* Given these facts, it seems highly likely that violent video games are exerting a destructive influence on today's youth.*claim*

Now we can see the problem: the specific circumstance—rising violence among children aged 12–16—is not a valid instance of the warrant's general circumstance: children being exposed to images of sadistic violence.

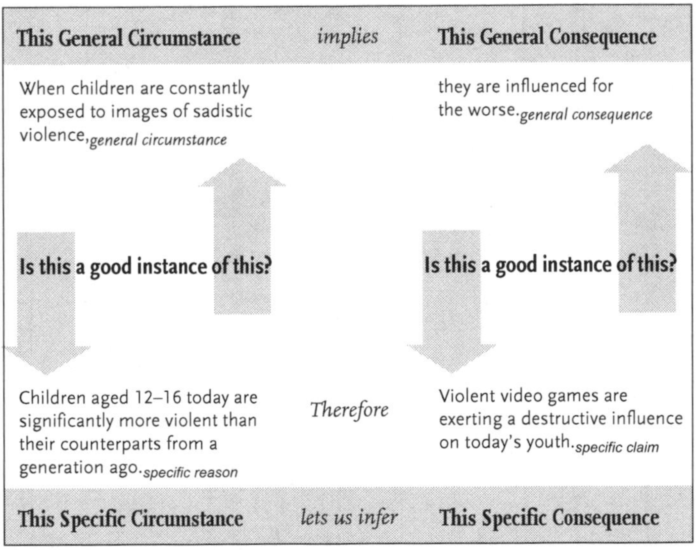
This General Circumstance
implies
This General Consequence
When children are constantly exposed to images of sadistic violence,general circumstance
they are influenced for the worse.general consequence
Is this a good instance of this?
Is this a good instance of this?
Children aged 12–16 today are significantly more violent than their counterparts from a generation ago.specific reason
Therefore
Violent video games are exerting a destructive influence on today's youth.specific claim
This Specific Circumstance
lets us infer
This Specific Consequence

So even if that statement about rising violence among children is true, it can't justify the claim. To fix that argument, we have to revise the reason to be a good instance of the warrant's general circumstance, which may also mean producing new evidence to support that new reason:

> **When children are constantly exposed to images of sadistic violence, they are influenced for the worse.**_warrant_ Over the past decade, video games have become a major source of children's exposure to violent imagery._new reason_ Jones (2014) shows that . . ._new evidence_ Given these facts, it seems highly likely that violent video games are exerting a destructive influence on today's youth, making them significantly more violent than their counterparts from a generation ago._claim_

Now the reason and claim seem closer to what the warrant covers or includes:

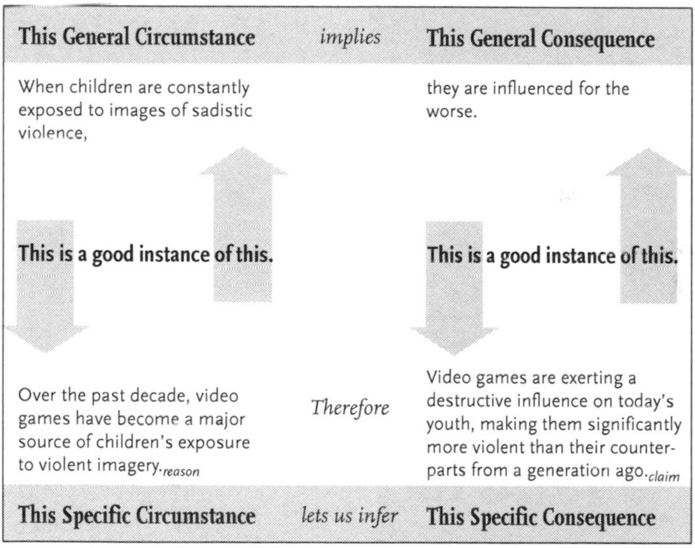
This General Circumstance
implies
This General Consequence
When children are constantly exposed to images of sadistic violence,
they are influenced for the worse.
This is a good instance of this.
This is a good instance of this.
Over the past decade, video games have become a major source of children's exposure to violent imagery.reason
Therefore
Video games are exerting a destructive influence on today's youth, making them significantly more violent than their counter-parts from a generation ago.claim
This Specific Circumstance
lets us infer
This Specific Consequence

But a reader keen to derail the argument might still object:

> Wait. All those images aren't "sadistic." Much of it is cartoon violence. And children aren't *constantly* exposed to it.

In response, the writer would have to deal with those issues.

Now you understand why important issues are so endlessly contested, why, even when you feel your case is airtight, your readers can still say, *Wait a minute. What about . . . ?* Readers can challenge reasons in two ways. They can object that your reasons are not grounded on sound evidence or that they seem irrelevant to a claim. To answer the first sort of objection, you must find better evidence. To answer the second sort, you must provide a warrant that makes your reasons relevant. If you can't, you must revise your argument.

11.7 CHALLENGING OTHERS' WARRANTS

The most difficult arguments to make are those that challenge not just the claims and evidence that a research community accepts but also the warrants it embraces. No argumentative task is harder, because when you challenge a community's warrants, you ask readers to change not just *what* they believe but *how* they reason. To challenge a warrant successfully, you must first imagine how those who accept it would defend it. Warrants can be based on different *kinds* of supporting arguments, so you have to challenge them in different ways.

11.7.1 Challenging Warrants Based on Experience

We base some warrants on our experience or on reports by others.

> When people habitually lie, we don't trust them.
>
> When insecticides leach into the ecosystem, eggshells of wild birds become so weak that fewer chicks hatch and the bird population falls.

To challenge those warrants, you have two choices, both difficult: (1) challenge the reliability of the experience, which is rarely easy; (2) find counterexamples that cannot be dismissed as special cases.

11.7.2 Challenging Warrants Based on Authority

We believe some people because of their expertise, position, or charisma.

> When authority X says Y, Y must be so.

The easiest—and friendliest—way to challenge an authority is to argue that, on the matter in question, the authority does not have all the evidence or reaches beyond its expertise. The most aggressive way is to argue that the source is in fact not an authority at all.

11.7.3 Challenging Warrants Based on Systems of Knowledge

These warrants are backed by systems of definitions, principles, or theories:

> FROM MATHEMATICS: When we add two odd numbers, we get an even one.
>
> FROM BIOLOGY: When an organism reproduces sexually, its individual offspring differ.
>
> FROM LAW: When we drive without a license, we commit a misdemeanor.

When you challenge these warrants, "facts" are largely irrelevant. You must either challenge the system, always difficult, or show that the case does not fall under the warrant.

11.7.4 Challenging General Cultural Warrants

These warrants are backed not by individual experience but by the common experience of an entire culture. To members of that culture, they seem unassailable "common sense."

> Out of sight, out of mind.
>
> An insult justifies retaliation.
>
> Handling toads causes warts.

Warrants like these may change over time, but slowly. You can challenge them, but readers will resist, because you seem to be challenging their heritage.

11.7.5 Challenging Methodological Warrants

Think of these as "meta-warrants," general patterns of thought with no content until applied to specific cases. We use them to explain abstract reasoning (they are the source of many proverbs):

GENERALIZATION: When every known case of X has quality Y, then all Xs probably have quality Y. (*Seen one, seen them all.*)

ANALOGY: When X is like Y in most respects, then X will be like Y in other respects. (*Like father, like son.*)

SIGN: When Y regularly occurs before, during, or after X, Y is a sign of X. (*Cold hands, warm heart.*)

Philosophers have questioned these warrants, but in matters of practical argumentation, we challenge only their application or point out limiting conditions: *Yes, we can analogize X to Y, but not if . . .*

11.7.6 Challenging Warrants Based on Articles of Faith

Some warrants are beyond challenge: Jefferson invoked one when he wrote, *We hold these truths to be self-evident, that all men are created equal. . . .* Others include

When a claim is experienced as revealed truth, it must be true.

When a claim is based on divine teaching, it must be true.

Such warrants are backed not by evidence but by the certainty of those who espouse them. It is pointless to challenge them, because they are statements of faith, impervious to argument or evidence. If you encounter them as you gather your data, ignore them or treat them not as a subject for research but as an inquiry into the meaning of life.

QUICK TIP **Reasons, Evidence, and Warrants**

You can justify your reasons in two ways: by offering evidence to support them or by deriving them from a warrant. Each of these ways leads to a different kind of argument. Researchers generally trust the first kind more than the second, so base your reasons on solid evidence when you can. Compare these two arguments:

> We should do what we can to discourage teenagers from texting and driving,*claim* because distracted driving is a leading cause of teenage deaths.*reason* According to the CDC, motor vehicle accidents are responsible for over a third of all fatalities among people aged 12–19, and texting while driving exponentially increases the likelihood that any driver will be involved in one. Moreover, . . .*evidence*

> We should do what we can to discourage teenagers from texting and driving,*claim* because when they do, their risk of having an accident increases.*reason 1* Driving is difficult and texting a distraction,*reason 2 supporting reason 1* and we know that when people are distracted while performing complex tasks, their performance suffers.*warrant linking reason 2 and reason 1*

If you are like most contemporary readers, you probably preferred the first of these arguments. That's because its warrant is not controversial (and therefore goes without saying) and its claim is supported by a reason based on solid evidence. That second argument is plausible because reason 1 and reason 2 are good instances of that warrant's general consequence and condition. But most readers still want evidence.

In particular, you can't support a claim of fact (see 8.1) with a warrant and reason alone:

> Texting and driving is a leading cause of teenage deaths,*claim of fact* because texting while driving is very distracting.*reason* When drivers are distracted, they increase their risk of having serious even fatal accidents.*warrant*

Are you thinking, *I could believe that, but I'd like some proof?* That commonsense response is telling. We can't just *reason* our way to the conclusion that texting while driving is a *leading* cause of teen fatalities, or even that it causes teen fatalities *at all*. Except in a few fields—some branches of mathematics, philosophy, theology—the way to demonstrate a claim of fact is to show with evidence that what you are claiming is, *in fact*, the case.

The lesson is this: whenever you can, rely not on elaborate lines of reasoning based on warrants but on hard evidence.

PART IV

Writing Your Argument

PROLOGUE
Planning Again

No formula can tell you when to start drafting. Many writers begin without a full plan, and as things become clearer, they have to discard good but irrelevant pages. Others can't get going without multiple outlines and summaries. And some of us compose drafts in our heads well before turning to a serious draft in writing. You have to find your own way to start a first draft, but you can prepare for that moment if you keep writing your way toward the paper from the start through summaries, analyses, and critiques.

Here's how you know when you're ready to plan a draft:

- You know who your readers are, what they know, and why they should care about your problem.
- You know the kind of ethos or character you want to project.
- You can sketch your question and its answer in two or three sentences.
- You can sketch the reasons and evidence supporting your claim.
- You know the questions, alternatives, and objections that your readers are likely to raise, and you can respond to them.
- You know when your readers may not see the relevance of a reason to a claim and can state the warrant that connects them.

Even when they have a plan and are ready to draft, though, experienced writers know that they won't march straight through to a finished product. They know they'll go down blind alleys, but also make new discoveries, maybe even rethink their whole project. They also know that a lot of their early drafting will not make

Sorting Out Terms: Hypothesis, Answer, Solution, Claim, Point

In part II we used the terms *answer, hypothesis,* and *solution* to name the sentence that resolved the central issue of your research. In part III we used the term *main claim* to refer to the answer, hypothesis, or solution that constitutes the key assertion that the rest of your argument supports. Here in part IV we use *point* to name the sentence that states the main claim in a paper (some use the term *thesis*). *Hypothesis, answer, solution, claim,* and *point*—all those terms refer to the same sentence. We use different terms because each defines the role of that sentence from a different angle.

it into their final draft, and so they start early enough to leave time for revision.

Part IV will lead you through the process of creating your final paper. In chapter 12 we walk through planning and drafting, then in chapter 13 organizing your argument. In chapter 14 we discuss the demanding task of incorporating and citing sources. In chapter 15 we discuss how to present quantitative data in visual form, and in chapter 16 how to write effective introductions and conclusions. Finally, in chapter 17 we deal with problems of writing in a clear and direct style.

12 Planning and Drafting

Once you've assembled your argument, you might be ready to draft it. But experienced writers know that time spent planning a first draft more than pays off when they start writing it. A plan helps you organize the elements of your argument into a form that will be both coherent and persuasive to your readers.

Some fields stipulate the plan of a research report. In the experimental sciences, for example, readers expect reports to follow a plan something like this:

> Introduction - Methods and Materials - Results - Discussion - Conclusion

If your field requires you to follow a conventional plan, ask your teacher for a model or find one in a secondary source. In most fields, however, you have to create a plan of your own, but that plan must still help readers find what they are looking for.

12.1 PLANNING YOUR PAPER

12.1.1 Sketch a Working Introduction

Writers are often advised to write their introductions last. A few writers can wait until they've written their last words before they write their first ones, but most of us need a working introduction to start us on the right track. Expect to write your introduction twice, a sketchy one for yourself right now, then later a final one for your readers. That final introduction will usually have three parts (see chapter 16), so you might as well sketch your working introduction to anticipate them.

1. **At the top of the first page of your storyboard, sketch a *brief* summary of *only* the key points in *only* those sources most relevant to your argument.** An account of marginally relevant

references has no place in your introduction. Summarize only the sources that you intend to challenge, modify, or expand on. Then order those sources in a way that is useful to your readers: chronologically, by quality, significance, point of view, and so on. Under *no* circumstances follow the order in which you happened to read them or record them in your notes. If you're sure what will go into this summary, just list the sources in a useful order.

2. **After your summary of sources, rephrase your question as a statement about a flaw or gap that you see in them:**

   Why is the Alamo story so important in our national mythology?

   → Few of these historians, however, have explained why the Alamo story has become so important in our national mythology.

3. **Sketch an answer to *So what if we don't find out?*** You may be only guessing but try to find *some* answer.

   If we understood how such stories become national legends, we would better understand our national values, perhaps even what makes us distinct.

If you can't think of any answer to *So what?*, skip it; we'll return to it in chapter 13.

4. **State the answer to your question as your point, or promise an answer in a launching point.** You have two choices here:
   - State the point of your paper at the end of your introduction to frame what follows and again near the beginning of your conclusion.
   - State it only in your conclusion, as a climax to your reasoning.

This is a crucial choice, because it creates your social contract with your readers. If you state your main point toward the end of your introduction, you put your readers in charge: *Reader, you control how to read this paper. You know my problem and its solution, my point. You can decide how—even whether—to read on. No surprises.* On the other hand, if you wait until your conclusion to state your main claim, you create a more controlling relationship: *Reader, you must follow me though every twist and turn until we reach the end, where I will finally reveal my point.* Most readers prefer to see your main point at the end of your introduction, because that lets them read what follows faster, understand its relevance better, and remember it all longer. Stating your claim early also helps keep *you* on track.

Some new researchers fear that if they reveal their main point too early, readers will be "bored" and stop reading. Others worry about repeating themselves. Both fears are baseless. If you ask an interesting question, readers will want to see how well you can answer it.

If you decide to announce your claim only in your conclusion, you still need a sentence at the end of your introduction that launches your reader into the body of your paper. That sentence should include terms that name the key concepts that will run through your paper (see 6.6.1, 8.2.1, 12.1.2). You'll be better prepared to write that launching sentence after you draft your final introduction. So for purposes of planning, put your main claim at the bottom of your storyboard's introduction page; you can move it later.

Some writers add a "road map" at the end their introduction:

> In part 1, I discuss the issue of . . . Part 2 addresses . . . Part 3 examines . . .

Road maps are common in the social sciences, but many in the humanities find them clumsy. You can add a road map to your storyboard to guide your drafting, then cut it from your final draft. If you keep it, make it short.

Here is how the first page of your storyboard might now look:

> Research has shown that female athletes under eighteen have almost twice the risk of sustaining concussions as male athletes of the same age who play the same sports.*context* [Summary of key sources follows.]
>
> But that research reveals little about the causes of this discrepancy.*question rephrased as gap in research*

> Until we understand why female athletes suffer proportionally more concussions than their male counterparts, we can't know the most effective ways to protect them.*consequences of question*
>
> The discrepancy appears to be due in part to differences in the protective equipment worn by male and female athletes as well as to different standards of monitoring, reporting, and care when injuries occur.*your tentative main point*

Sketchy as it is, this introduction is enough to start you on track. In your final draft, you'll revise it to state your problem more completely (see chapter 16).

12.1.2 Identify Key Concepts That Will Run Through Your Whole Paper

For your paper to seem coherent, readers must see a few key concepts running through all of its parts. You might find them among the terms you used to categorize your notes, but they must include keywords from the sentences stating your problem and main point. On the introduction page, circle four or five words that express those concepts. Ignore words that name your general topic; focus on those relevant to your specific question:

> employment, job satisfaction, recent SE Asian immigrants, cross-cultural, length of residence, prior economic level

If you find few key terms, your topic and point may be too general (review 8.2.1). List those key terms at the top of each storyboard page, and keep them in mind as you draft.

12.1.3 Plan the Body of Your Paper

1. **Sketch background and define terms.** After the introduction page of your storyboard, add a page on which you outline necessary background. You may have to define terms, spell out your problem or review research in more detail, set limits on your project, locate your problem in a larger historical or social context, and so on. Keep it short.
2. **Create a page for each major section of your paper.** At the top of each of these pages, write the point that the rest of that section

supports, develops, or explains. Usually, this will be a reason supporting your main claim.

3. **Find a suitable order.** When you assembled your argument (see 9.1), you ordered its parts in a way that may have been clear to you. But when you plan a draft, you must order them in a way that meets the needs of your readers. When you're not sure what that order should be, consider these options. The first two are based on your topic:
   - **Part-by-part.** If you can break your topic into its parts, you can deal with each in turn, but you must still order those parts in a way that helps readers understand them—by their functional relationships, hierarchy, and so on.
   - **Chronological.** This is the simplest: earlier to later or cause to effect.

   These next six are based on your readers' knowledge and understanding.
   - **Short to long, simple to complex.** Most readers prefer to deal with simple issues before they work through more complex ones.
   - **More familiar to less familiar.** Most readers prefer to read about more familiar issues before they read about new ones.
   - **Less contestable to more contestable.** Most readers move more easily from what they agree with to what they don't.
   - **More important to less important (or vice versa).** Readers prefer to read more important reasons first (but those reasons may have more impact if they come last).
   - **Earlier understanding to prepare for later understanding.** Readers may have to understand some events, principles, definitions, and so on before they understand something else.
   - **General analysis followed by specific applications.** Readers may have to understand the outlines of your overall position before they can follow how you apply it to specific texts, events, situations, and so on.

Often these principles cooperate: what readers agree with and easily understand might also be short and familiar. But these principles may also conflict: readers might reject most quickly reasons that are most important. Whatever your order, it must reflect *your readers'* needs, not the order that the material seems to impose on itself (as in an obvious compare-contrast organization), least of all the order in which those reasons occurred to you.

Finally, make the principle of order you choose clear by sketching at the top of each page words that show it: *First . . . , second . . .* ; *Later . . . , finally . . .* ; *More important . . .* ; *A more complex issue is . . .* ; *As a result . . .* Don't worry if these terms feel awkward. At this point, they're for your benefit, not your readers'. You can revise or even delete them from your final draft.

12.1.4 Plan Each Section and Subsection

1. **Highlight the key terms in each section and subsection.** Just as your paper needs an introduction, so does each of its sections. Earlier we told you to state the point of each section at the top of its storyboard page. Now, just as you picked out key terms to run through your whole paper, circle the ones that uniquely distinguish this section from all the others; they should be in the sentence that states the point of that section. If you cannot find terms to distinguish a section, look closely at how it contributes to the whole. It may offer little or nothing.
2. **Indicate where to put evidence, acknowledgments, warrants, and summaries.** Add these parts to the storyboard page for each section. They may, in turn, need to be supported by their own arguments.
   - **Evidence.** Most sections consist of evidence supporting a reason. If you have different kinds of evidence supporting the same reason, group and order them in a way that makes sense to readers. Note where you may have to explain your evidence—where it came from, why it's reliable, exactly how it supports a reason.
   - **Acknowledgments and responses.** Imagine what readers might object to, then outline a response. Responses may be subarguments with a claim, reasons, evidence, and even another response to an imagined response to your response.
   - **Warrants.** Generally speaking, if you need a warrant, state it before you offer its claim and supporting reason. This following

argument, for example, needs a warrant if it's intended for non-experts in Elizabethan social history:

> Since most students at Oxford University in 1580 signed documents with only their first and last names,*reason* most of them must have been commoners.*claim*

That argument is clearer to everyone (even experts) when introduced by a warrant:

> In late sixteenth-century England, when someone was not a gentleman but a commoner, he did not add "Mr." or "Esq." to his signature.*warrant* Most students at Oxford University in 1580 signed documents with only their first and last names,*reason* so most of them must have been commoners.*claim*

If you think readers might question your warrant, make an argument supporting it.

If your paper is long and "fact-heavy" with dates, names, events, or numbers, you might end each major section by briefly summarizing the progress of your argument. What have you established in that section? How does your argument shape up so far? If in your final draft those summaries seem clumsy, cut them.

12.1.5 Sketch a Working Conclusion

State your point again at the top of a conclusion page of your storyboard. After it, if you can, sketch its significance (another answer to *So what?*).

In doing all this, you may discover that you can't use all the notes you collected. That doesn't mean you wasted time. Research is like gold mining: dig up a lot, pick out a little, toss the rest. Ernest Hemingway said that you know you're writing well when you discard stuff you know is good—but not as good as what you keep.

12.2 AVOIDING THREE COMMON BUT FLAWED PLANS

Not all plans are equally good. Our first efforts often track our thinking or activities as researchers but not the experiences of readers.

1. **Do not organize your paper as a narrative of your thinking.** Few readers want to know what you found first, followed by the dead ends you hit, then the problems you overcame. They become especially annoyed when they have to slog through the history of your project to get to a main point you've saved for the end.

   To test your draft for this problem, look for sentences that refer not to the results of your research but to how you did it or to what you were thinking. You see signs of this in language like *The first issue was . . .* ; *Then I compared . . .* ; *Finally, I conclude.* If you discover more than a few such sentences, you may not be supporting a claim but rather telling the story of how you found it. If so, reorganize your paper around the core elements of your argument—your claim and the reasons supporting it.

2. **Do not assemble your paper as a patchwork of your sources.** Readers want *your* analysis, not a summary of your sources. Beginning researchers go wrong when they string together quotations, summaries, and loose paraphrases of sources into a patchwork that reflects little of their own thinking. Such "patch writing" invites the charge *This is all summary, no analysis.* It is a particular risk if you do most of your research online, because it is so easy to cut-and-paste from your sources. Experienced readers recognize patch writing, and you risk a charge of plagiarism (see 14.6).

   Advanced researchers rarely offer patchwork summaries, but they can follow sources too closely in another way: they map their paper on to the organization of a major source rather than create a new one that serves their argument better. If the key terms that run through your paper are the same as those in one or more sources, consider whether you are making your own argument or mimicking theirs.

3. **Do not map your paper directly on to the language of your assignment.** If you echo the language of your assignment in your first paragraph, your teacher may think that you've contributed no ideas of your own, as in this example:

ASSIGNMENT: Different theories of perception give different weight to cognitive mediation in processing sensory input. Some claim that input reaches the brain unmediated; others that receptive organs are subject to cognitive influence. Compare two theories of visual, aural, or tactile perception that take different positions on this matter.

PAPER'S OPENING PARAGRAPH: Different theorists of visual perception give different weight to the role of cognitive mediation in processing sensory input. In this paper I will compare two theories of visual perception, one of which . . .

If your assignment lists a series of issues to cover, avoid addressing them in the order given. If, for example, you were asked to "compare and contrast Freud and Jung on the imagination and unconscious," you would not have to organize your paper into two parts, the first on Freud and the second on Jung. That kind of organization too often results in a pair of unrelated summaries. Instead, try breaking the topics into their conceptual parts, such as elements of the unconscious and the imagination, their definitions, and so on; then order those parts in a way useful to your readers.

12.3 TURNING YOUR PLAN INTO A DRAFT

Some writers think that once they have an outline or a storyboard, they can just grind out sentences. Experienced writers know better. They know that drafting can be an act of discovery that planning can never replace, because it is then that we often experience one of research's most exciting moments: we discover ideas that we didn't have until we expressed them. But like other steps in the process, even surprises happen better with a plan.

12.3.1 Draft in a Way That Feels Comfortable

Many experienced writers begin to write long before they fill up their storyboard. They create a rough plan, use early drafts to explore what they think, then create a final plan based on what they discover. They know that much of that early writing will not

> ***Start Drafting as Soon as You Can***
> Deadlines come too soon: we long for another month, a week, just one more day. (We fought deadlines for every edition of this book.) In fact, some researchers seem never able to finish, thinking they have to keep working until their paper, dissertation, or book is perfect. That perfect paper has never been written and never will be. All you can do is to make yours as good as you can in the time available. When you've done that, you can say to yourself: *Reader, after my best efforts, here's what I believe—not the whole or final truth, but a truth important to me and I hope to you. I have tested and supported that truth as fully as time and my abilities allow, so that you might find my argument strong enough to consider, perhaps to accept, maybe even to change what you believe.*

survive, so they start early. Exploratory drafting can help you discover ideas you never imagined, but it works only if you have a distant deadline. If you are new to your topic or have a short deadline, draft when you have a clearer plan.

Once they have a plan, many writers draft quickly: they let the words flow, omitting quotations and data that they can plug in later, skipping ahead when they get stuck. If they don't remember a detail, they insert a "[?]" and keep writing until they run out of gas, then go back to look it up. But quick drafters need time to revise, so if you draft quickly, start early.

Other writers can work only slowly and carefully: they have to get every sentence right before they start the next one. To do that, they need a meticulous plan. So if you draft slowly, create a detailed outline or storyboard.

Most writers work best when they draft quickly, revise carefully, and toss what's irrelevant. But draft in any way that works for you.

12.3.2 Use Keywords to Keep Yourself on Track

One problem with drafting is staying on track. A storyboard helps, but you might also keep your key concepts in front of you and, from time to time, check how often you use them, especially those that distinguish each section. But don't let your storyboard or key terms stifle fresh thinking. If you find yourself wandering, follow the trail until you see where it takes you. You may be on the track of an interesting idea.

Even if papers in your field don't use headings and subheadings, we suggest that you do when you draft. Create each heading out of the words that are unique to the section or subsection it heads:

> Sam Houston as a Hero in Newspapers Outside of Texas

These headings also show the structure of your paper at a glance (numbered headings are common in some social sciences, rare in the humanities). If your field doesn't use heads, delete them from your final draft.

QUICK TIP Work Through Procrastination and Writer's Block

If you can't start writing or you struggle to draft even a few words, you may have writer's block. Some cases arise from anxieties about school and its pressures; if that might be you, see a counselor. But most cases have causes you can address:

- You feel so intimidated by the task that you don't know where to begin. If so, divide the process into small tasks; then focus on one step at a time.
- You have set no goals or goals that are too high. If so, create a routine that sets goals you can meet, then use devices such as a progress chart or regular meetings with a writing partner.
- You feel you must make every sentence or paragraph perfect before you move to the next one. You can avoid some obsession with perfection if you write informally along the way, telling yourself you are writing only to help you think on paper. In any event, know that every researcher compromises on perfection to get the job done.

If you have problems like these, go to the student learning center. Advisers there have worked with every kind of procrastinator and blocked writer and can give you advice tailored to your problem.

On the other hand, some cases of writer's block may really be opportunities to let your ideas simmer in your subconscious while they combine and recombine into something new and surprising. If you're stuck but have time (another reason to start early), let your unconscious work on the problem while you do something else for a day or two. Then return to the task to see if you can get back on track.

13 Organizing Your Argument

This chapter presents a procedure for organizing and revising your drafts so that your argument is as clear to your readers as it is to you. At first this procedure may seem a bit mechanical, but that's its virtue. If you follow it one step at a time, you can analyze and improve the organization of your draft efficiently and reliably.

Some new researchers think that once they've churned out a draft, they're done. The best writers know better. They write a first draft not to show to readers, but to discover what case they can actually make for their point and whether it stands up to their own scrutiny. Then they revise and revise until they think their readers will agree with their argument too. Revising for readers is hard, though, because we all know our own work too well to read it as others will. You must first know what readers look for, then determine whether your draft helps them find it. To do that, you have to analyze your draft objectively; otherwise, you'll just read into it what you want your readers to get out of it.

Some writers resist *any* revising for readers, fearing that if they accommodate their readers, they compromise their integrity. They think that the truth of their discovery should speak for itself, and if readers have a hard time understanding it, well, they just have to work harder. But revising for readers doesn't mean pandering to them. In fact, you only improve your ideas when you imagine drawing readers into an amiable conversation in which they engage your beliefs as you engage theirs.

In this chapter, we show you how to diagnose and revise your organization and argument so that readers get out of it what you think you put into it.

13.1 THINKING LIKE A READER

Readers do not read word by word, sentence by sentence, as if they were adding up beads on a string. They want to begin with a sense of the whole, its structure, and, most important, why they should read your paper in the first place. Then they use that sense of the whole and its aims to interpret its parts. So when you revise, it makes sense to attend first to your overall organization, then to sections, then to the coherence of your paragraphs and the clarity of your sentences, and, finally, to matters of spelling and punctuation. In reality, of course, no one revises so neatly. We all revise as we go, correcting spelling as we rearrange our argument, clarifying evidence as we revise a paragraph. But when you systematically revise top-down, from global structure to local sentences and words, you are more likely to read as your readers will than if you start at the bottom, with words and sentences, and work up. You will also revise more efficiently, because you won't spend time fine-tuning whole sections that you later decide to rearrange or even cut.

13.2 REVISING YOUR FRAME

Readers must recognize three things instantly and unambiguously:

- where your introduction ends
- where your conclusion begins
- what sentence in one or both states your main point

To ensure that readers recognize these, do this:

1. **Put an extra space after your introduction and before your conclusion.** If your field approves, put headings at those joints so that readers can't miss them.
2. **State your main point at or close to the end of your introduction.** Then compare that point with the one in your conclusion. They should at least not contradict each other. Nor should they be identical: make the one in your conclusion more specific and contestable.
3. **Include in the point sentence of your introduction key terms that name concepts and themes that run through your paper.** Do this not only when your point sentence announces your main claim but also if it is just a launching point (see 12.1.1, 16.4.2).

For example, consider this introductory paragraph (much abbreviated). What does it imply about the point of the paper?

> In the eleventh century, the Roman Catholic Church initiated several Crusades to recapture the Holy Land. In a letter to King Henry IV in the year 1074, Gregory VII urged a Crusade but failed to carry it out. In 1095 his successor, Pope Urban II, gave a speech at the Council of Clermont in which he also called for a Crusade, and in the next year, in 1096, he initiated the First Crusade. In this paper I will discuss the reasons for the Crusades.

The closest thing to a point sentence appears to be that vague last one. But it merely announces the Crusades as a topic.

Here are the first few sentences from the first paragraph of the conclusion (again, much abbreviated). What is its point?

> As these documents show, popes Urban II and Gregory VII did urge the Crusades to restore the Holy Land to Christian rule. But their efforts were also shrewd political moves to unify the Roman and Greek churches and to prevent the breakup of the empire from internal forces threatening to tear it apart. In so doing, they . . .

The point sentence in the conclusion seems to be the second one ("But their efforts . . . apart"). That point is specific, substantive, and plausibly contestable. We could add a shortened version of that point to the end of the introduction, or we could write a new sentence for the introduction that, while not revealing the full point, would at least introduce the key concepts of the paper more clearly:

> In a series of documents, the popes proposed their Crusades to restore Jerusalem to Christendom, but their words suggest other issues involving **political concerns** about European and Christian **unity** in the face of **internal forces** that were **dividing** them.

13.3 REVISING YOUR ARGUMENT

Once you determine that the outer frame of your paper will work for readers, analyze its argument section by section. We know this seems to repeat earlier steps, but once drafted, your argument may look different from the way it did in your storyboard or outline.

13.3.1 Identify the Substance of Your Argument

Does the structure of your argument match the structure of your paper?

1. **Is each reason supporting your main claim the point of a section of its own?** If not, the organizing points of your paper may conflict with the structure of your argument.
2. **Do you strike the right balance between reasons and evidence?** In each section, identify everything that counts as evidence, all the summaries, paraphrases, quotations, facts, figures, graphs, tables—whatever you report from a primary or secondary source. If what you identify as evidence and its explanation are less than a third or so of a section, you may not have enough evidence to support your reasons. If you have lots of evidence but few or no reasons, you may have just a data dump.

13.3.2 Evaluate the Quality of Your Argument

What might cause your readers to reject your argument?

1. **Is your evidence reliable?** In chapter 9, we said that evidence should be accurate and precise, sufficient and representative, and authoritative (see 9.4). If you are close to a final draft, it may be too late to find more or better evidence. But you can check other matters:
   - Check your data and quotations against your notes.
   - Make sure your readers see how quotations and data relate to your claim.
   - Be sure you haven't skipped intermediate subreasons between a major reason and its supporting evidence.

2. **Have you appropriately qualified your argument?** Can you drop in a few appropriate hedges like *probably, most, often, may,* and so on?

3. **Does your paper read like a conversation with peers or colleagues asking hard but friendly questions?** If it reads like a contest between competitors or if you haven't acknowledged alternative views or objections, go back through your argument and imagine a sympathetic but skeptical reader asking, *Why do you believe that? Are you really making that strong a point? Could you explain how this evidence relates to your point? But what about . . . ?* (Review 10.1–2.) Then answer the most important ones.
4. **Have you expressed all the warrants you should?** There is no easy test for this question. Once you identify each section and subsection of your argument, write in the margin its most important unstated warrant. Then ask whether readers will accept it. If not, you have to state and support it.

13.4 REVISING THE ORGANIZATION OF YOUR PAPER

Once you are confident about the outer frame of your paper and the substance of its argument, make sure that readers will find the whole paper coherent. To ensure that they do, check the following:

1. **Do key terms run through your whole paper?**
    - Circle key terms in the main point in your introduction and conclusion.
    - Circle those same terms in the body of your paper.
    - Underline other words related to concepts named by those circled terms.

Here again is that concluding paragraph about the Crusades, with its keywords circled:

> As these documents show, popes Urban II and Gregory VII did urge the Crusades to restore the Holy Land to Christian rule. But their efforts were also shrewd political moves to unify the Roman and Greek churches and to prevent the breakup of the empire from internal forces threatening to tear it apart.

If readers don't see at least one of those key terms in most paragraphs, they may think your paper wanders.

If you find a passage that lacks key terms, you might shoehorn a few in. If that's difficult, you may have gotten off track and need to rewrite or even discard that passage.

2. **Is the beginning of each section and subsection clearly signaled?** Could you quickly and confidently insert headings to mark where your major sections begin? If you can't, your readers probably won't recognize your organization. If you don't use headings, add an extra space at the major joints.
3. **Does each major section begin with words that signal how that section relates to the one before it?** Readers must not only recognize where sections begin and end, but understand why they are ordered as they are. Have you signaled the logic of your order with phrases such as *More important . . .*, *The other side of this issue is . . .*, *Some have objected that . . .*, *One complication is . . .*, or even just *First, . . . Second, . . .* ?
4. **Is it clear how each section relates to the whole?** For each section ask: *What question does this section answer?* If it doesn't answer one of the five questions whose answers constitute an argument (7.1), does it create a context, explain a background concept or issue, or help readers in some other way? If you can't explain how a section relates to your point, consider cutting it.
5. **Is the point of each section stated in a brief introduction (preferably) or in its conclusion?** If you have a choice, state the point of a section at the end of its introduction. Never bury it in the middle. If a section is longer than four or five pages, you might conclude by restating your point and summarizing your argument, especially if your argument is fact-heavy with names, dates, or numbers.
6. **Do terms that unify each section run through it?** Each section needs its own key terms to unify and uniquely distinguish it from the others. To test that, create a heading that uniquely distinguishes that section from all the others. Repeat step 1 for each section: find the point sentence and circle in it the key terms for that section (do not circle terms you circled in the main point

of the whole paper). Check whether those terms run through that section. If you find no terms that differ from those running through the whole, then your readers may not see what new ideas that section contributes. If you find that some of the terms also run through another section, the two sections may only repeat each another. If so, consider combining them.

13.5 CHECKING YOUR PARAGRAPHS

You may have learned that every paragraph should begin with a topic sentence and be directly relevant to the section in which it appears. Those are good rules of thumb, but applied too strictly they can make your writing seem stiff. The important thing is to structure and arrange your paragraphs so that they lead your readers through the conversation you are orchestrating. Open each paragraph with a sentence or two that signal its key concepts. Doing that will help readers better understand what follows. If your opening doesn't also state the paragraph's point, then your last sentence should. Never bury the point in the middle.

Paragraphs vary in length depending on the type of writing in which they appear. For example, they tend to be shorter in brief research reports and longer in, say, critical essays or book chapters. Paragraphs should be long enough to develop their points but not so long that readers lose focus, which is simply to say they should be "just right" (another Goldilocks moment). If you find yourself stringing together choppy paragraphs of just a few lines, it may mean your points are not well developed. If you find yourself rolling out very long paragraphs of more than a page, it may mean that you are digressing. You can sometimes vary the lengths of your paragraphs for effect: use short paragraphs to highlight transitions or statements that you want to emphasize.

Some writers find it more natural to think not about their paragraphs but about their paragraph breaks. Use your paragraph breaks as you would the pauses in a conversation, for example, to rest after you make a strong point, to give your reader a moment to process a complex passage, or to signal a transition to a new idea.

13.6 LETTING YOUR DRAFT COOL, THEN PARAPHRASING IT

If you start your project early, you'll have time to let your revised draft cool. What seems good one day often looks different the next. When you return to it, don't read straight through; skim its top-level parts: its introduction, the first paragraph of each major section, and its conclusion. Then, based only on what you've read, paraphrase it for someone who hasn't read it. Does the paraphrase hang together? Does it accurately sum up your argument? Even better, ask someone else to skim your paper and summarize it: how well that reader summarizes your argument will predict how well your final readers will understand it. Finally, always consider your reader's advice, even if you do not follow every suggestion.

QUICK TIP Abstracts

An abstract is a paragraph that tells readers what they will find in a paper, an article, or a report. It should be shorter than an introduction but do three things that an introduction does:

- state the research problem
- announce key themes
- state the main point or a launching point that anticipates the main point

Abstracts differ from field to field, and some fields don't use them at all. But most abstracts follow one of three patterns. To determine which suits your field, ask your teacher or look in a standard journal. Here are examples of these patterns, adapted from the abstract to a recent article in political science (the third is the original).

1. Context + Problem + Main Point

This kind of abstract is an abbreviated introduction. It begins with a sentence or two to establish the context of previous research, continues with a sentence or two to state the problem, and concludes with the main result of the research.

> Scholars have long assumed that democracy improves the quality of life for its citizens.*context* But recent research has called this orthodoxy into question, suggesting that there is little or no relationship between a country's regime type and its level of human development.*problem* In this article, we argue that democracy can be shown to advance human development, but only when considered as a historical phenomenon.*main point*

2. Context + Problem + Launching Point

This pattern is the same as the previous one, except that the abstract states not specific results, only their general nature (see 12.1.1).

> Scholars have long assumed that democracy improves the quality of life for its citizens,*context* but recent research has called this orthodoxy into question, suggesting that there is little or no relationship between a

> country's regime type and its level of human development.*problem* In this article, we review this body of work, develop a series of causal pathways through which democracy might improve social welfare, and test two hypotheses: (a) that a country's level of democracy in a given year affects its level of human development and (b) that its stock of democracy over the past century affects its level of human development.*launching point*

3. Summary

A summary also states the context and the problem; but before reporting the result, it summarizes the rest of the argument, focusing either on the evidence supporting the result or on the procedures and methods used to achieve it. Here is the abstract as it was published:

> Does democracy improve the quality of life for its citizens? Scholars have long assumed that it does,*context* but recent research has called this orthodoxy into question.*problem* This article reviews this body of work, develops a series of causal pathways through which democracy might improve social welfare, and tests two hypotheses: (a) that a country's level of democracy in a given year affects its level of human development and (b) that its stock of democracy over the past century affects its level of human development. Using infant mortality rates as a core measure of human development, we conduct a series of time-series—cross-national statistical tests of these two hypotheses. We find only slight evidence for the first proposition, but substantial support for the second.*summary* Thus, we argue that the best way to think about the relationship between democracy and development is as a time-dependent, historical phenomenon.*main point*

Since this version includes a summary, the statement of the problem is slightly abbreviated. Notice, too, the opening sentence. Rather than stating the context in standard fashion, this version begins with what seems to be a rhetorical question—"Does democracy improve the quality of life for its citizens?"—just so it can then upend the implied answer. Even as compressed a form as an abstract allows for the occasional stylistic flourish.

A final tip: if you publish your research, some researcher down the line may want to find it, using a search engine that looks for keywords. So imagine searching for your paper yourself. What keywords would you look for? Put them in your title and the first sentence of your abstract.

14 Incorporating Sources

Nothing sets the experienced researcher apart from the beginner more than the effective use of sources. But even a beginning researcher can project an ethos of credibility by following a few principles that show respect both for the writer's sources and for readers.

14.1 QUOTING, PARAPHRASING, AND SUMMARIZING APPROPRIATELY

You must build your paper out of your own words that reflect your own thinking. But you'll support much of that thinking with quotations, paraphrases, and summaries. As we've said, different fields use them differently: researchers in the humanities quote more than do social and natural scientists, who typically paraphrase and summarize. But you must decide each case for itself, depending on how you use the information. Here again are some principles:

- Summarize when details are irrelevant or a source isn't important enough to warrant much space.
- Paraphrase when you can state what a source says more clearly or concisely or when your argument depends on the details in a source but not on its specific words.
- Quote for these purposes:
  —The words themselves are evidence that backs up your reasons.
  —The words are from an authority who backs up your claims.
  —The words are strikingly original or express your key concepts so compellingly that the quotation can frame an extended discussion.
  —A passage states a view that you disagree with, and to be fair you want to state it exactly.

For every summary, paraphrase, or quotation you use, cite its bibliographic data in the appropriate style (see 14.5 and the Quick Tip). Under no circumstances stitch together downloads from the Web with a few sentences of your own. Teachers grind their teeth reading such papers, dismayed by their lack of original thinking. Readers of advanced projects reject such patchworks out of hand.

14.2 INTEGRATING DIRECT QUOTATIONS INTO YOUR TEXT

Signal direct quotations in one of two ways:

- For four or fewer quoted lines, run them into your text, surrounded by quotation marks.
- For five or more lines, set them off as an indented block.

You can insert run-in and block quotations in your text in three ways.

- Drop in the quotation with a few identifying words (*Author says, According to Author, As Author puts it,* etc.).

  > Diamond says, "The histories of the Fertile Crescent and China . . . hold a salutary lesson for the modern world: circumstances change, and past primacy is no guarantee of future primacy" (417).

- Introduce the quotation with a sentence that interprets or characterizes it.

  > Diamond suggests what we can learn from the past: "The histories of the Fertile Crescent and China . . . hold a salutary lesson for the modern world . . ." (417).

- Weave the grammar of the quotation into the grammar of your own sentence.

  > Diamond suggests that the chief "lesson for the modern world" in the history of the Fertile Crescent and China is that "circumstances change, and past primacy is no guarantee of future primacy" (417).

You can modify a quotation, so long as you don't change its meaning and you signal deletions with three dots (called *ellipses*) and changes with square brackets. This sentence quotes the original intact:

> Posner focuses on religion not for its spirituality, but for its social functions: "A notable feature of American society is religious pluralism,

and we should consider how this relates to the efficacy of governance by social norms in view of the historical importance of religion as both a source and enforcer of such norms" (299).

This version modifies the quotation to fit the grammar of the writer's sentence:

> In discussing religious pluralism, Posner says that "a notable feature of American society is [our] religious pluralism" and notes how social norms affect "the efficacy of governance . . . in view of the historical importance of religion as both a source and enforcer of such norms" (299).

14.3 SHOWING READERS HOW EVIDENCE IS RELEVANT

By this point you may be so sure that your evidence supports your reasons that you'll think readers can't miss its relevance. But evidence never speaks for itself, especially not long quotations or complex sets of numbers. You must speak for such evidence by introducing it with a sentence stating what you want your readers to get out of it. For example, this passage bases a claim about Hamlet on the evidence of the following quotation:

> When Hamlet comes upon his stepfather, Claudius, at prayer, he demonstrates cool rationality:*claim*
>
> Now might I do it [kill him] pat, now 'a is a-praying,
> And now I'll do't. And so 'a goes to heaven,
> And so am I reveng'd. . . . [Hamlet pauses to think]
> [But this] villain kills my father, and for that,
> I, his sole son, do this same villain send
> To heaven.
> Why, this is hire and salary, not revenge. (3.3)*report of evidence*

It is not clear how that quotation supports the claim, because nothing in it specifically refers to Hamlet's rationality. In contrast, compare this:

> When Hamlet comes upon his stepfather, Claudius, at prayer, he demonstrates cool rationality.*claim* **He impulsively wants to kill Claudius but**

pauses to reflect: if he kills Claudius while praying, he will send his soul to heaven, but he wants Claudius damned to hell, so he coolly decides to kill him later:*reason*

Now might I do it [kill him] pat, . . .*report of evidence*

Now we see the connection. (Do the same with tables and figures; see 15.3.1.)

Lacking a reason that explains the evidence, readers may not see what it *means*. So introduce complex evidence with a sentence explaining it.

14.4 THE SOCIAL IMPORTANCE OF CITING SOURCES

14.4.1 Citations Benefit You

Citations protect you from a charge of plagiarism, but beyond that narrow self-interest, correct citations contribute to your ethos. First, readers don't trust sources they can't find. If they can't find your sources because you failed to document them adequately, they won't trust your evidence; and if they don't trust your evidence, they won't trust your paper—or you. Second, many experienced researchers think that if a writer can't get the little things right, he can't be trusted on the big ones. Getting the details of citations right distinguishes reliable, experienced researchers from careless beginners. Finally, teachers assign research papers to help you learn how to integrate the research of others into your own thinking. Proper citations show that you have learned one important part of that process.

14.4.2 Citations Help Your Readers

Readers use citations before, while, and after they read your paper. Before, many experienced readers will preview your paper by skimming your list of sources to see whose work you read and whose you didn't. As they read, readers use citations to decide how much they can trust the reliability, currency, and completeness of your evidence. Papers with outdated or only very recent citations of sources found on the Internet alert readers to be skeptical. But papers whose citations show range and depth in engaging sources reassure readers. Finally, just as you depended on sources to start your bibliographical trail, so will some readers depend on *your* list to start theirs.

14.4.3 Citations Honor Your Sources

Finally, citations honor your sources. Few academic researchers get rich writing on topics such as "Ohio education, 1825–1850." Their reward isn't money; it's the reputation they earn for doing good work and the pleasure they take in knowing that colleagues respect it enough to cite it—even in disagreement. Your sources may never know you cited them, but that doesn't matter. When you cite sources, you honor them by acknowledging your intellectual debts.

In short, when you cite sources fully and accurately, you sustain and enrich the sense of community that gives written research both its scholarly and social value.

14.5 FOUR COMMON CITATION STYLES

It would be easier if we all cited sources in the same style, but we don't. For academic research, there are two basic patterns, each with two common versions. The many differences among the styles can seem picky and irrelevant, but they matter to readers. So be sure to find out which style you should use, and consult the proper guide for your style. (You can also find reliable online guides.)

Many researchers today use citation software that automatically generates citations in the style they choose. Some teachers encourage this practice. Others feel that students should not rely on such assistance, but rather learn the details. If you don't know where your teacher stands on the issue, ask.

14.5.1 Two Basic Patterns: Author-Title and Author-Date

All citation forms begin with the name of the author, editor, or whoever else is responsible for the source. We distinguish styles by what follows the author. If the title follows the author, the style is called *author-title*.

Anes, Lee J. *A Story of Ohio: Its Early Days.* Boston: Hobson Press, 1988.

This pattern is common in the humanities.

If the date follows the author, the style is called *author-date.*

Anes, Lee. 1988. *A story of Ohio: Its early days.* Boston: Hobson Press.

This pattern is used in the natural sciences and most of the social sciences, because in those rapidly changing fields, readers want to know quickly how old a source is. They can spot dates more easily when they come at the beginning of a citation.

14.5.2 Two Author-Title Styles

There are two versions of author-title style, each based on a well-known style manual.

- **Chicago Author-Title Style:** *The Chicago Manual of Style*, 16th ed. (Chicago: University of Chicago Press, 2010). It is sometimes called Turabian style, based on a widely used condensed manual: Kate L. Turabian, *A Manual for Writers of Research Papers, Theses, and Dissertations*, 8th ed. (Chicago: University of Chicago Press, 2013). When using this style, you list your sources in a bibliography and cite them in your text with footnotes or endnotes.
- **MLA Style:** *MLA Handbook for Writers of Research Papers*, 8th ed. (New York: Modern Language Association, 2016). You are mostly likely to learn MLA (Modern Language Association) style in a literature or composition course. In this style, you give a list of works cited and cite your sources parenthetically in your text.

These styles differ only in minor details, but those details matter, so be sure to consult the proper style guide.

14.5.3 Two Author-Date Styles

There are two versions of author-date style, each based on a well-known style manual.

- **Chicago Author-Date Style:** This style is also described in *The Chicago Manual of Style* and sometimes called Turabian style. When using it, you list your sources in a bibliography but cite them parenthetically in your text.
- **APA Style:** *Publication Manual of the American Psychological Association*, 6th ed. (Washington, DC: American Psychological Association, 2009). This style uses parenthetical citations as well.

Like the author-title styles, these styles differ only in minor details. But again, those details matter, so be sure to follow the prescriptions of the style you use down to the last comma, space, and capital letter.

14.6 GUARDING AGAINST INADVERTENT PLAGIARISM

It will be as you draft that you risk the worst mistake a researcher can make: you lead readers to think that you're trying to pass off as your own the work of another writer. Do that and you risk an accusation of plagiarism, a charge that, if sustained, could mean, for a professional writer, an irreparably damaged reputation or, for a student writer, a failing grade or even expulsion. Students know they cheat when they put their name on a paper purchased on the Internet or copied from a fraternity or sorority file. Most also know they cheat when they pass off as their own long passages copied directly from their sources. For those cases, there's nothing to say beyond *Don't.*

But many inexperienced writers don't realize when they risk being charged with plagiarism because they are careless or misinformed. You run that risk when you do any of the following:

- You quote, paraphrase, or summarize a source but fail to cite it.
- You use ideas or methods from a source but fail to cite it.
- You use the exact words of a source and you do cite it, but you fail to put those words in quotation marks or in a block quotation.
- You paraphrase a source and cite it, but you use words so similar to those of the source that anyone can see that as you paraphrased, you followed the source word by word.

14.6.1 Cite the Source of Every Quotation, Paraphrase, or Summary

You must cite your source every time you use its words, even if you only paraphrase or summarize them. If the quotations, paraphrases, or summaries come from different pages of your sources, cite each one individually. If a paraphrase or summary extends over several paragraphs, cite it only once at the end. (See the Quick Tip at the end of this chapter for guidance on citing sources in your text.)

The most common problem is not that students don't know that they should cite a source, but that they lose track of which words are theirs and which are borrowed. That's why we urged you in chapter 6 to distinguish in your notes between quotations, paraphrases, and summaries of sources and your own analyses, thoughts, and commentary. Always include the citation as soon as you add a quotation because you may not remember to do so later. Be especially careful to cite a paraphrase or summary as you draft it; otherwise, you may not even remember that it originated with a source.

14.6.2 Signal Every Quotation, Even When You Cite Its Source

Even if you cite the source, readers must know exactly which words are not yours, even if they are *as few as a single line.* It gets complicated, however, when you copy less than a line. Read this:

> "Because technology begets more technology, the importance of an invention's diffusion potentially exceeds the importance of the original invention. Technology's history exemplifies what is termed an autocatalytic process: that is, one that speeds up at a rate that increases with time, because the process catalyzes itself" (Diamond 1998, 301).

If you were writing about Jared Diamond's ideas, you would probably have to use some of his words, such as *the importance of an invention.* But you wouldn't put that phrase in quotation marks, because it shows no originality of thought or expression.

Two of his phrases, however, are so striking that they do require quotation marks: *technology begets more technology* and *autocatalytic process.* For example:

> The power of technology goes beyond individual inventions because "technology begets more technology." It is, as Diamond puts it, an "autocatalytic process" (301).

Once you cite those words, you can use them again without quotation marks or citation:

> As one invention begets another one and that one still another, the process becomes a self-sustaining catalysis that spreads across national boundaries.

This is a gray area: words that seem striking to some are not to others. If you put quotation marks around too many ordinary phrases, readers might think you're naive, but if you fail to use them when readers think you should, they may suspect you of plagiarism. Since it's better to seem naive than dishonest, especially early in your career, use quotation marks freely. (You must, however, follow the standard practices of your field. Lawyers, for example, often use the exact language of a statute or judicial opinion with no quotation marks.)

14.6.3 Don't Paraphrase Too Closely

You paraphrase appropriately when you represent an idea in your own words more clearly or pointedly than the source does. But readers will think that you plagiarize if they can match your words and phrasing with those of your source.

For example, here is a passage from Malcolm Gladwell's *Outliers: The Story of Success*:

> "Achievement is talent plus preparation. The problem with this view is that the closer psychologists look at the careers of the gifted, the smaller the role innate talent seems to play and the bigger the role preparation seems to play" (38).

This too-close paraphrase is plagiarism:

> Success seems to depend on a combination of talent and preparation. However, when psychologists closely examine the gifted and their

> careers, they discover that innate talent plays a much smaller role than preparation (Gladwell 38).

This paraphrase does not plagiarize:

> As Gladwell observes, summarizing studies on the highly successful, we tend to overestimate the role of talent and underestimate that of preparation (38).

This phrasing is not a close match to the original. And notice that we chose not to put *talent* or *preparation* in quotes. We decided that those words are common enough to use as our own.

To avoid seeming to plagiarize, read the passage, look away, think about it for a moment; *then still looking away*, paraphrase it in your own words. Then check whether you can run your finger along your sentence and find synonyms for the same ideas in the same order in your source. If you can, try again.

14.6.4 Usually Cite a Source for Ideas Not Your Own

Most of our ideas are based on sources somewhere in history. But readers don't expect you to cite a source for the idea that the world is round. They do, however, expect you to cite a source for an idea when (1) the idea is associated with a specific person *and* (2) it's new enough *not* to be part of a field's common knowledge. For example, psychologists claim that we think and feel in different parts of our brains. But no reader would expect you to cite a source for that idea, because it's so familiar that no one would think you are implying it is yours. On the other hand, some psychologists argue that emotions are crucial to rational decision making. That idea is so new and tied to particular researchers that you'd have to cite them.

14.6.5 Don't Plead Ignorance, Misunderstanding, or Innocent Intentions

Some students sincerely believe that they don't have to cite material downloaded from the Web because it's free and publicly available. They are wrong. Other students defend themselves by claiming

Why the Fuss over Honest Mistakes?

Some students wonder why teachers are so unforgiving of honest slip-ups. *What's the harm?*

First, they harm your credibility. One failure to acknowledge a source can lead readers to doubt your honesty, a career-ending judgment for an advanced student. But they matter even to a beginner. Your teacher is preparing you to write not for her but for others who will have only your words to judge your ethos. She needs to see that you know not only how to use sources thoughtfully but how to acknowledge them carefully and completely.

Other students think plagiarism is a victimless offense. It is not. Recently, two young scholars were praised when they used in a new way methods and ideas published twenty years earlier. They mentioned their source in passing but failed to acknowledge their specific debt fully. In doing so, they not only claimed undeserved credit but deprived the older scholar of credit he deserved. Worse, by omitting the bibliographical trail that led to his work, they kept readers from rediscovering it. The credit he lost cost him not only reputation but also perhaps grants, promotions, and ultimately higher pay.

they didn't *intend* to mislead. Well, we read words, not minds. Here is how to think about this issue: If the person you borrowed from read your writing, would she recognize your words or ideas as her own, including paraphrases, summaries, or even general ideas or methods? If so, you must cite that source and enclose any of her exact words in quotation marks or set them off in a block quotation. No exceptions, no excuses.

QUICK TIP Indicating Citations in Your Paper

You must indicate in your paper every place where you use a source. The three of the four most common citation styles—Chicago author-date style, MLA style, and APA style (see 14.5)—use parenthetical citations that direct readers to specific pages in the source, with enough information to find the corresponding entry in a list of sources.

> Some have claimed that Castro would reform Cuban politics (Smith 1999, 233).

If you use Chicago author-title style, you may instead use a raised number, or superscript, that directs readers to a correspondingly numbered note at the bottom of the page or at the end of the paper.

> Some have claimed that Castro would reform Cuban politics.[5]
>
> 5. George Smith, *Travels in Cuba* (Boston: Hasbro Press, 1999), 233.

PARENTHETICAL CITATIONS

A parenthetical (or in-text) citation includes only the information a reader needs to locate the source in a list of sources at the end of your paper. Depending on your field, that list will be called your bibliography, references, or works cited. What you include in an in-text citation depends first on whether you use author-title or author-date citation style. For example, here are the author-title forms for citing a single-author work if you do not mention the author in your sentences and you have only one work by that author in your list of sources:

> **Chicago Author-Title** (Author, page[s])
> Only one writer provides data on this matter (Kay, 220).
>
> **MLA** (Author page[s])
> Only one writer provides data on this matter (Kay 220).

If in your list of sources you list more than one publication for an author, you must add a short title so that readers will know which publication you are citing. In this case, the format in both styles is the same:

Chicago Author-Title and MLA (Author, *Short Title*, page[s])
Only one writer provides data on this matter (Kay, *A Life*, 220).

In author-date style, you must add the date to every citation:

Chicago Author-Date (Author date, page[s])
Only one writer provides data on this matter (Kay 2006, 220).

APA (Author, date, p. xxx)
Only one writer provides data on this matter (Kay, 2006, p. 220).

If you have mentioned the author, drop the name from the citation:

Chicago Author-Date: Kay is the only writer who provides data on this matter (2006, 220).

MLA: Kay is the only writer who provides data on this matter (220).

APA: Kay is the only writer who provides data on this matter (2006, p. 220).

There are additional rules for citations if a work has more than one author, if you cite more than one work by the same author, and so on. For these, consult the appropriate guide.

NOTES AND BIBLIOGRAPHY

In Chicago author-title style, you use notes—footnotes at the bottom of the page or endnotes following the paper—to direct readers to sources in a bibliography. Notes include the same information as a bibliography entry, but the form differs in three ways: notes list names not last name, first name, but first name last name; individual elements of a note are separated by commas rather than periods; and publication data are in parentheses.

NOTE FORM: 5. George Smith, *Travels in Cuba* (Boston: Hasbro Press, 1999), 233.

BIBLIOGRAPHY FORM: Smith, George. *Travels in Cuba*. Boston: Hasbro Press, 1999.

For details, consult the Turabian guide or *The Chicago Manual of Style.*

Researchers are increasingly using parenthetical citations rather than notes, because notes duplicate the information listed in a bibliography. If in doubt, ask your teacher.

15 Communicating Evidence Visually

Most readers grasp quantitative evidence more easily in tables, charts, and graphs than they do in words. But some visual forms suit particular data and messages better than others. In this chapter, we show you how to choose the graphic form that best helps readers both grasp your data and understand how they support your argument.

15.1 CHOOSING VISUAL OR VERBAL REPRESENTATIONS

When the data are few and simple, readers can grasp them as easily in a sentence as in a table:

> In 2013, on average, men earned $50,033 a year and women $39,157, a difference of $10,876.

TABLE 15.1. Male-female salaries ($), 2013

Men	50,033
Women	39,157
Difference	10,876

But if you present more than a few numbers, readers will struggle to keep them straight:

> Between 1970 and 2010, the structure of families changed in two ways. In 1970, 85 percent of families had two parents, but in 1980 that number declined to 77 percent, then to 73 percent in 1990, to 68 percent in 2000, and to 64 percent in 2010. The number of one-parent families rose, particularly families headed by a mother. In 1970, 11 percent of families were headed by a single mother. In 1980, that number rose to 18 percent, in 1990 to 22 percent, and to 23 percent in 2000. There were some marginal changes among single fathers (headed 1 percent of the families in 1970, 2 percent in 1980, 3 percent in 1990, and 4 percent in 2000). Families headed by no adult remained stable at 3–4 percent.

A note on terminology: We use the term *graphics* for all visual representations of data. Traditionally, graphics are divided into *tables* and *figures*. A table is a grid with columns and rows. Figures are all other graphic forms, including graphs, charts, photographs, drawings, and diagrams. Figures that present quantitative data are divided into *charts* and *graphs*. Charts typically consist of bars, circles, points, or other shapes; graphs consist of continuous lines.

15.2 CHOOSING THE MOST EFFECTIVE GRAPHIC

When you graphically present data as complex as in that paragraph, the most common choices are tables, bar charts, and line graphs, each of which has a distinctive rhetorical effect.

A table seems precise and objective. It emphasizes discrete numbers and requires readers to infer relationships or trends on their own (unless you state them in an introductory sentence).

TABLE 15.2. Changes in U.S. family structure, 1970–2010

Percentage of total families					
Family type	1970	1980	1990	2000	2010
2 parents	85	77	73	68	64
Mother	11	18	22	23	27
Father	1	2	3	4	4
No adult	3	4	3	4	4

Charts and line graphs present a visual image that communicates values less precisely than do the exact numbers of a table but with more impact. But charts and graphs also differ. A bar chart emphasizes contrasts among discrete items:

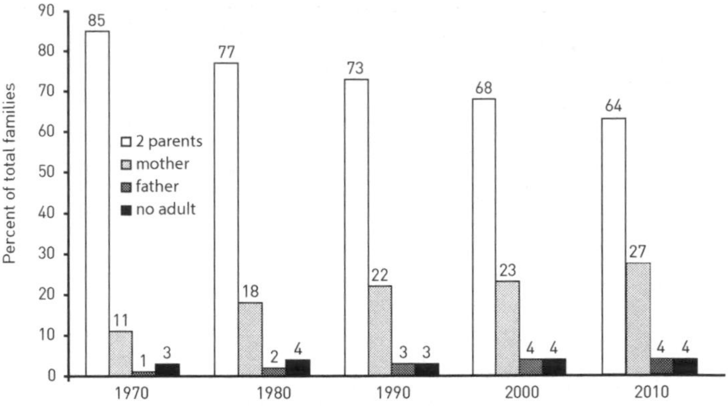

FIGURE 15.1. Changes in U.S. family structure, 1970–2000

A line graph suggests continuous change over time:

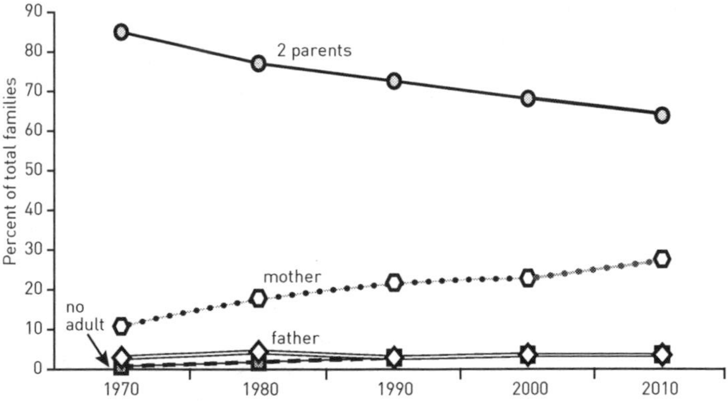

FIGURE 15.2. Changes in U.S. family structure, 1970–2000

Choose the form that achieves the effect you want, not the one that comes to mind first.

How many choices you should consider depends on your experience. If you're new to quantitative research, limit your choices to basic tables, bar charts, and line graphs. Your computer software offers more choices, but ignore those that you aren't familiar with. If you're doing advanced research, readers will expect you to draw from a larger range of graphics favored in your field. In that case, consult table 15.7, which describes the rhetorical uses of other common forms. You may have to consider even more creative ways of representing data if you are writing a dissertation or article in a field that routinely displays complex relationships in large data sets. (See the bibliography for additional resources.)

What follows is a guide to the basics of tables, charts, and graphs.

15.3 DESIGNING TABLES, CHARTS, AND GRAPHS

Computer programs create graphics so dazzling that many writers let their software determine their design. That's a mistake. Readers don't care how fancy a graphic looks if it doesn't communicate your point clearly. Here are some principles for designing effective graphics. To follow them, you may have to change default settings in your graphics software.

15.3.1 Frame Each Graphic to Help Readers Understand It

A graphic representing complex numbers rarely speaks for itself. You must frame it to show readers what to see in it and how to understand its relevance to your argument:

1. Label every graphic in a way that describes its data. For a table, the label is called a *title* and is set flush left above the table; for a figure, the label is called a *legend* and is set flush left below the figure. Keep titles and legends short but descriptive enough to distinguish every graphic from every other one.

    - Avoid making the title or legend a general topic.

      NOT: Heads of households

      BUT: Changes in one- and two-parent heads of households, 1970–2010

    - Do not give background information or characterize what the data imply.

      NOT: Weaker effects of counseling on depressed children before professionalization of staff, 1995–2004

      BUT: Effect of counseling on depressed children, 1995–2004

- Be sure labels distinguish graphics presenting similar data.

  NOT: Risk factors for high blood pressure

  BUT: Risk factors for high blood pressure among men in Cairo, Illinois

  OR: Risk factors for high blood pressure among men in St. Louis, Missouri

2. Insert into the table or figure information that helps readers see how the data support your point. For example, if numbers in a table show a trend and the size of the trend matters, indicate the change in a final column. If a line on a graph changes in response to an influence not mentioned on the graph, add text to the image to explain it.

   Although reading and math scores declined by almost 100 points following redistricting, that trend reversed when supplemental math and reading programs were introduced.

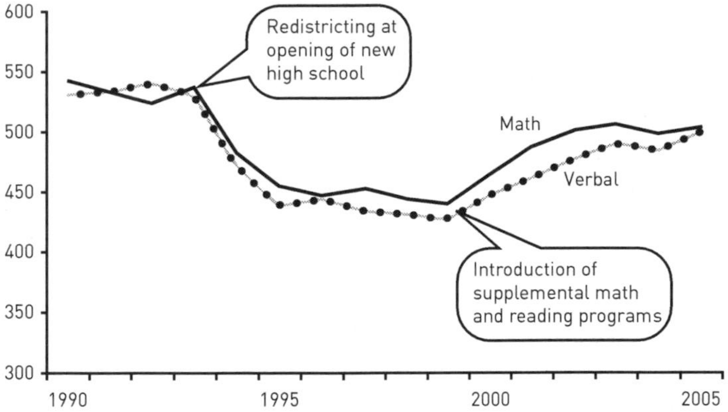

FIGURE 15.3. SAT scores for Mid-City High, 1990–2005

3. Introduce the table or figure with a sentence that explains how to interpret it. Then highlight what it is in the table or figure that you want readers to focus on, particularly any number or relationship mentioned in that introductory sentence. For example, we have to study table 15.3 to understand how it supports the sentence before it:

Most predictions about increased gasoline consumption have proved wrong.

TABLE 15.3. Gasoline consumption

	1970	1980	1990	2000
Annual miles (000)	9.5	10.3	10.5	11.7
Annual consumption (gal.)	760	760	520	533

We need a sentence to explain how the numbers support or explain the claim, a more informative title, and visual help that highlights what we should see in the table:

Gasoline consumption has not grown as predicted. Though Americans drove 23 percent more miles in 2000 than in 1970, they used 32 percent less fuel.

TABLE 15.4. Per capita mileage and gasoline consumption, 1970–2000

	1970	1980	1990	2000
Annual miles (000)	9.5	10.3	10.5	11.7
(% change vs. 1970)		8.4%	10.5%	23.1%
Annual consumption (gal.)	760	760	520	533
(% change vs. 1970)		0%	(31.5%)	(31.6%)

The added sentence tells us how to interpret the key data in table 15.4, and the shading tells us where to find them.

15.3.2 Keep All Graphics as Simple as Their Content Allows

Some guides encourage you to cram as much data as you can into a graphic. But readers want to see only the data relevant to your point, free of distractions. For all graphics:

1. Include only relevant data. If you include data only for the record, label it accordingly and put it in an appendix.
2. Keep the visual impact simple.
   - Box a graphic only if you group two or more figures.
   - Do not color or shade the background.

FOR TABLES

- Never use both horizontal and vertical dark lines to divide columns and rows. Use light gray lines only if the table is complex or you want to direct your reader's eyes in one direction to compare data.
- For tables with many rows, lightly shade every fifth row.

FOR CHARTS AND GRAPHS

- Use background grid lines only if the graphic is complex or readers need to see precise numbers. Make them light gray.
- Color or shade lines or bars only to show a contrast. Use color only if the text will be printed in color and not photocopied later. (Black-and-white photocopies make many colors look alike.)
- Never use iconic bars (for example, images of cars to represent automobile production) or add a third dimension merely for effect. Both look amateurish and can distort how readers judge values.
- Plot data on three dimensions only when your readers are familiar with such graphs and you cannot display the data in any other way.

3. Use clear labels.

- Label all rows and columns in tables and both axes in charts and graphs.
- Use tick marks and labels to indicate intervals on the vertical axis of a graph.
- If possible, label lines, bar segments, and the like on the image rather than in a legend set to the side. Use a legend only if labels would make the image too complex to read.
- When specific numbers matter, add them to bars or segments in charts or to dots on lines in graphs.

15.4 SPECIFIC GUIDELINES FOR TABLES, BAR CHARTS, AND LINE GRAPHS

15.4.1 Tables

Tables with lots of data can seem dense, so organize them to help readers.

- Order the rows and columns by a principle that lets readers quickly find what you want them to see. Do not automatically choose alphabetic order.
- Round numbers to a relevant value. If differences of less than 1,000 don't matter, then 2,123,499 is irrelevantly precise.
- Sum totals at the bottom of a column or at the end of a row, not at the top or left.

Compare tables 15.5 and 15.6.

TABLE 15.5. Unemployment in major industrial nations, 1990 2000

	1990	2001	Change
Australia	6.7	6.5	(0.2)
Canada	7.7	5.9	(1.8)
France	9.1	8.8	(0.3)
Germany	5.0	8.1	3.1
Italy	7.0	9.9	2.9
Japan	2.1	4.8	2.7
Sweden	1.8	5.1	3.3
UK	6.9	5.1	(1.8)
USA	5.6	4.2	(1.6)

Table 15.5 looks cluttered and its items aren't helpfully organized. In contrast, table 15.6 is clearer because it has an informative title, less visual clutter, and items organized to let us see the pattern more easily.

TABLE 15.6. Changes in unemployment rates of industrial nations, 1990–2000

English-speaking vs. non-English-speaking nations

	1990	2001	Change
Canada	7.7	5.9	(1.8)
UK	6.9	5.1	(1.8)
USA	5.6	4.2	(1.6)
Australia	6.7	6.5	(0.2)
France	9.1	8.8	(0.3)
Japan	2.1	4.8	2.7
Italy	7.0	9.9	2.9
Germany	5.0	8.1	3.1
Sweden	1.8	5.1	3.3

15.4.2 Bar Charts

Bar charts communicate as much by visual impact as by specific numbers. But bars arranged in no pattern imply no point. If possible, group and arrange bars to create an image that matches your message. For example, look at figure 15.4 in the context of the explanatory sentence before it. The items are listed alphabetically, an order that doesn't help readers see the point.

Most of the world's deserts are concentrated in North Africa and the Middle East.

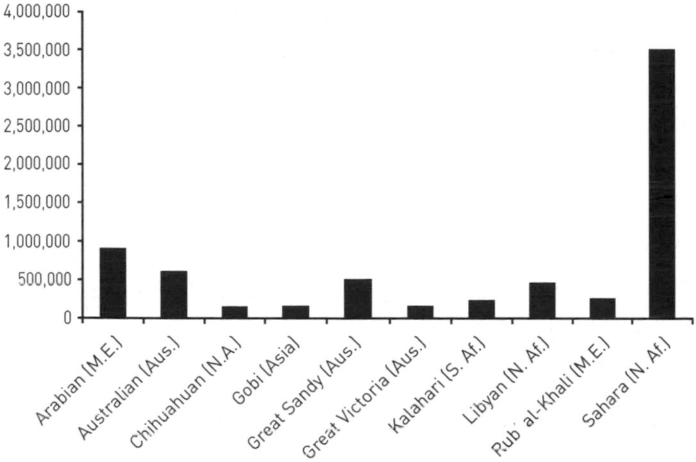

FIGURE 15.4. World's ten largest deserts

In contrast, figure 15.5 supports the claim with a coherent image.

Most of the world's deserts are concentrated in North Africa and the Middle East.

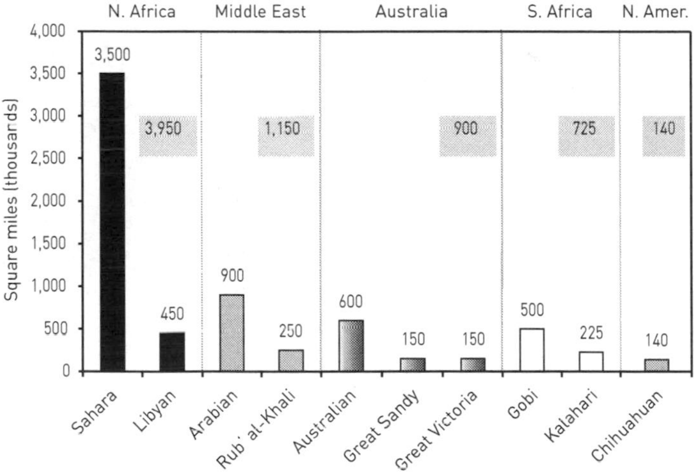

FIGURE 15.5. World distribution of large deserts

In standard bar charts, each bar represents 100 percent of a whole. But sometimes readers need to see specific numbers for parts of the whole. You can do that in two ways:

- Divide the bars into proportional parts, creating a "stacked" bar.
- Give each part of the whole its own bar, then group the parts into clusters.

Use stacked bars only when you want readers to compare whole values for different bars rather than their divided segments, because readers can't easily compare the proportions of segments by eye alone. If you do use stacked bars, do this:

- Arrange segments in a logical order. If possible, put the largest segment at the bottom in the darkest shade.
- Label segments with specific numbers and to assist comparisons; connect corresponding segments with gray lines.

Compare figures 15.6 and 15.7:

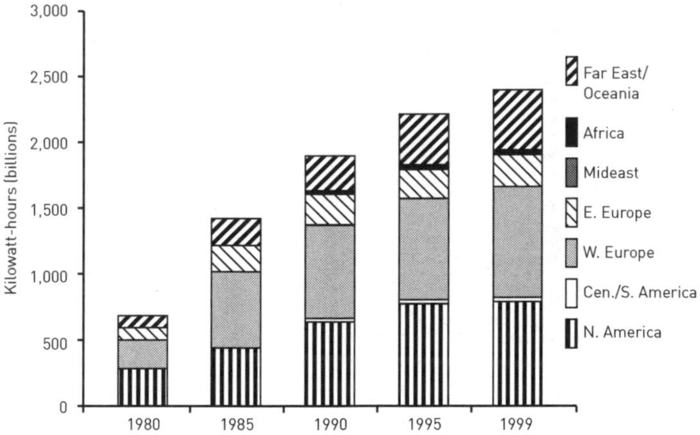

FIGURE 15.6. World generation of nuclear energy, 1980–1999

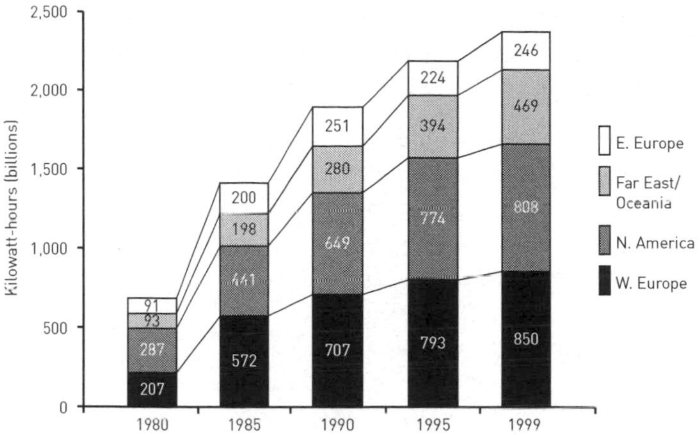

FIGURE 15.7. Largest generators of nuclear energy, 1980–1999

If you group bars because segments are as important as the wholes, do this:

- Arrange groups in a logical order; if possible put bars of similar size next to one another (order bars in the same way through all the groups).
- Label groups with the number for the whole, either above each group or below the labels on the bottom.

Most data that fit a bar chart can also be shown in a pie chart. Pie charts are popular in magazines, tabloids, and annual reports. While splashy, they are harder to read than bar charts. Readers must compare proportions of segments whose sizes are often hard to judge. But pie charts have their place, especially to communicate qualitative impressions about the comparative size of data, either to show that one segment is disproportionately larger than the rest or that the data is divided into many small segments. Avoid using pie charts to convey quantitative data, however. Use bar charts instead.

15.4.3 Line Graphs

Because a line graph emphasizes trends, readers must see a clear image to interpret it correctly. Do the following:

- Choose the variable that makes the line go in the direction, up or down, that supports your point. If the good news is a reduction (down) in high school dropouts, you can more effectively represent the same data as a rising line indicating increase in retention (up). If you want to emphasize bad news, find a way to represent your data as a falling line.
- Plot more than six lines on one graph only if you cannot make your point in any other way.
- If you have fewer than ten or so data points, indicate them with dots. If only a few are relevant, insert numbers to show their exact value.
- Do not depend on different shades of gray to distinguish lines, as in figure 15.8.

Compare figure 15.8 and figure 15.9:

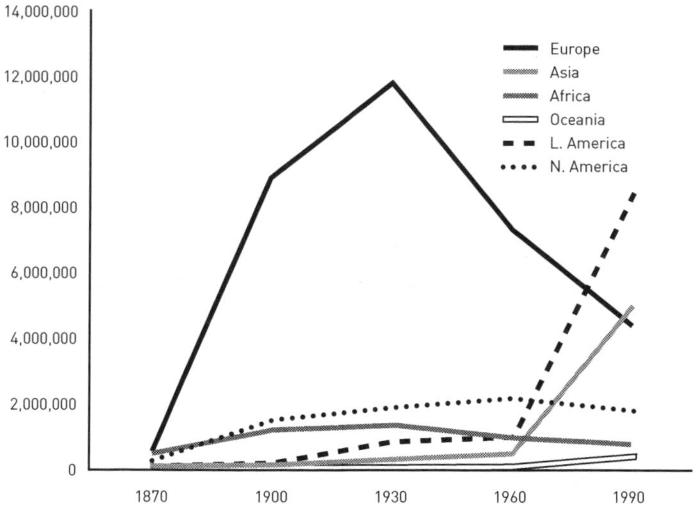

FIGURE 15.8. Foreign-born residents in the United States, 1870–1990

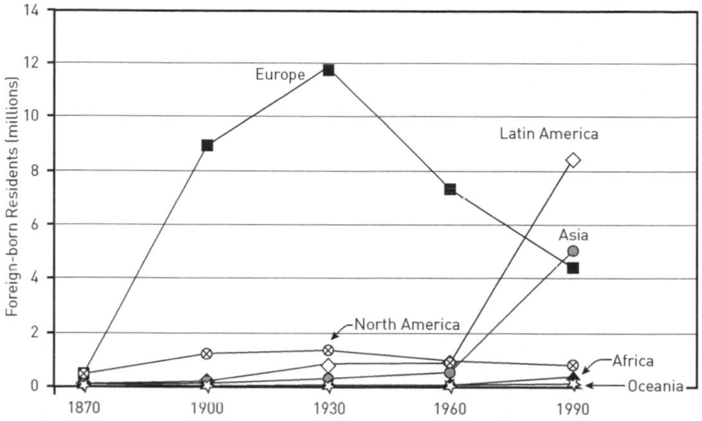

FIGURE 15.9. Foreign-born residents in the United States, 1870–1990

Figure 15.8 is harder to read because the shades of gray do not distinguish the lines well against the background and because our eyes have to flick back and forth to connect the lines to the legend. Figure 15.9 makes those connections clearer.

These different ways of showing the same data can be confusing. To cut through that confusion, test different ways of representing the same data. Construct alternative graphics; then ask someone unfamiliar with the data to judge them for impact and clarity. Be sure to introduce the figures with a sentence that states the claim you want the figure to support.

15.5 COMMUNICATING DATA ETHICALLY

Your graphic must be not only clear and accurate, but honest. Do not distort the image of the data to make your point. For example, the two bar charts below display identical data, yet imply different messages:

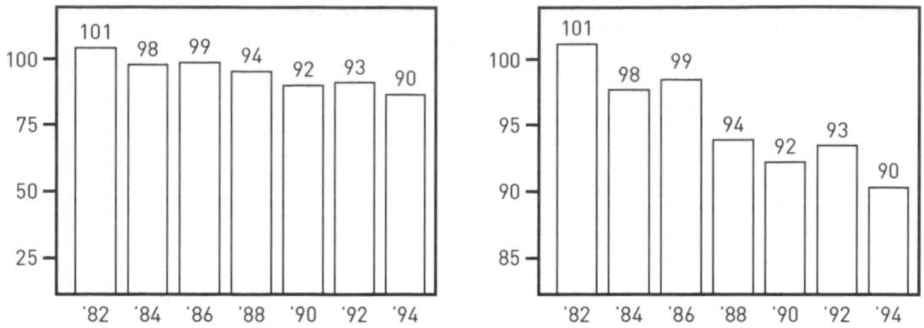

FIGURE 15.10. Capitol City pollution index, 1982–1994

The 0–100 scale in the figure on the left creates a fairly flat slope, which makes the drop in pollution seem small. The vertical scale in the figure on the right, however, begins not at 0 but at 80. When a scale is so truncated, it creates a sharper slope that exaggerates small contrasts.

Graphs can also mislead by implying false correlations. Someone might claim that unemployment goes down as union membership goes down and offer figure 15.11 as evidence. And indeed, in that graph, union membership and the unemployment rate do seem to move together so closely that a reader might infer one causes the other:

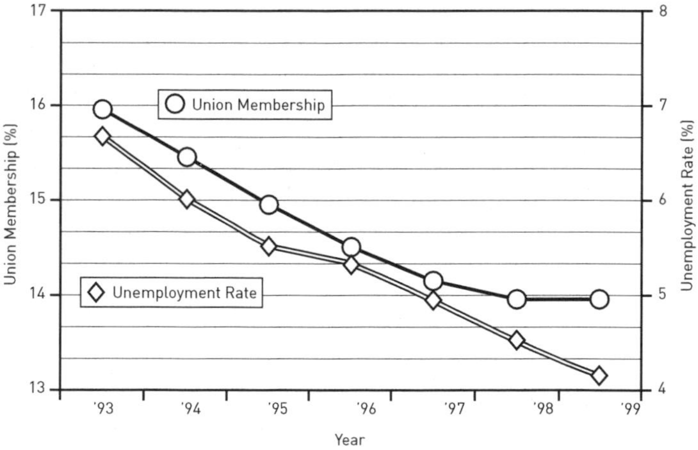

FIGURE 15.11. Union membership and unemployment rate, 1993–1999

But the scale for the left axis (union membership) differs from the scale for the right axis (the unemployment rate), making it seem that the two trends could be causally related. They may be, but that distorted image doesn't prove it.

Graphs can also mislead when the image encourages readers to misjudge values. The two charts in figure 15.12 represent exactly the same data but seem to communicate different messages:

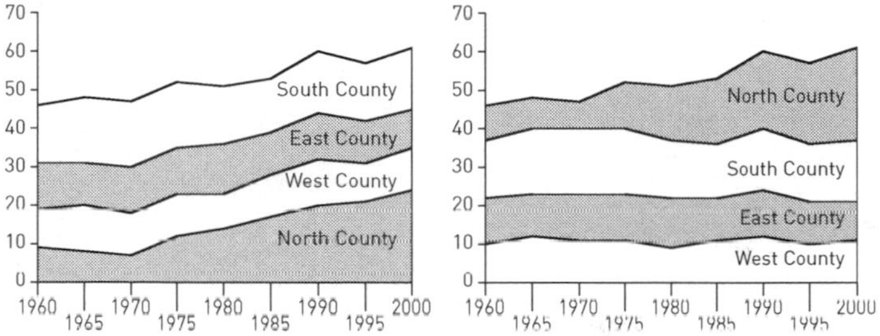

FIGURE 15.12. Representation of suburban counties in state university undergraduates (percent of total)

The charts in figure 15.12 are both stacked area charts. Despite their visual differences, they represent the same data. Area charts such as these represent changes in values not by the *angles* of the lines, but by the areas *between* them. In both charts, the bands for south, east, and west are roughly the same width throughout, indicating little change in the values they represent. The band for the north, however, widens sharply, representing a sharp increase in the numbers it represents. In the chart on the left, readers could easily misjudge the top three bands, because they are on top of the rising north band, making those bands seem to rise as well. In the chart on the right, on the other hand, those three bands do not rise because they are on the bottom. Now only the band for the north rises.

Here are four guidelines for avoiding visual misrepresentation:

- Do not manipulate a scale to magnify or reduce a contrast.
- Do not use a figure whose image distorts values.
- Do not make a table or figure unnecessarily complex or misleadingly simple.
- If the table or figure supports a point, state it.

TABLE 15.7. Common graphic forms and their uses

	Data	Rhetorical Uses
Bar Chart		
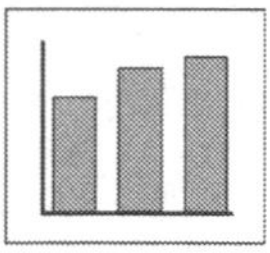	Compares the value of one variable across a series of items called cases (e.g., average salaries for service workers$_{variable}$ in six companies$_{cases}$).	Creates strong visual contrasts among individual cases, emphasizing individual cases. For specific values, add numbers to bars. Can show ranks or trends. Vertical bars (called *columns*) are most common but can be horizontal if cases are numerous or have complex labels. See 15.4.2.
Bar Chart, Grouped or Split		
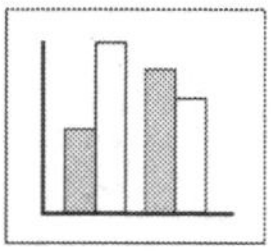	Compares the value of one variable, divided into subsets, across a series of cases (e.g., average salaries$_{variable}$ for men and women service workers$_{subsets}$ in six companies$_{cases}$).	Contrasts subsets within and across individual cases; not useful for comparing total values for cases. For specific values, add numbers to bars. Grouped bars show ranking or trends poorly; useful for time series only if trends are unimportant. See 15.4.2.
Bar Chart, Stacked		
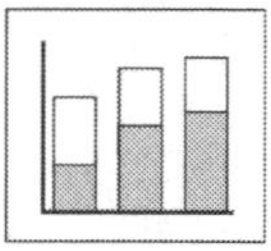	Compares the value of one variable, divided into two or more subsets, across a series of cases (e.g., harassment complaints$_{variable}$ segmented by region$_{subsets}$ in six industries$_{cases}$).	Best for comparing totals across cases and subsets *within* cases; difficult to compare subsets across cases (use grouped bars). For specific values, add numbers to bars and segments. Useful for time series. Can show ranks or trends for total values only. See 15.4.2.
Histogram		
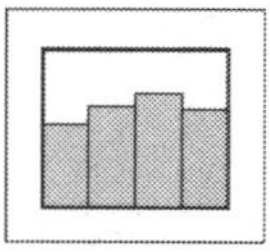	Compares two variables, with one segmented into ranges that function like the cases in a bar graph (e.g., service workers$_{continuous\ variable}$ whose salary is $0–5,000, $5,001–10,000, $10,001–15,000, etc.$_{segmented\ variable}$).	Best for comparing segments within continuous data sets. Shows trends but emphasizes segments (e.g., a sudden spike at $5,000–10,000 representing part-time workers). For specific values, add numbers to bars.
Image Chart		
	Shows value of one or more variables for cases displayed on a map, diagram, or other image (e.g., states$_{cases}$ colored red or blue to show voting patterns$_{variable}$).	Shows the distribution of the data in relation to preexisting categories; de-emphasizes specific values. Best when the image is familiar, as in a map or diagram of a process.
Pie Chart		
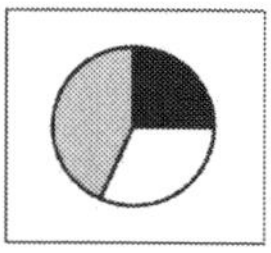	Shows the proportion of a single variable for a series of cases (e.g., the budget share$_{variable}$ of U.S. cabinet departments$_{cases}$).	Best for comparing one segment to the whole. Useful only with few segments or segments that are very different in size; otherwise comparisons among segments are difficult. For specific values, add numbers to segments. Common in popular venues, frowned on by professionals. See 15.4.2.

TABLE 15.7. *(continued)*

	Data	Rhetorical Uses
Line Graph		
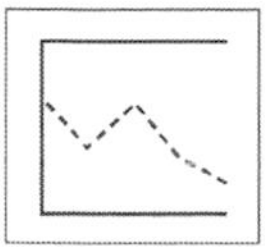	Compares continuous variables for one or more cases (e.g., temperature$_{variable}$ and viscosity$_{variable}$ in two fluids$_{cases}$).	Best for showing trends; deemphasizes specific values. Useful for time series. To show specific values, add numbers to data points. To show the significance of a trend, segment the grid (e.g., below- or above-average performance). See 15.4.3.
Area Chart		
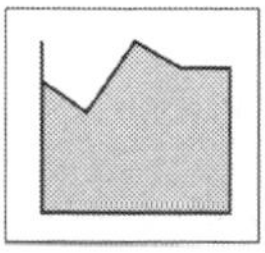	Compares two continuous variables for one or more cases (e.g., reading test scores$_{variable}$ over time$_{variable}$ in a school district$_{case}$).	Shows trends; deemphasizes specific values. Can be used for time series. To show specific values, add numbers to data points. Areas below the lines add no information but will lead some readers to misjudge values. Confusing with multiple lines/areas.
Area Chart, Stacked		
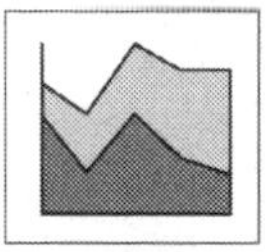	Compares two continuous variables for two or more cases (e.g., profit$_{variable}$ over time$_{variable}$ for several products$_{cases}$).	Shows the trend for the total of all cases, plus how much each case contributes to that total. Likely to mislead readers on the value or the trend for any individual case, as explained in 15.5.
Scatterplot		
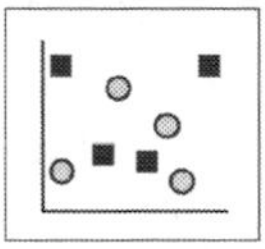	Compares two variables at multiple data points for a single case (e.g., housing sales$_{variable}$ and distance from downtown$_{variable}$ in one city$_{case}$) or at one data point for multiple cases (e.g., brand loyalty$_{variable}$ and repair frequency$_{variable}$ for ten manufacturers$_{cases}$).	Best for showing the distribution of data, especially when there is no clear trend or when the focus is on outlying data points. If only a few data points are plotted, it allows a focus on individual values.
Bubble Chart		
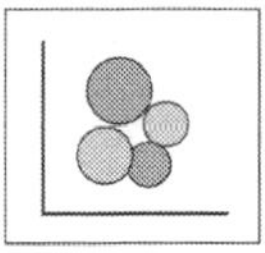	Compares three variables at multiple data points for a single case (e.g., housing sales,$_{variable}$ and distance from downtown,$_{variable}$ prices$_{variable}$ in one city$_{case}$) or at one data point for multiple cases (e.g., image advertising,$_{variable}$ repair frequency,$_{variable}$ and brand loyalty$_{variable}$ for ten manufacturers$_{cases}$).	Emphasizes the relationship between the third variable (bubbles) and the first two; most useful when the question is whether the third variable is a product of the others. Readers easily misjudge relative values shown by bubbles; adding numbers mitigates that problem.

16 Introductions and Conclusions

A good introduction encourages readers to read your work with interest and prepares them to understand it better. A good conclusion leaves them with a clear statement of your point and renewed appreciation of its significance. In this chapter, we show you how to write both. The time you spend revising your introduction and conclusion may be the most important revision you do.

Once you think you have a draft that works, you're ready to write your final introduction and conclusion. Some writers think that means following the standard advice: *Grab their attention with something snappy or cute.* That's not useless advice, but readers want more than cute and snappy. In part II, we showed you how to develop a project around a research problem. Here, we show you how to use that problem to engage your readers. What seizes their attention is a problem they think needs a solution, and what holds it is a promise that you've found it. As we've said, you can always work with readers who say, *I don't agree.* What you can't survive are those who shrug and say, *I don't care.*

16.1 THE COMMON STRUCTURE OF INTRODUCTIONS

As we've emphasized, different research communities do things in different ways, but nowhere do those differences seem greater than in their introductions. These three condensed examples are from the fields of cultural criticism, computer design, and legal history. But while they look different on the surface, their underlying structures are identical.

(1) Why can't a machine be more like a man? In almost every episode of *Star Trek: The Next Generation*, the android Data wonders what makes a person a person. In the original *Star Trek*, similar questions were raised by the half-Vulcan Mr. Spock, whose status as a person was undermined by his machinelike logic and lack of emotion. In fact, Data and

Spock are only the most recent "quasi-persons" who have explored the nature of humanity. The same question has been raised by and about creatures ranging from Frankenstein's monster to the Terminator. But the real question is why these characters who struggle to be persons are always white and male. As cultural interpreters, do they tacitly reinforce destructive stereotypes of what it means to be "normal"? The model person seems in fact to be defined by Western criteria that exclude most of the people in the world.

(2) As part of its program of Continuous Quality Improvement (CQI), Motodyne Computers plans to redesign the user interface for its Unidyne™ online help system. The specifications for its interface call for self-explanatory icons that let users identify their function without verbal labels. Motodyne has three years' experience with its current icon set, but it has no data showing which icons are self-explanatory. Lacking such data, we cannot determine which icons to redesign. This report provides data for eleven icons, showing that five of them are not self-explanatory.

(3) In today's society, would Major John André, a British spy in civilian clothes captured behind American lines in 1780, be hanged? Though considered a noble patriot, he suffered the punishment mandated by military law. Over time our traditions have changed, but the punishment for spying has not. It is the only offense that mandates death. Recently, however, the Supreme Court has rejected mandatory death sentences in civilian cases, creating an ambiguity in their application to military cases. If Supreme Court decisions apply to the military, will Congress have to revise the Uniform Code of Military Justice? This article concludes that it will.

The topics and problems posed in those three introductions differ as much as their intended readers, but behind them is a shared pattern that readers look for in all introductions, regardless of field. That common structure consists of three elements:

- contextualizing background
- statement of the problem
- response to the problem

Not every introduction has all three elements, but most do.

Here is that pattern of *Context* + *Problem* + *Response* in each of those introductions:

> (1) **CONTEXT:** Why can't a machine be more like a man? . . . The same question has been raised by and about creatures ranging from Frankenstein's monster to the Terminator.
> **PROBLEM:** But the real question is . . . do they tacitly reinforce destructive stereotypes of what it means to be "normal"?
> **RESPONSE:** The model person seems in fact to be defined by Western criteria that exclude most of the people in the world.
>
> (2) **CONTEXT:** As part of its program of Continuous Quality Improvement (CQI), Motodyne Computers plans to redesign the user interface. . . . Motodyne has three years' experience with its current icon set . . .
> **PROBLEM:** but it has no data showing which icons are self-explanatory. Lacking such data, we cannot determine which icons to redesign.
> **RESPONSE:** This report provides data for eleven icons, showing that five of them are not self-explanatory.
>
> (3) **CONTEXT:** In today's society, would Major John André . . . be hanged [for spying]? . . . It is the only offense that mandates death.
> **PROBLEM:** Recently, however, the Supreme Court has rejected mandatory death sentences in civilian cases, creating an ambiguity in their application to military cases. . . . Will Congress have to revise the Uniform Code of Military Justice?
> **RESPONSE:** This article concludes that it will.

Each of those elements plays it own role not only in motivating readers to read your paper, but in helping them understand it.

16.2 STEP 1: ESTABLISHING A CONTEXT

The opening context establishes *common ground*, a shared understanding between reader and writer about the larger issue the writer will address. But it does more, illustrated by the opening of a fairy tale:

> One sunny morning Little Red Riding Hood was skipping through the forest on her way to Grandmother's house.*stable context [imagine butterflies dancing around her head to flutes and violins]*

Like the opening to most fairy tales, this one establishes an unproblematic, even happy context, just so that it can be disrupted with a problem:

> . . . when suddenly Hungry Wolf jumped out from behind a tree *disrupting condition [imagine trombones and tubas]* frightening her [and, if they've lost themselves in the story, little children as well]. *cost*

The rest of the story elaborates that problem and then resolves it.

Unlikely though it may seem, most introductions follow the same strategy. They open with the stable context of a common ground—some apparently unproblematic account of research already known. The writer then disrupts it with a problem, saying in effect: *Reader, you may think you know something,* ***but*** *your knowledge is flawed or incomplete.*

> (3) STABLE CONTEXT: In today's society, would Major John André, a British spy . . . be hanged? . . . [Spying] is the only offense that mandates death.
>
> DISRUPTING PROBLEM: Recently, **however**, the Supreme Court has rejected mandatory death sentences. . . .

Not every research paper opens with common ground. This one opens directly with a problem:

> Recently the chemical processes that thin the ozone layer have been found to be less well understood than once thought. We may have labeled hydrofluorocarbons as the chief cause incorrectly.

Some readers might find that problem disturbing enough to motivate their reading, but we can heighten its punch by introducing it with the seemingly unproblematic context of prior research, *specifically so that we can disrupt it*:

> As we have investigated environmental threats, our understanding of chemical processes in acid rain and the buildup of carbon dioxide has improved, allowing us to understand better their effects on the biosphere. *stable context* [*Sounds good.*] **But recently the processes that thin the ozone layer have been found to be less well understood than once**

> **thought.***destabilizing condition* We may have labeled hydrofluorocarbons as the chief cause incorrectly.*consequence*

Readers now have not one reason to see their self-interest in the problem, but two: not just the problem itself, but also their incomplete understanding of the whole matter.

Your context can describe a misunderstanding:

> **The Crusades are widely believed to have been motivated by religious zeal to restore the Holy Land to Christendom.***stable context* **In fact**, the motives were at least partly, if not largely, political.

It can survey flawed research:

> **Few sociological concepts have fallen out of favor as fast as Catholicism's alleged protective influence against suicide. Once one of sociology's basic beliefs, it has been called into question by a series of studies in both Europe and North America**. . . .*stable context* **However**, certain studies still find an effect of religion . . .

Or it can point to a misunderstanding about the problem itself:

> **American education has focused on teaching children to think critically, to ask questions and test answers.***stable context* **But** the field of critical thinking has been taken over by fads and special interests.

Some inexperienced researchers skimp on common ground, opening their paper as if they were picking up a class conversation where it left off. Their introductions are so sketchy that only others in the course would understand them:

> In view of Hofstadter's failure to respect the differences among math, music, and art, it is not surprising that the response to *The Embodied Mind* would be stormy. It is less clear what caused the controversy. I will argue that any account of the human mind must be interdisciplinary. . . .

When you draft your introduction, imagine you are writing to someone who has read some of the same sources as you and is generally interested in the same issues, but does not know what specifically happened in your class.

Others make the opposite mistake, thinking they should list every source they read that remotely touches their topic. Survey only those sources whose findings you will *directly* modify. Add more *only* if you need to locate the problem in a wider context.

16.3 STEP 2: STATING YOUR PROBLEM

Once you establish a stable context or common ground, disrupt it with a problem. As we've said, the statement of a research problem has two parts (see chapter 4):

- a *condition* of incomplete knowledge or understanding, and
- the *consequences* of that condition, a more significant gap in understanding

You can state the condition directly:

> . . . but Motodyne has no data showing which icons are self-explanatory.

Or you can imply it in an indirect question:

> The real question is why these characters are always white and male.

You make this condition of ignorance or flawed understanding part of a *full* research problem *only* when you imagine someone asking, *So what?*, and then spell out as an answer the *consequence* of that flawed understanding. You can state that consequence as a direct cost:

> Lacking such data, we cannot determine which icons to redesign.$_{cost}$

Or you can transform the cost into a benefit:

> With such data, we could determine which icons to redesign.$_{benefit}$

The choice between stating a cost and stating a benefit is not just a matter of style. Some research indicates that readers are more motivated by a real cost than by a potential benefit. Our suggestion: state costs or consequences when presenting your problem; state benefits to intensify your solution.

That's the straightforward version of stating a problem; there are variations.

16.3.1 When Should You State the Condition of a Problem Explicitly?

Occasionally, you tackle a problem so familiar that its name implies both its condition and consequence to those in the field: *the role of DNA in personality*; *Shakespeare's knowledge of foreign languages*. Likewise, in some fields like mathematics and the natural sciences, many research problems are widely known, so just stating the condition is enough to bring to mind its consequence. Here again is that (condensed) introduction to Crick and Watson's landmark account of the double-helix structure of DNA:

> We wish to suggest a structure for the salt of deoxyribose nucleic acid (D.N.A.). This structure has novel features which are of considerable biological interest. A structure for nucleic acid has already been proposed by Pauling and Corey. They kindly made their manuscript available to us in advance of publication. Their model consists of three intertwined chains, with the phosphates near the fibre axis, and the bases on the outside. In our opinion, this structure is unsatisfactory. . . .

It was enough for them merely to "suggest" a structure for DNA, because they knew everyone wanted to know what it was. (Note, though, that they do raise a problem by mentioning Pauling and Corey's *incorrect* model.)

In the natural sciences and most social sciences, researchers usually address questions familiar to their readers. In that case, you might think you do not need to spell out your problem. But readers won't know the *particular* flaw in their knowledge that your research will correct unless you tell them.

In the humanities and some social sciences, researchers more often pose questions that they alone have found or even invented, questions that readers find new and often surprising. In that case, you must explicitly describe the gap in knowledge or flawed understanding that you intend to resolve.

16.3.2 Should You Spell Out Consequences and Benefits?

To convince readers that they should take your problem seriously, you must state the cost *they* will pay if it is not resolved or the benefits *they* gain if it is. Sometimes you can describe tangible costs that your research helps your readers avoid (see 4.1):

> Last year the River City Supervisors agreed that River City should add the Bayside development to its tax base. Their plan, however, was based on little economic analysis. If the Board votes to annex Bayside without understanding what it will cost the city, **the Board risks worsening River City's already shaky fiscal situation.** When the burden of bringing sewer and water service up to city code are included in the analysis, the annexation will cost more than the Board assumes.

This is the kind of problem that motivates *applied* research. The area of ignorance (no economic analysis) has tangible consequences (higher costs).

In pure research, you formulate the same kind of problem when you explain the consequence not in money, but as misunderstanding or, alternatively, as the possible benefit of better understanding:

> Since 1972 American cities have annexed upscale neighborhoods to prop up tax bases, often bringing disappointing economic benefits. But those results could have been predicted had they done basic economic analysis. The annexation movement is a case study of how political decisions at the local level fail to use expert information. What is puzzling is why cities do not seek out that expertise. **If we can discover why cities fail to rely on basic economic analyses, we might better understand why their decision making fails so often in other areas as well.** This paper analyzes the decision-making process of three cities that annexed surrounding areas without consideration of economic consequences.

16.3.3 Testing Conditions and Consequences

In chapter 4 we suggested a way to test how clearly you articulate the consequences of not solving a problem: after the sentences that best state your readers' condition of ignorance or misunderstanding, ask, *So what?*

> Motodyne has no data showing which icons are self-explanatory. [*So what?*] Without such data, it cannot determine which icons to redesign.

> Stories about the Alamo in Mexican and U.S. versions differ in obvious ways, but U.S. versions from different eras also differ. [*So what?*] Well . . .

Answering *So what?* can be exasperating, even dismaying. If you fall in love with stories about the Battle of the Alamo, you can pursue them to your heart's content, without having to answer to anyone but yourself: *I just like reading about them.* But for others to appreciate your research, you have to "sell" them on its significance. Otherwise, why should they spend time on it?

To convince readers to care about your work, you have to show them that your problem is their problem—even if they don't know it yet. You have to convince them that if they go on not knowing, say, how Hollywood turned the Alamo story into myth, they will fail to understand something more important about national identity. To be sure, some readers will ask again, *So what? I don't care about national identity.* To which you can only shrug and think, *Wrong audience.* Successful researchers know how to find and solve interesting problems, but they also know how to find (or create) an audience interested in the problems they solve.

If you are sure your readers know the consequences of your problem, you might decide not to state them explicitly. Crick and Watson did not specify the cost of not knowing the structure of DNA, because they knew their readers already recognized that without understanding the structure of DNA, they could not understand genetics (something more important). Had Crick and Watson spelled out that consequence, it might have seemed redundant or condescending.

If you are tackling your first research project, no reasonable teacher will expect you to state the consequences of your problem in detail, because you probably don't yet know why other researchers think it is significant. But you take a big step in that direction when you can state your own incomplete knowledge or flawed understanding in a way that shows you are committed to improving it. You take an even bigger step when you can show that by better understanding one thing, you better understand something much more important, even if only to you.

16.4 STEP 3: STATING YOUR RESPONSE

Once you disrupt your readers' stable context with a problem, they expect you to resolve it in one of two ways: by stating your solution or main point or by promising that you will do so later on. Readers look for this statement or promise in the last few sentences of your introduction.

16.4.1 State the Gist of Your Solution

You can state your main point/solution explicitly toward the end of your introduction:

> As we have investigated environmental threats, our understanding of chemical processes in acid rain and the buildup of carbon dioxide has improved, allowing us to understand better their effects on the biosphere.*stable context* [*Sounds good.*] But recently the chemical processes that thin the ozone layer have been found to be less well understood than once thought.*condition* [*So what?*] We may have labeled hydrofluorocarbons as the chief cause incorrectly.*consequence* **We have found that the bonding of carbon** . . .*gist of solution/main point*

16.4.2 Promise a Solution

Alternatively, you can delay your main point by stating toward the end of your introduction only where your paper is headed, implying that you will present that point in your conclusion. This approach provides a launching point and creates a point-last paper:

> As we have investigated environmental threats, our understanding . . . has improved. . . . But recently the chemical processes . . . have been found to be less well understood. . . . [*So what?*] We may have labeled hydrofluorocarbons as the chief cause incorrectly. [*Well, what* have *you found?*] **In this report we describe a hitherto unexpected chemical bonding between** . . .*promise of point to come*

This introduction launches us into the paper, not with its main point but with a promise of one to come.

The weakest promise is one that merely announces a vague topic:

> This study investigates processes leading to ozone depletion.

When you save your point for the end of your paper, you ask your readers to trust that getting to it is worth their effort. You build this trust in your introduction by giving them not just a general topic but an outline of your solution or a plan for your argument (or both).

> There are many designs for hydroelectric turbine intakes and diversion screens, but on-site evaluation is not cost-effective. A more viable alternative is computer modeling. **To evaluate hydroelectric diversion screens, this study will evaluate three computer models—Quattro, AVOC, and Turbo-plex—to determine which is most cost-effective in reliability, speed, and ease of use.**

This kind of plan is common in social sciences, but less frequent in the humanities, where many consider it a bit heavy-handed.

16.5 SETTING THE RIGHT PACE

When crafting your introduction, you must decide how quickly to raise your problem. That depends on how much your readers know. In this next example, the writer devotes one sentence to announcing a consensus among well-informed engineers and then briskly disrupts it:

> Fluid-film forces in squeeze-film dampers (SFDs) are usually obtained from the Reynolds equation of classical lubrication theory. **However, the increasing size of rotating machinery requires the inclusion of fluid inertia effects in the design of SFDs. Without them** . . .

(We have no idea what any of that means, but the structure of *Context* + *Problem* is clear.)

This next writer also addresses technical concepts but patiently lays them out for readers who have little technical knowledge:

> A method of protecting migrating fish at hydroelectric power developments is diversion by screening turbine intakes . . . [*another 110 words explaining screens*]. Since the efficiency of screens is determined by the interaction of fish behavior and hydraulic flow, screen design can be evaluated by determining its hydraulic performance . . . [*40 more words explaining hydraulics*]. **This study provides a better understanding of the hydraulic features of this technique, which may guide future designs.**

The pace of an introduction varies by field. Researchers whose problems are already familiar to their research communities can open quickly; those who work in fields where problems are not widely shared must start more slowly. But the pace of your introduction signals something else as well. When you open quickly, you imply an audience of peers; when you open slowly, you imply readers who know less than you. If your readers are knowledgeable and you open slowly, they may think *you* know too little. But if they know little and you open quickly, they may think you are inconsiderate of their needs.

16.6 ORGANIZING THE WHOLE INTRODUCTION

When organizing your introduction, you have many choices, but they are not as complicated as they might seem. They all follow what is in fact a simple "grammar." A full introduction consists of just three elements:

> Context + Problem + Response

You don't need all three in every introduction:

- If the problem is well known, omit the common ground.
- If the consequences of the problem are well known, omit them.
- If you want readers to follow your thinking before they know your answer, offer a launching point at the end of your introduction and state your main point in your conclusion.

All this may seem formulaic, but it's what readers expect. And when you master a rhetorical pattern like this, you have more than a formula for writing. You also have a tool for thinking. To write a full statement of your shared context and problem, you have to think hard about what your readers know, what they don't, and, in particular, what they should know and why.

16.7 FINDING YOUR FIRST FEW WORDS

Many writers find the first sentence or two especially difficult to write, and so they fall into clichés.

- Don't repeat the language of your assignment. If you are struggling to start, prime your pump by paraphrasing it, but when you revise, rewrite it.
- Don't start with a dictionary entry: "*Webster's* defines *ethics* as . . ." If a word is important enough to define, a dictionary definition won't serve.
- Don't start grandly: "The most profound philosophers have for centuries wrestled with the important question of . . ." If your subject is grand, it will speak its own importance.

These miscues arise from a good impulse: they are attempts to establish a shared context or common ground with a community of readers. The problem in all cases is that it is the wrong community. In that first example, the community is too narrow: it is just the student's teacher. In the other examples, the community is too broad: those writers are groping for a context that all of humanity could agree to. To avoid these missteps, open in a way that is likely to appeal to the *specific community of readers* you hope to interest.

Here are three standard choices for your first sentence or two.

16.7.1 Open with a Striking Fact Relevant to Your Problem

> Those who think that tax cuts for the rich stimulate the economy should contemplate the fact that the top 1 percent of Americans control one-third of America's total wealth.

16.7.2 Open with a Striking Quotation

Do this only if its words anticipate key terms in the rest of your introduction:

"From the sheer sensuous beauty of a genuine Jan van Eyck there emanates a **strange fascination** not unlike that which we experience when permitting ourselves to be **hypnotized** by **precious stones**." Edwin Panofsky suggests here something **strangely magical** in Jan van Eyck's works. His images hold a **jewel-like** fascination. . . .

16.7.3 Open with a Relevant Anecdote

Do this only if its language anticipates your topic and vividly illustrates your problem. Here are the opening sentences of an article recounting the rise and fall of a Chicago street gang:

> On a park bench in July 1996, Cynthia, Laurie, and other senior officers of the Black Sisters United (BSU)—Chicago's largest federation of "girl gangs"—reflected on their efforts to sustain an organization that could represent and act on behalf of young African-American women in the city. "We was so close!" Cynthia said with deep anguish, sitting upright and looking about to see if anyone had heard her.

16.8 WRITING YOUR CONCLUSION

Even if your argument doesn't have a section labeled *Conclusion*, it will have a paragraph or two that serve as one. Your conclusion is an occasion to sum up your argument, but just as important, it is an opportunity to extend your research community's conversation by suggesting new questions your research has allowed you to see. You may be happy to know that you can write your conclusion using the same elements in your introduction, in reverse order.

16.8.1 Start with Your Main Point

State your main point near the beginning of your conclusion. If you already stated it in your introduction, repeat it here but more fully; do not simply repeat it word-for-word.

16.8.2 Add a New Significance or Application

After your point, say why it's significant, preferably with a new answer to *So what?* For example, the writer of this conclusion introduces an additional consequence of the Supreme Court's decision on military death sentences:

> In light of recent Supreme Court decisions rejecting mandatory capital punishment, the mandatory death penalty for treason is apparently unconstitutional and must therefore be revised by Congress. **More significantly, though, if the Uniform Code of Military Justice is changed, it will challenge the fundamental value of military culture that ultimate betrayal requires the ultimate penalty. Congress will then have to deal with the military's sense of what is just.**

This observation belongs in the conclusion rather than in the introduction because it suggests *further questions* the article doesn't take up: *How exactly will the military respond to that challenge to its values? How should Congress respond in turn?* Just as in your introduction you increase the punch of your problem by stating its consequences, so in your conclusion you can increase the significance of your solution by noting its additional implications.

16.8.3 Call for More Research

Just as your opening context surveys research already done, so your conclusion can call for research still to do:

> These differences between novice and expert diagnosticians define their maturation and development. But while we know how novices and experts think differently, **we do not understand which elements in the social experience of novices contribute to that development and how. We need longitudinal studies on how mentoring and coaching affect outcomes and whether active explanation and critique help novices become skilled diagnosticians more quickly.**

When you state what remains to do, you keep the conversation alive. So before you write your last words, imagine someone fascinated by your work who wants to follow up on it: What more would *you* like to know? What research would you suggest they do? After all, that may have been how you found your own problem.

QUICK TIP Titles

The first thing readers read—and the last thing you should write—is your title. Beginning writers just attach a few words to suggest the topics of their papers. That's a mistake: a title is useful when it helps readers understand *specifically* what is to come. Compare these three titles:

> Microfinance
>
> Microfinance and Economic Development
>
> Microfinance as a Strategy for Economic Development: Realizing Its Potential for Improving the Standing of Women

Put into your title the keywords in your main point, the ones you circled when you checked for the continuity of conceptual themes (6.6.1, 8.2.1, 12.1.1, 12.3.2, 13.4). When readers see those concepts turn up again in your main point and again through the body of your paper, they will feel that your text has met their expectations. (Two-line titles give you more room for key terms. End the first line with a colon that introduces a more specific second line.)

17 Revising Style

TELLING YOUR STORY CLEARLY

So far we have focused on the argument and organization of your paper. In this chapter, we show you how to revise your sentences so that readers will think they are clear and direct.

Readers will accept your claim only if they understand your argument, but they won't understand your argument if they can't understand your sentences. Once you revise your paper so that readers will judge its argument to be sound and well organized, find time to make a last pass to make your sentences as easy to read as the complexity of your ideas allows. But again, you face a familiar problem: you can't know which sentences need revising just by reading them. Since you already know what you want them to mean, you will read into them what you want your readers to get out of them. To ensure that your sentences will be as clear to your readers as they are to you, you need a way to identify difficult sentences even when they seem fine to you.

17.1 JUDGING STYLE

If you had to read an article in the style of one of the following examples, which would you choose?

1a. Conventional management practice assumes that interaction and collaboration enhance organizational performance by improving employee creativity and productivity. But unless collaboration is punctuated by isolation, and unless workspace configurations provide isolation opportunities, erosion rather than enhancement of organizational effectiveness may result.

1b. Managers want the people who work for them to interact and collaborate. When they do this, they become more creative and productive.

The organization then performs better. But people also need opportunities to work alone, and workplaces need to provide these opportunities. Otherwise, the organization may become less effective.

1c. Managers conventionally assume that when employees interact and collaborate, they become more creative and productive, thus leading the whole organization to perform better. But unless employees also have opportunities to work alone, and unless workspaces are configured to provide them, the organization may become less rather than more effective.

Few readers choose (1a): it sounds dense, abstract, opaque. Some choose (1b), but it sounds simpleminded, like an adult speaking slowly to a child. Most choose (1c), which sounds like one colleague speaking to another. One of the worst problems in academic writing today is that too many researchers sound like (1a).

A few researchers prefer (1a), claiming that heavy thinking demands heavy writing, that when they try to make complicated ideas clear, they sacrifice nuances and complexity of thought for too-easy understanding. If readers don't understand, too bad; they should work harder.

Perhaps. Everyone who reads philosophers like Immanuel Kant or Friedrich Hegel struggles with their complex prose style, at least at first. But what they have to say proves to be worth the effort. The problem is, few of us think as well as Kant or Hegel. For most of us most of the time, our dense writing indicates not the irreducible difficulty of a work of genius, but the sloppy thinking of writers who aren't considering their readers. And even when complex thought does require a complex style (which is less often than we think), every sentence profits from a second look (and truth be told, Kant and Hegel would have benefited from a good editor).

Some writers do go too far in avoiding a complex style, using simplistic sentences like those in (1b) above. But we assume that most of you do not have that problem, and that you need little help with spelling and grammar. (If you think you do, talk to a writing tutor.) We address here the problem of a style that is too "academic," which is to say, more difficult than it has to be. Convoluted and indirect prose is not what good writers aim for, but what thoughtless ones get away with.

This problem especially afflicts those just starting advanced work because they are hit by double trouble. First, when any of us writes about new and complex ideas that challenge our understanding, we write less clearly than we ordinarily can. This problem afflicts even the most experienced researchers. But new researchers compound that problem when they believe that a complex style bespeaks academic success and they imitate the tangled prose they read. That we can avoid.

17.2 THE FIRST TWO PRINCIPLES OF CLEAR WRITING

17.2.1 Distinguishing Impressions from Their Causes

If we asked you to explain how you chose between (1a) and (1c) above, you would probably describe (1a) with words like *unclear, wordy*, and *dense*; (1c) with words like *clear, concise*, and *direct.* But those words refer not to those sentences on the page, but to how you *felt* as you read them. If you said that (1a) was *dense*, you were really saying that *you* had a hard time getting through it; if you said (1c) was *clear*, you were saying that *you* found it easy to understand.

There's nothing wrong with using impressionistic words to describe your feelings, but they don't help you *fix* unclear sentences like (1a), because they don't explain *what it is on the page or screen that makes you feel as you do.* For that, you need a way to think about sentences that connects an impression like *confusing* to what it is *in the sentence* that confuses you. More important, you have to know how to revise your own sentences when they are clear to you but won't be to your readers.

There are a few principles that distinguish the felt complexity of (1a) from the mature clarity of (1c). These principles focus on only two parts of a sentence: the first six or seven words and the last four or five. Get those words straight, and the rest of the sentence will (usually) take care of itself. To use these principles, though, you must understand five grammatical terms: *simple subject, whole subject, verb, noun,* and *clause.* (If you haven't used those terms for a while, review them before you read on.)

This is important: don't try to apply these principles as you write new sentences. If you follow them *as you draft,* you may tie yourself in knots. Rather, let them guide you when you revise sentences you have already written.

17.2.2 Subjects and Characters

The first principle may remind you of something you learned in grammar school. At the heart of every sentence are its subject and verb. In grammar school you probably learned that subjects are the "doers" or agents of an action. But that's not always true, because subjects can be things other than doers, even actions. Compare these two sentences (the whole subject in each clause is underlined):

> 2a. Locke frequently repeated himself because he did not trust the power of words to name things accurately.
>
> 2b. The reason for Locke's frequent repetition lies in his distrust of the accuracy of the naming power of words.

The two subjects in (2a)—*Locke* and *he*—fit that grammar-school definition: they are doers. But the subject of (2b)—*The reason for Locke's frequent repetition*—does not, because *reason* doesn't really *do* anything here. The real doer is still Locke.

To get beyond sixth-grade definitions, we have to think not only about the grammar of a sentence—its subjects and verbs—but also about the *stories* they tell—about doers and their actions. Here is a story about rain forests and the biosphere:

> 3a. If rain forests are stripped to serve short-term economic interests, the earth's biosphere may be damaged.
>
> 3b. The stripping of rain forests in the service of short-term economic interests could result in damage to the earth's biosphere.

In the clearer version, (3a), look at the whole subjects of each clause:

3a. If rain forests$_{subject}$ are stripped$_{verb}$ . . . the earth's biosphere$_{subject}$ may be damaged.$_{verb}$

Those subjects name the main characters in that story in a few short, concrete words: *rain forests* and *the earth's biosphere*. Compare (3b):

3b. The stripping of rain forests in the service of short-term economic interests$_{subject}$ could result$_{verb}$ in damage to the earth's biosphere.

In (3b) the simple subject (*stripping*) names not a concrete character but rather an action; it is only part of the long abstract phrase that is the whole subject: *the* ***stripping*** *of rain forests in the service of short-term economic interests.*

Now we can see why grammar-school definitions may be bad language theory but good advice about writing. The first principle of clear writing is this:

> Readers will judge your sentences to be clear and readable to the degree that you make their subjects name the main characters in your story. When you do this, your subjects will be short, specific, and concrete.

17.2.3 Verbs, Nouns, and Actions

There is a second difference between clear and unclear prose: it is in the way writers express the crucial *actions* in their stories—as verbs or as nouns. For example, look again at the pairs of sentences (2) and (3) below. (Words naming actions are boldfaced; actions that are verbs are underlined; actions that are nouns are double-underlined.)

2a. Locke frequently **repeated** himself because he did not **trust** the power of words to **name** things accurately.

2b. The reason for Locke's frequent **repetition** lies in his **distrust** of the accuracy of the **naming** power of words.

3a. If rain forests are **stripped** to **serve** short-term economic interests, the earth's biosphere may be **damaged**.

3b. The **stripping** of rain forests in the **service** of short-term economic interests could result in **damage** to the earth's biosphere.

Sentences (2a) and (3a) are clearer than (2b) and (3b) because their subjects are characters, but also because their actions are expressed not as nouns but as verbs.

There is a technical term for turning a verb (or adjective) into a noun: we *nominalize* it. (This term defines itself: when we nominalize the verb *nominalize*, we create the nominalization *nominalization*.) Most nominalizations end with suffixes such as *-tion, -ness, -ment, -ence, -ity*.

Verb →	Nominalization	Adjective →	Nominalization
decide	decision	precise	precision
fail	failure	frequent	frequency
resist	resistance	intelligent	intelligence

But some are spelled like the verb: *change → change; delay → delay; report → report.*

(We'll discuss passive verbs like *are stripped* and *be damaged* in 17.4.)

When you express actions not with verbs but with abstract nouns, you also clutter a sentence with articles and prepositions. Look at all the articles and prepositions (boldfaced) in (4b) that (4a) doesn't need:

4a. Having standardized indices for measuring mood disorders, we now can quantify patients' responses to different treatments.

4b. The standardization **of** indices **for the** measurement **of** mood disorders has now made possible **the** quantification **of** patient response **as a** function **of** treatment differences.

Sentence (4b) adds one *a*, *as*, and *for*; two *the*s, and four *of*s, all because four verbs were turned into nouns: *standardize → stan-*

dardization, measure → measurement, quantify → quantification, respond → response.

When you turn adjectives and verbs into nouns, you can tangle up your sentences in two more ways:

- You have to add verbs that are less specific than the verbs you could have used. In (4b), instead of the specific verbs *standardize, measure, quantify,* and *respond,* we have the single vague verb *made.*
- You are likely to make the characters in your story modifiers of nouns or objects of prepositions or to drop them from a sentence altogether: in (4b), the character *we* becomes *our,* and thereafter the rest of the characters are missing in action.

So here are two principles of a clear style:

- Express crucial actions in verbs.
- Make your central characters the subjects of those verbs; keep those subjects short, concrete, and specific.

17.2.4 Diagnosis and Revision

Given how readers judge sentences, we can offer ways to diagnose and revise yours.

To diagnose:

1. Underline the first six or seven words of every clause, whether main or subordinate.
2. Perform two tests:
   - Are the underlined subjects concrete characters, not abstractions?
   - Do the underlined verbs name specific actions, not general ones like *have, make, do, be,* and so on?
3. If the sentence fails either test, you should probably revise.

To revise:

1. Find the characters you want to tell a story about. If you can't, invent them.

2. Find what those characters are doing. If their actions are in nouns, change them into verbs.
3. Create clauses with your main characters as subjects and their actions as verbs.

You will probably have to recast your sentence in some version of *If X, then Y*; *X, because Y*; *Although X, Y*; *When X, then Y*; and so on.

That's the simple version of revising dense prose into something clearer. Here is a more nuanced one.

17.2.5 Who or What Can Be a Character?

You may have wondered why we called *rain forests* and *the earth's biosphere* "characters" when we usually think of characters as flesh-and-blood people. For our purposes, a character is anything that can be the subject of a lot of verbs in a sequence of sentences. This means that we can also tell stories whose characters are things like *rain forests* and even abstractions like *thought disorders*. In your kind of research, you may have to tell a story about *demographic changes*, *social mobility*, *isotherms*, or *gene pools*.

Sometimes you have a choice: a paper in economics might tell a story about real or virtual people, such as *consumers* and the *Federal Reserve Board*, or about abstractions associated with them, such as *savings* and *monetary policy*. Note, however, that you can still make those abstract characters part of a story with action verbs:

> 5a. When consumers **save** more, the Federal Reserve **changes** its monetary policy to influence how banks **lend** money.
>
> 5b. When consumer **savings rise**, Federal Reserve monetary policy **adapts** to **influence** bank **lending** practices.

A passage might be about real people or about abstractions associated with them: *banks* vs. *lending practices*, *savers* vs. *microeconomics*, or *analysts* vs. *predictions*. All things being equal, though, readers prefer characters to be at least concrete things or, better, flesh-and-blood people.

Experts, however, like to tell stories about abstractions (boldfaced; subjects are underlined).

6. Standardized indices to measure **mood disorders** help us quantify how patients respond to different **treatments**. These **measurements** suggest that **treatments** requiring long-term **hospitalization** are no more effective than outpatient **care** for most patients.

The abstract nominalizations in the second sentence—*measurements, treatments, hospitalization, care*—refer to concepts as familiar to its intended readers as *doctors* and *patients*. Given those readers, the writer would not need to revise them.

In a way, that example undercuts our advice about avoiding nouns made out of verbs, because now instead of revising every abstract noun into a verb, you have to choose which ones to change and which ones to leave as nouns. For example, the abstract nouns in the second sentence of (6) are the same as the first three in (7a):

7a. The **hospitalization** of patients without appropriate **treatment** results in the unreliable **measurement** of outcomes.

But we would improve that sentence if we revised those abstract nouns into verbs:

7b. We cannot **measure** outcomes reliably when patients **are hospitalized** but not **treated** appropriately.

So what we offer here is no iron rule of writing, but rather a principle of diagnosis and revision that you must apply judiciously. In general, though, readers prefer sentences whose subjects are short, specific, and concrete. And that usually means flesh-and-blood characters.

17.2.6 Avoiding Excessive Abstraction

You create the worst problems for readers when you make abstract nouns your main character and subjects of your sentences, then sprinkle more abstractions around them. Here is a passage about two abstract characters, *democracy* and *institutionalization*. Nevertheless, the passage is still clear, at least for its intended readers, because its writers focused on their characters in subjects and avoided additional abstractions, especially nominalizations (main characters are italicized; whole subjects are underlined; verbs are boldfaced):

> 8a. We **expect** that older *democracies* **will benefit** from greater *institutionalization* in the political sphere. Although political *institutionalization* **is** difficult to define, there **seems** to be general consensus that procedures in a well-institutionalized polity **are** functionally **differentiated**, **regularized** (and hence predictable), **professionalized** (including meritocratic methods of recruitment and promotion), **rationalized** (explicable, rule based, and non-arbitrary), and **infused** with value. Most long-standing *democracies* **fit** this description.

Note how the story becomes less clear when those main characters are displaced from subjects and when the key abstraction *institutionalization* is surrounded by other abstract nouns (main characters are italicized; whole subjects are underlined; the additional abstractions are boldfaced):

> 8b. Our **expectation** is that greater *institutionalization* in the political sphere will be of **benefit** to older *democracies*. Although **definition** of political *institutionalization* is difficult, there seems to be general consensus that functional **differentiation**, **regularization** (and hence predictable), **professionalization** (including meritocratic methods of recruitment and promotion), **rationalization** (explicable, rule based, and nonarbitrary), and the **infusion** of value are characteristic of procedures in a well-institutionalized polity. This description is a **fit** for most long-standing *democracies*.

We're not suggesting that you change every abstract noun into a verb. This story about democracy and institutionalization would be difficult to transpose into one about a flesh-and-blood character like *citizens* or *you*. (If you don't believe us, give it a try.) If your best main characters are abstractions, use them. But avoid other abstractions you don't need. As always, the trick is knowing which ones you need and which you don't (usually fewer than you think). Knowing one from the other is a skill that comes only from practice—and criticism.

17.2.7 Creating Main Characters

Having qualified our principle once, we complicate it again. If your sentences are readable, your characters will be the subjects of verbs that express the crucial actions those characters are involved in. But most stories have several characters, any one of whom you can turn into a main character by making it the subject of sentences. Take the sentence about rain forests:

> 9. If rain forests are stripped to serve short-term economic interests, the earth's biosphere may be damaged.

That sentence tells a story that implies other characters but does not specify them: Who is stripping the forests? More important, does it matter? This story could focus on them, but who are they?

> 9a. If developers strip rain forests to serve short-term economic interests, they may damage the earth's biosphere.
>
> 9b. If loggers strip rain forests to serve short-term economic interests, they may damage the earth's biosphere.
>
> 9c. If Brazil strips its rain forests to serve short-term economic interests, it may damage the earth's biosphere.

Which is best? It depends on whom you want *your readers to think* the story is about. As you revise sentences, put characters in subjects and actions in verbs, when you can. But be sure that the character is your *central* character, if only for that sentence.

17.3 A THIRD PRINCIPLE: OLD BEFORE NEW

There is a third principle of reading and revising even more important than the first two. Fortunately, all three principles are related. Compare the (a) and (b) versions in the following. Which seems clearer? Why? (Hint: Look at the beginnings of sentences, this time not just for characters as subjects, but whether those subjects express information that is familiar or information that is new and therefore unexpected.)

> 10a. Because the naming power of words was distrusted by Locke, he repeated himself often. Seventeenth-century theories of language,

especially Wilkins's scheme for a universal language involving the creation of countless symbols for countless meanings, had centered on this naming power. A new era in the study of language that focused on the ambiguous relationship between sense and reference begins with Locke's distrust.

10b. Locke often repeated himself because he distrusted the naming power of words. This naming power had been central to seventeenth-century theories of language, especially Wilkins's scheme for a universal language involving the creation of countless symbols for countless meanings. Locke's distrust begins a new era in the study of language, one that focused on the ambiguous relationship between sense and reference.

Most readers prefer (10b), saying not just that (10a) is *too complex* or *inflated*, but that it's also *disjointed*; it doesn't *flow*—impressionistic words that again describe not what we see on the page but how we *feel* about it.

We can explain what causes those impressions if we again apply the "first six or seven words" test. In the disjointed (a) version, the sentences after the first one begin with information that a reader could not predict:

the naming power of words

Seventeenth-century theories of language

A new era in the study of language

In contrast, the sentences after the first one in (10b) begin with information that readers would find familiar:

Locke

This naming power [repeated from the previous sentence]

Locke's distrust [a useful abstract noun because it repeats something from the previous sentence]

In (10a) each sentence begins unpredictably, so we can't easily see the "topic" of the whole passage. In (10b) each sentence after the first opens with words referring to ideas that readers recall from the previous sentence.

Readers follow a story most easily if they can begin each sentence with a character or idea that is familiar to them, either because it was already mentioned or because it comes from the context. From this principle of reading, we can infer principles of diagnosis and revision.

To diagnose:

1. Underline the first six or seven words of every sentence.
2. Have you underlined words that your readers will find familiar and easy to understand (usually words used before)?
3. If not, revise.

To revise:

1. Make the first six or seven words refer to familiar information, usually something you have mentioned before (typically your main characters).
2. Put at the ends of sentences information that your readers will find unpredictable or complex and therefore harder to understand.

This old-new principle happily cooperates with the ones about characters and subjects, because older information usually names a character (after you introduce it, usually at the *end* of a prior sentence). But should you ever have to choose between beginning a sentence with a character or with old information, *always choose the principle of old before new.*

17.4 CHOOSING BETWEEN THE ACTIVE AND PASSIVE VOICE

You may have noted that some of the clearer sentences had passive verbs. This seems to contradict familiar advice from English teachers to avoid them. Followed mindlessly, that advice will make your sentences *less* clear. Rather than worry about active and passive, ask a simpler question: Do your sentences begin with familiar information, preferably a main character? If you put familiar characters in your subjects, you will use the active and passive properly.

For example, which of these two passages "flows" more easily?

11a. The quality of our air and even the climate of the world depend on healthy rain forests in Asia, Africa, and South America. But the increasing demand for more land for agricultural use and for wood products for construction worldwide now threatens these forests with destruction.

11b. The quality of our air and even the climate of the world depend on healthy rain forests in Asia, Africa, and South America. But these rain forests are now threatened with destruction by the increasing demand for more land for agricultural use and for wood products used in construction worldwide.

Most readers think (11b) flows more easily. Why? Note that the beginning of the second sentence in (11b) picks up on the character introduced at the end of the first sentence:

11b. . . . rain forests in Asia, Africa, and South America. But these rain forests . . .

The second sentence of (11a), on the other hand, opens with information completely unconnected to the first sentence:

11a. . . . rain forests in Asia, Africa, and South America. But the increasing demand for more land . . .

In other words, the passive allowed us to move the older, more familiar information from the end of its sentence to its beginning, where it belongs. And that's the main function of the passive: to build sentences that begin with older information. If we don't use the passive when we should, our sentences won't flow as well as they could.

In English classes, students are told that they should use only active verbs, but they hear the opposite in engineering, the natural sciences, and some social sciences. There teachers demand the passive, thinking that it makes writing more objective. Most of that advice is equally misleading. Compare the passive (12a) with the active (12b):

12a. Eye movements **were measured** at tenth-of-second intervals.

12b. We **measured** eye movements at tenth-of-second intervals.

These sentences offer equally objective information, but their *stories* differ: one is about eye movements, the other about a person measuring them, who happens also to be the author. The first is supposed to be more "objective" because it ignores the person and focuses on the movements. But just avoiding *I* or *we* doesn't make writing more "objective." It simply changes the story.

In fact, the issue of the passive is still more complicated. When a scientist uses the passive to describe a *process*, she implies that the process can be repeated by anyone. In this case, the passive is the right choice, because anyone who wanted to repeat the research would have to measure eye movements.

On the other hand, consider this pair of sentences:

13a. It **can be concluded** that the fluctuations result from the Burnes effect.

13b. We **conclude** that the fluctuations result from the Burnes effect.

The active verb in (13b), *conclude*, and its first-person subject, *we*, are not only common in the sciences, but appropriate. The difference? It has to do with the kind of action the verb names. The active (and therefore first person) is appropriate when authors refer to actions that only the *writer/researcher* can perform—not only rhetorical actions, such as *suggest, conclude, argue*, or *show*, but also those for which they get credit as scientists, such as *design* experiments, *solve* problems, or *prove* results. Everyone can *measure*, but only author/researchers are entitled to *claim* what their research means.

Scientists typically use the first person and active verbs at the beginning of journal articles, where they describe how *they* discovered their problem and at the end where they describe how *they* solved it. In between, when they describe processes that anyone can perform, they regularly use the passive.

17.5 A FINAL PRINCIPLE: COMPLEXITY LAST

We have focused on how clauses begin. Now we look at how they end. You can anticipate the principle for ending sentences: if familiar information goes first, the newest, most complex information goes last. This principle is particularly important in three contexts:

- when you introduce a new technical term
- when you present a unit of information that is long and complex
- when you introduce a concept that you intend to develop in what follows

17.5.1 Introducing Technical Terms

When you introduce technical terms that are new to your readers, construct your sentences so that those terms appear in the last few words. Compare these two:

> 14a. The monoamine hypothesis has been the leading biological account of depression for over three decades. According to this hypothesis, deficits in monoamines including dopamine, epinephrine, norepinephrine, and serotonin are associated with depression. Monoamine concentrations in neural synapses are regulated in different ways by different types of antidepressants.

> 14b. For over three decades, the leading biological account of depression has been the monoamine hypothesis. According to this hypothesis, depression is associated with deficits in neurotransmitters called monoamines, including dopamine, epinephrine, norepinephrine, and serotonin. Different types of antidepressants work in different ways to regulate concentrations of monoamines in neural synapses.

In (14a) all the technical-sounding terms appear early in the sentences; in (14b) the technical terms appear at the end of the sentences.

17.5.2 Introducing Complex Information

Put complex bundles of ideas that require long phrases or clauses at the end of a sentence, never at the beginning. Compare (11a) and (11b) again:

> 11a. The quality of our air and even the climate of the world depend on healthy rain forests in Asia, Africa, and South America. But the increas-

ing demand for more land for agricultural use and for wood products for construction worldwide now threatens these forests with destruction.

11b. The quality of our air and even the climate of the world depend on healthy rain forests in Asia, Africa, and South America. But these rain forests are now threatened with destruction by the increasing demand for more land for agricultural use and for wood products used in construction worldwide.

In (11a) the second sentence begins with a long, complex unit of information, a subject that runs on for more than a line. In contrast, the subject of the second sentence in (11b), *these rain forests*, is short, simple, and easy to read, again because the passive verb (*are now threatened*) lets us flip the short and familiar information to the beginning and the long and complex part to the end.

In short, don't begin your sentences with complexity; save it for the end. Unfortunately that's not easy to do, because you may be so familiar with your ideas that you can't distinguish what is *for your readers* old and simple from what's new and complex.

17.5.3 Introducing What Follows

When you start a paragraph, put the key terms that appear in the rest of the paragraph at the end of the first or second sentence. Which of these two sentences would best introduce the rest of the paragraph that follows?

15a. The political situation changed, because disputes over succession to the throne plagued seven of the eight reigns of the Romanov line after Peter the Great.

15b. The political situation changed, because after Peter the Great seven of the eight reigns of the Romanov line were plagued by turmoil over disputed succession to the throne.

The problems began in 1722, when Peter the Great passed a law of succession that terminated the principle of heredity and required the sovereign to appoint a successor. But because many tsars, including Peter, died before they named successors, those who aspired to rule had no authority by appointment, and so their succession was often disputed by lower-level aristocrats. There was turmoil even when successors were appointed.

Most readers feel that (15b) is more closely connected to the rest of the passage. The last few words of (15a) seem unimportant in relation to what follows (in another context, of course, they might be crucial).

So once you've checked the first six or seven words in every sentence, check the last five or six as well. If those words are not the most important, complex, or weighty, revise so that they are. Look especially at the ends of sentences that introduce paragraphs or even sections.

17.6 SPIT AND POLISH

We've focused on those issues of sentence style relevant to writing research papers, and on principles of diagnosis and revision that help make prose as readable as possible. There are other principles—sentence length, the right choice of words, concision, and so on. But those are issues pertinent to writing of all kinds and are addressed by many books. And, of course, readability alone is not enough. After you revise your style, you still have to check your grammar, spelling, and punctuation. Then you have to make sure that you have observed the accepted conventions for representing numbers, proper names, foreign words, and so on. Though important, those matters fall outside the purview of this book.

QUICK TIP **The Quickest Revision Strategy**

Our advice about revision may seem overly detailed, but if you revise in steps, it's not difficult to follow. The first step is the most important: as you draft, remember to forget these steps (except for this one about remembering). Your first job is to draft something to revise. You will never do that if you keep asking yourself whether you should have just used a verb or a noun. If you don't have time to look at every sentence, start with passages where you found it hard to explain your ideas. When you struggle to write about confusing content, your sentences tend toward confusion as well.

For Clarity and Flow

To diagnose:

1. Highlight the first six or seven words in every sentence. Ignore short introductory phrases such as *At first, For the most part,* and so on.
2. Run your eye down the page, checking whether you highlighted a consistent set of related words. The words that begin a series of sentences need not be identical, but they should name people or concepts that your readers will see are clearly related. If not, revise.
3. Check the highlighted words in each sentence. They should include a subject that names a character and a verb that names an important action. If not, revise.

To revise:

1. Identify your main characters, real or conceptual. Make them the subjects of verbs.
2. Look for nouns ending in *-tion, -ment, -ence,* and so on. If they are the subjects of verbs, turn them into verbs.
3. Make sure that each sentence begins with familiar information, preferably a character you have mentioned before.

For Emphasis

To diagnose:

1. Underline the last five or six words in every sentence.
2. You should have underlined
    - technical-sounding words that you are using for the first time
    - the newest, most complex information
    - information that is most emphatic
    - concepts that the next several sentences will develop
3. If you do not see that information there, revise: put those words last in the sentence.

PART V

Some Last Considerations

The Ethics of Research

In the last few hundred pages, we've offered a lot of practical advice, but also much preaching about creating social contracts with your readers, projecting an ethos that will encourage their trust, guarding against biases in collecting and reporting evidence, avoiding plagiarism, and so on. Now we want to share with you the underlying ethical issues that shape our advice, hoping that when you close this book, you'll give them more thought.

Everything we've said about research reflects our belief that it is a profoundly *social* activity that connects you both to those who will use your research and to those who might benefit—or suffer—from that use. But it also connects you and your readers to everyone whose research you used and beyond them to everyone whose research they used. To understand our responsibility to those in that network, now and in the future, we have to move beyond mere technique to think about the ethics of civil communication.

We start with two broad conceptions of the word *ethics*: the forging of bonds that create a community and the moral choices we face when we act in that community. The term *ethical* comes from the Greek *ethos*, meaning either a community's shared *customs* or an individual's *character*, good or bad. So far, we have focused on the community-building aspects of research, the bonds we create with our readers and our sources. But as does any social activity, research challenges us to define our individual ethical principles and then to make choices that honor or violate them.

At first glance, a purely academic researcher seems on relatively safe ethical ground—we are less tempted to sacrifice principle for gain than, say, a Wall Street analyst evaluating a stock that her firm wants her to push on investors, or a scientist paid by a drug company to "prove" that a product is safe (regardless of whether it works). No teacher will pay you to write a paper supporting her views, and you probably won't have occasion to fake results to gain fame—like the American researcher who became famous (and powerful) for discovering an HIV virus, when he had in fact "borrowed" it from a laboratory in France.

Even so, you will face such choices from the very beginning of your project. Some are the obvious *Thou shalt not*s for ethical researchers:

- They do not plagiarize or claim credit for the results of others.
- They do not misreport sources, invent data, or fake results.
- They do not submit data whose accuracy they don't trust, unless they say so.
- They do not conceal objections that they cannot rebut.
- They do not caricature or distort opposing views.
- They do not destroy data or conceal sources important for those who follow.

We apply these principles easily enough to obvious cases: the biologist who used india ink to fake "genetic" marks on his mice, the Enron accountants and their auditors at Arthur Andersen who shredded source documents, the government political advisers who erase e-mails, or the student who submits a paper purchased on the Internet.

More challenging are those occasions when ethical principles take us beyond a simple *Do not* to what we should affirmatively *Do*. When we think about ethical choices in that way, we move beyond simple conflicts between our own self-interest and the honest pursuit of truth, or between what we want for ourselves and what is good for or at least not harmful to others. If reporting research is genuinely a collaborative effort between readers and writers to find the best solution to shared problems, then the challenge is to find ways to create ethical partnerships to make ethical choices (what we traditionally call *character*) that can help build ethical communities.

Such a challenge raises more questions than we can answer here. Some of those questions have answers that we all agree on; others are controversial. The five of us answer some of them differently. But one thing we agree on is that research offers every researcher an ethical invitation that, when not just dutifully accepted but *embraced*, can serve the best interests of both researchers and their readers.

- When you create, however briefly, a community of shared understanding and interest, you set a standard for your work higher than any you could set for yourself alone.
- When you explain to others why your research *should* change their understanding and beliefs, you must examine not only your own understanding and interests, but your responsibility to them if you convince them to change theirs.
- When you acknowledge your readers' alternative views, including their strongest objections and reservations, you move closer not just to more reliable knowledge, better understanding, and sounder beliefs, but to honoring the dignity and human needs of your readers.

In other words, when you do research and report it as a conversation among equals working toward greater knowledge and better understanding, the ethical demands you place on yourself should redound to the benefit of all—even when we cannot all agree on a common good. When you decline that conversation, you risk harming yourself and possibly those who depend on your work.

It is this concern for the integrity of the common work of a community that underscores why researchers condemn plagiarism so strongly. Plagiarism is theft, but of more than words. By not acknowledging a source, the plagiarist steals the modest recognition that honest researchers should receive, the respect that a researcher spends a lifetime struggling to earn. And that weakens the community as a whole, by reducing the value of research to those who follow.

That is true in all research communities, including the undergraduate classroom. The student plagiarist steals not only from his sources, but from his colleagues by making their work seem lesser by comparison to what was bought or stolen. When such intellectual thievery becomes common, the community grows suspicious, then distrustful, then cynical: *Everyone does it. I'll fall behind if I don't.* Teachers must then worry as much about not being tricked as about teaching and learning. What's worse, the plagiarist compromises her own education and so steals from the larger society that devotes its resources to training her and her generation to do reliable work later, work that the community will depend on.

In short, when you report your research ethically, you join a community in a search for some common good. When you respect sources, preserve and acknowledge data that run against your results, assert claims only as strongly as warranted, acknowledge the limits of your certainty, and meet all the other ethical obligations you have as a researcher and writer, you move beyond gaining a grade or other material goods—you earn the larger benefit that comes from creating a bond with your readers. You discover that research focused on the best interests of others is also in your own.

A Postscript for Teachers

In this postscript we want to make explicit what has been implicit throughout. We hope you will join in an effort to improve the national "research scene." Too many teachers of undergraduates say, *I've given up teaching the research paper.* Colleagues tell us that the ones they get are boring patchworks, that students aren't up to the task, that in any event the dead-tree research paper is a relic of pre-digital days, and even that no one but ivory-tower academics does research anymore.

We think otherwise, of course. We think doing research is the best way to learn to read and think critically. And we know for a fact that the vast majority of our students will have careers in which, if they do not do their own research, they will have to evaluate and depend on the research of others. We also know that most of that research will be in written form, even if it happens to be delivered online. And we can think of no way to prepare for that responsibility better than doing research of one's own.

We wrote this book for those who agree, and believe—or will at least consider—two propositions:

- Students learn to do research well and report it clearly when they take the perspective of their readers and of the community whose values and practices define competent research and its reporting.
- They learn to manage an important part of that mental and social process when they understand how a few key formal features of their reports influence how their readers read and judge them.

These two propositions, we believe, are closely related. By understanding the complementary processes of reading and writing, students plan, perform, and report their research better. They can use the features that readers expect to guide themselves through not only the process of drafting, but all the stages of their project. And by understanding what their readers look for in a report, they learn to read the reports of others more critically. The two processes, reading and writing, are mutually supporting.

THE RISKS OF IMPOSING FORMAL RULES

Emphasizing formal features, though, has its risks, especially with new researchers. It is easy to reduce formal structure to empty drill. Those who teach dancers only to hit their marks or pianists only to find the right keys deprive students of the deep pleasures of dance or music. Those who teach research *by the numbers,* as if it were merely learning the proper forms for footnotes and bibliography, deprive students of the pleasures of discovery, students who might otherwise have blessed the world with their own good research.

If students are shown how to approach research in the right spirit, the features of argument become not empty forms but answers to questions that stimulate and reward hard thinking. They help students recognize what is important in the relationship between a researcher, her sources, her disciplinary colleagues and readers. This recognition is a crucial prerequisite to creative and original research.

Forms empty of meaning encourage empty imitation, especially when teachers fail to create in their classrooms a rhetorical context that dramatizes for students their social role as researchers, even if at first only in simulation or role-playing. No textbook can fully create that context, because it requires a class experience that only imaginative teachers can orchestrate.

Only a teacher, understanding his unique students, can devise assignments that create situations whose social dynamic gives point and purpose to research and whose expectations students can recognize and understand. The less experience students have, the more social support teachers must provide before their students can use formal structures in productive ways.

ON ASSIGNMENT SCENARIOS: CREATING A GROUND FOR CURIOSITY

Teachers have found many ways to construct research assignments that give students this necessary support. The most successful have these features:

1. Good assignments establish outcomes beyond a product to be evaluated. Good teachers ask students to raise a question or problem that at least *they* want to resolve, and to support that resolution with reliable and relevant evidence. Good research assignments then ask students to translate that private interest into a public one, so that they can experience, or at least imagine, readers who need the understanding that only they can provide.

The best assignments ask students to write for those who actually need to know or understand something better. Those readers might be a transient community of researchers that a problem creates, as when students do their research for a client outside of class. A senior design class, for example, might address a problem of a local company or civic organization; a music class might write program notes; a history class might investigate the origins of some part of their university or an institution in their local community.

Less experienced students might write for their classmates, but they might also write for students in another class who could actually use the information that a beginning researcher could provide. They might do preliminary research for those senior design students or for students in a graduate seminar; or they might even write reports back to students still in high school.

Next best are assignments that simulate such situations, in which students assume that other students or a client or even other researchers have a problem that the student researcher can resolve. Even in large classes, students can work in small groups whose members serve as readers with interests that beginning researchers can reasonably address.

2. Good assignments help students learn about their readers. Most students have trouble imagining readers whom they have never met and whose situation they have never experienced. Biology students with no knowledge or experience working with a government agency will be unlikely to write a plausible report that meets the concerns of a state EPA administrator. But teachers can help by urging students to imagine those distant readers. Alternatively, they can turn the class into its own audience by letting students decide what problems need solving, what questions need answering. If students can define the problems they're interested in, they will make the best possible readers for one another's research.

3. Good assignments create scenarios that are rich in contextual information. When students write to solve the problems of readers known and accessible to them, the assignment presents a scenario rich in detail. Students can investigate, interrogate, and analyze the situation for as long as time and ingenuity allow.

But when it's not practical to locate the project in a real context, the assignment should create as much of an imagined context as possible. It's impossible to predict everything students need to know about such a scenario, so it is important to make analysis and discussion of it a part of the writing process. Only when students are working in a social context do they have meaningful choices and good reasons to make them. Only then are those choices rhetorically significant. And only when writers can make rhetorically significant choices will they understand that at the heart of every real writing project is the anticipation of their readers' responses. When students have no choices because their project has no rhetorical "scene" and so is only a mechanical drill, doing research and writing it up become merely make-work—for you as much as for them.

Again we stress the importance of lively discussion among the students, either in class, if the class is small enough, or in subgroups if the class is large.

4. Good assignments provide interim readers. Few professional researchers call a report finished before they have solicited responses, something students need even more. Encourage students to solicit early responses from colleagues, friends, family, even from you. And build opportunities for response into the assignment itself. Other students can play this role reasonably well, but not if they think that their task is just "editing"—which for them often means rearranging a sentence here and fixing a misspelling there. Have student responders work through some of the steps in chapters 12–17; you can even create teams of responders, each with responsibility for specific features of the text. Those who provide interim responses must participate in the scenario as imagined readers.

5. As with any real project, good assignments give students time and a schedule of interim deadlines. Research is messy, so it does no good to march students through it lockstep: (1) select topic, (2) state thesis, (3) write outline, (4) collect bibliography, (5) read and take notes, (6) write report. That caricatures real research. But students need some framework, a schedule of tasks that helps them monitor their progress. They need time for false starts and blind alleys, for revision and reconsideration. They need interim deadlines and stages for sharing and criticizing their progress. Those stages can reflect the various sequences outlined in this book.

RECOGNIZING AND TOLERATING THE INEVITABLE MESSINESS OF LEARNING

Students also seriously—sometimes desperately—need other kinds of support, especially recognition of what can be expected of them and tolerance for the predictable missteps of even experienced researchers. Beginners behave in awkward ways, taking suggestions and principles as inflexible rules that they apply mechanically. They work through a topic to a question to their library's online catalog to a few websites, marching on and on to a feeble conclusion, not because they lack imagination or creativity, but because they are struggling to acquire a skill that to them is surpassingly strange. Such awkwardness is an inevitable stage in learning any skill. It passes, but too often only after they have moved on to other classes.

We urge you not to be troubled when a whole class of beginning students produces reports that look alike. We have had to learn to be patient with students, as we wait for the delayed gratification that comes when the learners arrive at genuine originality—knowing it will likely come when we are no longer there to see it.

We try to assure students that even if they do not solve their problem, they succeed if they can pose it in a way that convinces us that it is new—at least to them—and arguably *needs* a solution. Proving that there is a problem to be solved often requires more research and more critical ability than solving it, certainly more than one in which a student can ask a simple question and answer it.

We know that some students use research assignments simply to gather information on a topic, to review a field just to gain control over it. To them, the demand for a significant problem seems artificial. You can only ask them to imagine that they are writing for a reader who is intelligent and possibly interested in their topic but does not have the time to do any research, a reader who is, indeed, in the circumstance they are in.

Finally, different students stand in different relations to the research practices you teach. Advanced students should strive toward the full quality of your own disciplinary practices. But few beginners are yet committed to any research community or to the values that underlie everything in this book. Some will make that commitment early, but most will not. Some never will.

In sum, to teach research well, we teachers must adapt the steps we've outlined here to fit the particular circumstances and needs of the individuals before us in class. We can only hope that students at all levels learn these steps, learn to identify them in other writing projects, and then attempt them on their own. Maybe then they can move toward the kind of sound research and reasoned decision-making that our society so badly needs but too seldom gets.

Appendix
BIBLIOGRAPHICAL RESOURCES

There is a large literature on finding and presenting information, only some of which can be listed here. For a larger and more current selection, consult the Library of Congress catalog or an online bookseller. URLs are provided here for sources that are available online (in addition to or in place of traditional print formats). Other sources may also be available online or in an e-book format; consult your library. This list is divided as follows:

INTERNET DATABASES (BIBLIOGRAPHIES AND INDEXES)

General 282
Humanities 283
Social Sciences 283
Natural Sciences 284

PRINT AND ELECTRONIC RESOURCES

General 284
Visual Representation of Data (Tables, Figures, Posters, etc.) 286

Humanities

General 287
Art 288
History 289
Literary Studies 290
Music 291
Philosophy 292

Social Sciences

General 293
Anthropology 294
Business 295
Communication, Journalism, and Media Studies 296
Economics 297

Education 298
Geography 299
Law 299
Political Science 300
Psychology 301
Religion 302
Sociology 303
Women's Studies 304

Natural Sciences
General 305
Biology 306
Chemistry 307
Computer Sciences 308
Geology and Earth Sciences 308
Mathematics 309
Physics 310

For most of those areas, six kinds of resources are listed:

1. specialized dictionaries that offer short essays defining concepts in a field
2. general and specialized encyclopedias that offer more extensive overviews of a topic
3. guides to finding resources in different fields and using their methodologies
4. bibliographies, abstracts, and indexes that list past and current publications in different fields
5. writing manuals for different fields
6. style manuals that describe required features of citations in different fields

INTERNET DATABASES (BIBLIOGRAPHIES AND INDEXES)

GENERAL

Academic OneFile. Farmington Hills, MI: Gale Cengage Learning, 2006–. http://www.gale.cengage.com/.

ArticleFirst. Dublin, OH: OCLC, 1990–. http://www.oclc.org/.

Booklist Online. Chicago: American Library Association, 2006–. http://www.booklistonline.com/.

Clase and Periódica. Mexico City: UNAM, 2003–. http://www.oclc.org/.

ERIC. Educational Resources Information Center. Washington, DC: US Department of Education, Institute of Education Sciences, 2004–. http://www.eric.ed.gov/.

Essay and General Literature Index (H. W. Wilson). Ipswich, MA: EBSCO Publishing, 2000s–. http://www.ebscohost.com/wilson/.

General OneFile. Farmington Hills, MI: Gale Cengage Learning, 2006–. http://www.gale.cengage.com/.

ISI Web of Science (formerly *Web of Knowledge*). New York: Thomson Reuters, 1990s–. http://wokinfo.com/.

LexisNexis Academic. Dayton, OH: LexisNexis, 1984–. http://www.lexisnexis.com/.

Library Literature and Information Science Full Text (H. W. Wilson). Ipswich, MA: EBSCO Publishing, 1999–. http://www.ebscohost.com/wilson/.

Library of Congress Online Catalog. Washington, DC: Library of Congress. http://catalog.loc.gov/.

Omnifile Full Text Select (H. W. Wilson). Ipswich, MA: EBSCO Publishing, 1990–. http://www.ebscohost.com/wilson/.

Periodicals Index Online. ProQuest Information and Learning, 1990–. http://www.proquest.com.

ProQuest Dissertations and Theses. Ann Arbor, MI: ProQuest Information and Learning, 2004–. http://www.proquest.com/.

ProQuest Research Library. Ann Arbor, MI: ProQuest Information and Learning, 1998–. http://www.proquest.com/.

Reference Reviews. Bradford, UK: MCB University Press, 1997–. http://www.emeraldinsight.com/journals.htm?issn=0950-4125.

WorldCat. Dublin, OH: Online Computer Library Center. http://www.oclc.org/worldcat/.

HUMANITIES

Arts and Humanities Citation Index. Philadelphia: Institute for Scientific Information, 1990s–. http://www.thomsonscientific.com.

Humanities Full Text (H. W. Wilson). Ipswich, MA: EBSCO Publishing, 2011–. http://www.ebscohost.com/wilson/.

Humanities International Index. (formerly *American Humanities Index*). Ipswich, MA: EBSCO Publishing, 2005–. http://www.ebscohost.com/academic/.

U.S. History in Context. Farmington Hills, MI: Gale Group, 2007–. http://www.gale.cengage.com/.

SOCIAL SCIENCES

Anthropological Literature. Cambridge, MA: Tozzer Library, Harvard University, 1984–. http://hcl.harvard.edu/libraries/tozzer/anthrolit/anthrolit.cfm.

AnthroSource. American Anthropological Association. Arlington, VA. http://www.aaanet.org/publications/anthrosource/.

Anthropology Plus. Rutgers, NJ: Rutgers University Library. http://www.libraries.rutgers.edu/indexes/anthropology_plus.

APA PsycNET. Washington, DC: American Psychological Association, 1990s–. http://www.apa.org/pubs/databases/psycnet/.

ASSIA: Applied Social Sciences Index and Abstracts. Rutgers, NJ: Rutgers University Library. http://www.libraries.rutgers.edu/indexes/assia.

PAIS International with Archive. Public Affairs Information Service; CSA Illumina. Bethesda, MD: CSA, 1915–. http://www.csa.com/.

Political Science. Research Guide. Ann Arbor: University of Michigan. http://guides.lib.umich.edu/polisci/.

Social Sciences Abstracts (H. W. Wilson). Ipswich, MA: EBSCO Publishing, 1990s–. http://www.ebscohost.com/wilson/.

Social Sciences Citation Index. Philadelphia: Institute for Scientific Information, 1990s–. http://wokinfo.com/.

Sociological Abstracts. Sociological Abstracts; Cambridge Scientific Abstracts. Bethesda, MD: ProQuest CSA, 1990s–. http://www.csa.com/.

NATURAL SCIENCES

Applied Science and Technology Index (H. W. Wilson). Ipswich, MA: EBSCO Publishing, 1997–. http://www.ebscohost.com/wilson/.

NAL Catalog (AGRICOLA). Washington, DC: National Agricultural Library, 1970–. http://agricola.nal.usda.gov/.

PubMed.gov. US National Library of Medicine, National Institutes of Health. http://www.ncbi.nlm.nih.gov/pubmed.

Science Citation Index. Philadelphia: Institute for Scientific Information, 1990s–. http://wokinfo.com/

PRINT AND ELECTRONIC RESOURCES

GENERAL

1. *American National Biography.* New York: Oxford University Press, 2000–. http://www.anb.org/

1. Bowman, John S., ed. *The Cambridge Dictionary of American Biography.* Cambridge: Cambridge University Press, 1995.

1. *World Biographical Information System.* [Munich:] Thomson Gale, n.d. http://db.saur.de/WBIS/.

1. Matthew, H. C. G., and Brian Howard Harrison, eds. *Oxford Dictionary of National Biography, in Association with the British Academy: From the Earliest Times to the Year 2000.* New York: Oxford University Press, 2004. Also at http://www.oxforddnb.com/.

2. Jackson, Kenneth T., Karen Markoe, and Arnie Markoe, eds. *The Scribner Encyclopedia of American Lives.* 8 vols. covering 1981–2008. New York: Charles Scribner's Sons, 1998–2010.

2. Lagassé, Paul, ed. *The Columbia Encyclopedia.* 6th ed. New York: Columbia University Press, 2008.

2. *New Encyclopaedia Britannica.* 16th ed. 32 vols. Chicago: Encyclopaedia Britannica, 2010. Also at http://www.eb.com/.

3. Abbott, Andrew Delano. *Digital Paper: A Manual for Research and Writing with Library and Internet Materials.* Chicago: University of Chicago Press, 2014.

3. Balay, Robert, ed. *Guide to Reference Books.* 11th ed. Chicago: American Library Association, 1996.

3. Hacker, Diana, and Barbara Fister. *Research and Documentation in the Electronic Age.* 5th ed. Boston: Bedford/St. Martin's, 2015. Also at http://bcs.bedfordstmartins.com/resdoc5e/.

3. Kane, Eileen, and Mary O'Reilly-de Brún. *Doing Your Own Research.* London: Marion Boyars, 2005.

3. Kieft, Robert, ed. *Guide to Reference.* Chicago: American Library Association, 2008–. http://www.guidetoreference.org/.

3. Lipson, Charles. *Doing Honest Work in College: How to Prepare Citations, Avoid Plagiarism, and Achieve Real Academic Success.* 2nd ed. Chicago: University of Chicago Press, 2008.

3. Mann, Thomas. *Oxford Guide to Library Research.* 3rd ed. New York: Oxford University Press, 2005.

3. *Reference Universe.* Sterling, VA: Paratext, 2002–. http://refuniv.odyssi.com/.

3. Rowely, Jennifer, and John Farrow. *Organizing Knowledge: An Introduction to Managing Access to Information.* 3rd ed. Aldershot, Hampshire, UK: Gower, 2000.

3. Sears, Jean L., and Marilyn K. Moody. *Using Government Information Sources: Electronic and Print.* 3rd ed. Phoenix: Oryx Press, 2001.

4. *Alternative Press Index.* Chicago: Alternative Press Centre; Ipswich, MA: EBSCO Publishing, 1969–.

4. *Bibliographic Index Plus.* Ipswich, MA: EBSCO Publishing; Bronx: H. W. Wilson, 2003.

4. *Book Review Digest Plus.* New York: H. W. Wilson; Ipswich, MA: EBSCO Publishing, 2002–. http://www.ebscohost.com/wilson/.

4. *Book Review Digest Retrospective: 1908–1982 (H. W. Wilson).* Bronx: H. W. Wilson Co.; Ipswich, MA: EBSCO Publishing, 2011–. http://www.ebscohost.com/wilson/.

4. *Book Review Index.* Detroit: Gale Research, 1965–. Also at http://www.gale.cengage.com.

4. *Books in Print.* New Providence, NJ: R. R. Bowker, 2011. Also at http://www.booksinprint.com/.

4. Brigham, Clarence S. *History and Bibliography of American Newspapers, 1690–1820.* 2 vols. Westport, CT: Greenwood Press, 1976.

4. *Conference Papers Index.* Bethesda, MD: Cambridge Scientific Abstracts, 1978–.

4. Farber, Evan Ira, ed. *Combined Retrospective Index to Book Reviews in Scholarly Journals, 1886–1974.* 15 vols. Arlington, VA: Carrollton Press, 1979–82.

4. Gregory, Winifred, ed. *American Newspapers, 1821–1936: A Union List of Files Available in the United States and Canada.* New York: H. W. Wilson, 1937.

4. *Kirkus Reviews.* New York: Kirkus Media, 1933–. Also at http://www.kirkusreviews.com/.

4. *National Newspaper Index.* Menlo Park, CA: Information Access, 1982–2011.

4. *Newspapers in Microform.* Washington, DC: Library of Congress, 1948–83. Also at http://www.loc.gov/.

4. *New York Times Index*. New York: New York Times, 1913–.

4. *Periodicals Index Online*. Ann Arbor, MI: ProQuest Information and Learning, 1990–. http://pio.chadwyck.co.uk/.

4. Poole, William Frederick, and William Isaac Fletcher. *Poole's Index to Periodical Literature*. Rev. ed. Gloucester, MA: Peter Smith, 1971.

4. *Popular Periodical Index*. Camden, NJ: Rutgers University, 1973–93.

4. *Readers' Guide to Periodical Literature (H. W. Wilson)*. Ipswich, MA: EBSCO Publishing, 2003–. http://www.ebscohost.com/wilson/.

4. *Reference Books Bulletin*. Chicago: American Library Association, 1989. Also at http://www.ala.org/offices/reference-books-bulletin.

4. *Serials Review*. San Diego: Pergamon, 1975–. Also at http://www.sciencedirect.com/science/journal/00987913.

4. *Subject Guide to Books in Print*. New York: R. R. Bowker, 1957–. Also at http://www.booksinprint.com/.

4. *Wall Street Journal*. New York: Dow Jones, 1889–. Also at http://www.proquest.com/.

5. Bolker, Joan. *Writing Your Dissertation in Fifteen Minutes a Day: A Guide to Starting, Revising, and Finishing Your Doctoral Thesis*. New York: H. Holt, 1998.

5. Crews, Kenneth D. *Copyright Law and Graduate Research: New Media, New Rights, and Your Dissertation*. Ann Arbor, MI: UMI, 2002.

5. Few, Stephen. *Show Me the Numbers: Designing Tables and Graphs to Enlighten*. Burlingame, CA: Analytics Press, 2012.

5. Miller, Jane E. *The Chicago Guide to Writing about Numbers*. 2nd ed. Chicago: University of Chicago Press, 2015.

5. Sternberg, David. *How to Complete and Survive a Doctoral Dissertation*. New York: St. Martin's Griffin, 1981.

5. Strunk, William, and E. B. White. *The Elements of Style*. 50th anniversary ed. New York: Pearson Longman, 2009.

5. Williams, Joseph M., and Joseph Bizup. *Style: Lessons in Clarity and Grace*. 11th ed. Boston: Pearson Longman, 2014.

6. *The Chicago Manual of Style*. 16th ed. Chicago: University of Chicago Press, 2010. Also at http://www.chicagomanualofstyle.org/.

VISUAL REPRESENTATION OF DATA (TABLES, FIGURES, POSTERS, ETC.)

2. Harris, Robert L. *Information Graphics: A Comprehensive Illustrated Reference*. New York: Oxford University Press, 2000.

3. Cleveland, William S. *The Elements of Graphing Data*. Rev. ed. Summit, NJ: Hobart Press, 1994.

3. Cleveland, William S. *Visualizing Data*. Summit, NJ: Hobart Press, 1993.

3. Monmonier, Mark. *Mapping It Out: Expository Cartography for the Humanities and Social Sciences*. Chicago: University of Chicago Press, 1993.

3. Tufte, Edward R. *Envisioning Information*. Cheshire, CT: Graphics, 1990.

3. Tufte, Edward R. *The Visual Display of Quantitative Information.* 2nd ed. Cheshire, CT: Graphics Press, 2001.

3. Tufte, Edward R. *Visual and Statistical Thinking: Displays of Evidence for Making Decisions.* Cheshire, CT: Graphics Press, 1997.

3. Wainer, Howard. *Visual Revelations: Graphical Tales of Fate and Deception from Napoleon Bonaparte to Ross Perot.* New York: Psychology Press, 2014.

5. Alley, Michael. *The Craft of Scientific Presentations: Critical Steps to Succeed and Critical Errors to Avoid.* 2nd ed. New York: Springer, 2013.

5. Briscoe, Mary Helen. *Preparing Scientific Illustrations: A Guide to Better Posters, Presentations, and Publications.* 2nd ed. New York: Springer, 1996.

5. Esposito, Mona, Kaye Marshall, and Fredricka L. Stoller. "Poster Sessions by Experts." In *New Ways in Content-Based Instruction,* edited by Donna M. Brinton and Peter Master, 115–18. Alexandria, VA: Teachers of English to Speakers of Other Languages, 1997.

5. Kosslyn, Stephen M. *Elements of Graph Design.* New York: W. H. Freeman, 1994.

5. Larkin, Greg. "Storyboarding: A Concrete Way to Generate Effective Visuals." *Journal of Technical Writing and Communication* 26, no. 3 (1996): 273–89.

5. Nicol, Adelheid A. M., and Penny M. Pexman. *Displaying Your Findings: A Practical Guide for Creating Figures, Posters, and Presentations.* 6th ed. Washington, DC: American Psychological Association, 2010.

5. Nicol, Adelheid A. M., and Penny M. Pexman. *Presenting Your Findings: A Practical Guide for Creating Tables.* 6th ed. Washington, DC: American Psychological Association, 2010.

5. Rice University, Cain Project in Engineering and Professional Communication. "Designing Scientific and Engineering Posters" [2003]. http://www.owlnet.rice.edu/~cainproj/ih_posters.html.

5. Robbins, Naomi B. *Creating More Effective Graphs.* New York: John Wiley and Sons, 2005. Paperback reprint, Houston, TX: Chart House, 2013.

5. Ross, Ted. *The Art of Music Engraving and Processing: A Complete Manual, Reference, and Text Book on Preparing Music for Reproduction and Print.* Miami: Hansen Books, 1970.

5. Zweifel, Frances W. *A Handbook of Biological Illustration.* 2nd ed. Chicago: University of Chicago Press, 1988.

6. CBE Scientific Illustration Committee. *Illustrating Science: Standards for Publication.* Bethesda, MD: Council of Biology Editors, 1988.

HUMANITIES

GENERAL

1. Hornblower, Simon, and Antony Spawforth, eds. *The Oxford Classical Dictionary.* 4th ed. Oxford: Oxford University Press, 2012. Also at http://www.oxford-classicaldictionary3.com/.

1. Murphy, Bruce, ed. *Benét's Reader's Encyclopedia*. 5th ed. New York: HarperCollins, 2008.

3. Kirkham, Sandi. *How to Find Information in the Humanities*. London: Library Association, 1989.

4. *Arts and Humanities Citation Index*. Philadelphia: Institute for Scientific Information, 1976–. Compact disc ed. 1994. Also at http://wokinfo.com/.

4. Blazek, Ron, and Elizabeth Aversa. *The Humanities: A Selective Guide to Information Sources*. 5th ed. Englewood, CO: Libraries Unlimited, 2000.

4. *British Humanities Index*. London: Library Association; Bethesda, MD: Cambridge Scientific Abstracts, 1963–. Also at http://www.proquest.com/.

4. Harzfeld, Lois A. *Periodical Indexes in the Social Sciences and Humanities: A Subject Guide*. Metuchen, NJ: Scarecrow Press, 1978.

4. *An Index to Book Reviews in the Humanities*. Williamston, MI: P. Thomson, 1960–90.

4. *Index to Social Sciences and Humanities Proceedings*. Philadelphia: Institute for Scientific Information, 1979–. Also at http://wokinfo.com/.

4. *L'année philologique*. Paris: Belles Lettres, 1928–. Also at http://www.annee-philologique.com/.

4. *Walford's Guide to Reference Material*. Vol. 3, *Generalia, Language and Literature, the Arts*, edited by Anthony Chalcraft, Ray Prytherch, and Stephen Willis. 8th ed. London: Library Association, 2000.

5. Northey, Margot, and Maurice Legris. *Making Sense in the Humanities: A Student's Guide to Writing and Style*. Toronto: Oxford University Press, 1990.

ART

1. Chilvers, Ian, and Harold Osborne, eds. *The Oxford Dictionary of Art and Artists*. 4th ed. Oxford: Oxford University Press, 2009.

1. Myers, Bernard L., and Trewin Copplestone, eds. *The Macmillan Encyclopedia of Art*. Rev. ed. London: Basingstroke Macmillan, 1981.

1. Myers, Bernard S., and Shirley D. Myers, eds. *McGraw-Hill Dictionary of Art*. 5 vols. New York: McGraw-Hill, 1969.

1. *Oxford Art Online*. Oxford: Oxford University Press, 2007–. http://www.oxfordartonline.com/.

1. *Oxford Reference Online: Art and Architecture*. Oxford: Oxford University Press, 2002–. http://www.oxfordreference.com/.

1. Sorensen, Lee. *Dictionary of Art Historians*. Durham, NC: Duke University Press. http://www.dictionaryofarthistorians.org/.

2. Myers, Bernard S., ed. *Encyclopedia of World Art*. 17 vols. New York: McGraw-Hill, 1959–87.

3. Arntzen, Etta, and Robert Rainwater. *Guide to the Literature of Art History*. Chicago: American Library Association, 1980.

3. Jones, Lois Swan. *Art Information and the Internet: How to Find It, How to Use It*. Phoenix: Oryx Press, 1999.

3. Jones, Lois Swan. *Art Information: Research Methods and Resources*. 3rd ed. Dubuque, IA: Kendall/Hunt, 1994.

3. Marmor, Max, and Alex Ross. *Guide to the Literature of Art History 2.* Chicago: American Library Association, 2005.

3. Minor, Vernon Hyde. *Art History's History.* 2nd ed. Upper Saddle River, NJ: Prentice Hall; London: Pearson Education [distributor], 2009.

4. *Art Abstracts (H. W. Wilson).* Ipswich, MA: EBSCO Publishing, 1990s–. http://www.ebscohost.com/wilson/.

4. *Art Index (H. W. Wilson).* Ipswich, MA: EBSCO Publishing, 1990s–. http://www.ebscohost.com/wilson/.

4. *Art Index Retrospective: 1929–1984 (H. W. Wilson).* Ipswich, MA: EBSCO Publishing, 1990s. http://www.ebscohost.com/wilson/.

4. *International Bibliography of Art.* Lost Angeles: J. Paul Getty Trust; Ann Arbor, MI: ProQuest CSA, 2008–. http://www.csa.com/.

5. Barnet, Sylvan. *A Short Guide to Writing about Art.* 11th ed. Upper Saddle River, NJ: Prentice Hall, 2015.

HISTORY

1. Cook, Chris. *A Dictionary of Historical Terms.* 3rd ed. Houndmills, UK: Macmillan, 1998.

1. Ritter, Harry. *Dictionary of Concepts in History.* Westport, CT: Greenwood Press, 1986.

2. Bjork, Robert E., ed. *The Oxford Dictionary of the Middle Ages.* 4 vols. Oxford: Oxford University Press, 2010.

2. Breisach, Ernst. *Historiography: Ancient, Medieval, and Modern.* 3rd ed. Chicago: University of Chicago Press, 2007.

2. *The Cambridge Ancient History.* 14 vols. Cambridge: Cambridge University Press, 1970–2005. Also at http://histories.cambridge.org/.

2. Grendler, Paul F., ed. *Encyclopedia of the Renaissance.* 6 vols. New York: Scribner's, 1999.

2. Hillerbrand, Hans J., ed. *The Oxford Encyclopedia of the Reformation.* 4 vols. New York: Oxford University Press, 1996.

2. *The New Cambridge Medieval History.* 7 vols. Cambridge: Cambridge University Press, 1995–2005.

2. *The New Cambridge Modern History.* 14 vols. Cambridge: Cambridge University Press, 1957–90.

3. Benjamin, Jules R. *A Student's Guide to History.* 12th ed. Boston: Bedford/St. Martin's, 2013.

3. Bentley, Michael, ed. *Companion to Historiography.* London: Routledge, 1997.

3. Brundage, Anthony. *Going to the Sources: A Guide to Historical Research and Writing.* 5th ed. Chichester, UK: Wiley-Blackwell, 2013.

3. Frick, Elizabeth. *History: Illustrated Search Strategy and Sources.* 2nd ed. Ann Arbor, MI: Pierian Press, 1995.

3. Fritze, Ronald H., Brian E. Coutts, and Louis Andrew Vyhnanek. *Reference Sources in History: An Introductory Guide.* 2nd ed. Santa Barbara, CA: ABC-Clio, 2004.

3. Higginbotham, Evelyn Brooks, Leon F. Litwack, and Darlene Clark Hine, eds. *The Harvard Guide to African-American History*. Cambridge, MA: Harvard University Press, 2001.

3. Kyvig, David E., and Myron A. Marty. *Nearby History: Exploring the Past around You*. 3rd ed. Walnut Creek, CA: AltaMira Press, 2010.

3. Norton, Mary Beth, and Pamela Gerardi, eds. *The American Historical Association's Guide to Historical Literature*. 3rd ed. 2 vols. New York: Oxford University Press, 1995.

3. Prucha, Francis Paul. *Handbook for Research in American History: A Guide to Bibliographies and Other Reference Works*. 2nd ed. rev. Lincoln: University of Nebraska Press, 1996.

4. *America: History and Life*. Ipswich, MA: EBSCO Publishing, 1990s–. http://www.ebscohost.com/academic/.

4. Blazek, Ron, and Anna H. Perrault. *United States History: A Multicultural, Interdisciplinary Guide to Information Sources*. 2nd ed. Westport, CT: Libraries Unlimited, 2003.

4. Danky, James Philip, and Maureen E. Hady. *African-American Newspapers and Periodicals: A National Bibliography*. Cambridge, MA: Harvard University Press, 1998.

4. *Historical Abstracts*. Ipswich, MA: EBSCO Publishing, 1990s–. http://www.ebscohost.com/academic/.

4. Kinnell, Susan K., ed. *Historiography: An Annotated Bibliography of Journal Articles, Books, and Dissertations*. 2 vols. Santa Barbara, CA: ABC-Clio, 1987.

4. Mott, Frank Luther. *A History of American Magazines*. 5 vols. Cambridge, MA: Harvard University Press, 1930–68.

5. Barzun, Jacques, and Henry F. Graff. *The Modern Researcher*. 6th ed. Belmont, CA: Thomson/Wadsworth, 2004.

5. Marius, Richard, and Melvin E. Page. *A Short Guide to Writing about History*. 9th ed. New York: Pearson Longman, 2015.

LITERARY STUDIES

1. Abrams, M. H., and Geoffrey Galt Harpham. *A Glossary of Literary Terms*. 11th ed. Boston: Wadsworth Cengage Learning, 2015.

1. Baldick, Chris, ed. *The Concise Oxford Dictionary of Literary Terms*. 3rd ed. Oxford: Oxford University Press, 2008.

1. Brogan, Terry V. F., ed. *The New Princeton Handbook of Poetic Terms*. Princeton, NJ: Princeton University Press, 1994.

1. Cavanagh, Clare, et al. *The Princeton Encyclopedia of Poetry and Poetics*. Princeton, NJ: Princeton University Press, 2012. eBook 2012.

1. Groden, Michael, Martin Kreiswirth, and Imre Szeman, eds. *The Johns Hopkins Guide to Literary Theory and Criticism*. 2nd ed. Baltimore: Johns Hopkins University Press, 2005. Also at http://litguide.press.jhu.edu/.

2. Birch, Dinah, ed. *The Oxford Companion to English Literature*. 7th ed.

New York: Oxford University Press, 2009. Also at http://www.oxfordreference.com/.

2. Hart, James D., and Phillip W. Leininger, eds. *The Oxford Companion to American Literature*. 7th ed. New York: Oxford University Press, 2009. Also at http://www.oxfordreference.com/.

2. Lentricchia, Frank, and Thomas McLaughlin, eds. *Critical Terms for Literary Study*. 2nd ed. Chicago: University of Chicago Press, 1995. eBook, 2012.

2. Parini, Jay, ed. *The Oxford Encyclopedia of American Literature*. 4 vols. New York: Oxford University Press, 2004. Also at http://www.oxfordreference.com/.

2. Ward, Sir Adolphus William, A. R. Waller, William Peterfield Trent, John Erskine, Stuart Pratt Sherman, and Carl Van Doren. *The Cambridge History of English and American Literature: An Encyclopedia in Eighteen Volumes*. New York: G. P. Putnam's Sons, 1907–21. Bartleby.com, 2000. At http://www.bartleby.com/cambridge/.

3. Altick, Richard Daniel, and John J. Fenstermaker. *The Art of Literary Research*. 4th ed. New York: W. W. Norton, 1993.

3. Harner, James L. *Literary Research Guide: An Annotated Listing of Reference Sources in English Literary Studies*. 5th ed. New York: Modern Language Association of America, 2008.

3. Klarer, Mario. *An Introduction to Literary Studies*. 2nd ed. London: Routledge, 2004.

3. Vitale, Philip H. *Basic Tools of Research: An Annotated Guide for Students of English*. 3rd ed., rev. and enl. New York: Barron's Educational Series, 1975.

4. *Abstracts of English Studies*. Boulder, CO: National Council of Teachers of English, 1958–91. Reprint, New Castle, DE: Oak Knoll Press, 2003. Also at http://catalog.hathitrust.org/Record/000521812.

4. Blanck, Jacob, Virginia L. Smyers, and Michael Winship. *Bibliography of American Literature*. 9 vols. New Haven, CT: Yale University Press, 1955–91. Also at http://collections.chadwyck.co.uk/.

4. *Index of American Periodical Verse*. Metuchen, NJ: Scarecrow Press, 1971–2006.

4. *MLA International Bibliography*. New York: Modern Language Association of America. http://www.mla.org/bibliography/.

5. Barnet, Sylvan, and William E. Cain. *A Short Guide to Writing about Literature*. 12th ed. New York: Longman/Pearson, 2011.

5. Griffith, Kelley. *Writing Essays about Literature: A Guide and Style Sheet*. 9th ed. Boston: Wadsworth Cengage Learning, 2014.

6. *MLA Handbook for Writers of Research Papers*. 8th ed. New York: Modern Language Association of America, 2016.

MUSIC

1. *Oxford Music Online*. New York: Oxford University Press, 2001–. Includes *Grove Music Online*. http://www.oxfordmusiconline.com/.

1. Randel, Don Michael, ed. *The Harvard Dictionary of Music*. 4th ed. Cambridge, MA: Belknap Press of Harvard University Press, 2003.

1. Sadie, Stanley, and John Tyrrell, eds. *The New Grove Dictionary of Music and Musicians*. 2nd ed. 29 vols. New York: Grove, 2001. Also at http://www.oxfordmusiconline.com/ (as part of *Grove Music Online*).

2. Netti, Bruno, Ruth M. Stone, James Porter, and Timothy Rice, eds. *The Garland Encyclopedia of World Music*. 10 vols. New York: Garland, 1998–2013. Also at http://alexanderstreet.com/.

3. Brockman, William S. *Music: A Guide to the Reference Literature*. Littleton, CO: Libraries Unlimited, 1987.

3. Duckles, Vincent H., Ida Reed, and Michael A. Keller, eds. *Music Reference and Research Materials: An Annotated Bibliography*. 5th ed. New York: Schirmer Books, 1997.

4. *The Music Index*. Ipswich, MA: EBSCO Publishing, 2000s–. http://www.ebscohost.com/academic/.

4. *RILM Abstracts of Music Literature*. New York: RILM, 1967–. Also at http://www.ebscohost.com/academic/.

5. Druesedow, John E., Jr. *Library Research Guide to Music: Illustrated Search Strategy and Sources*. Ann Arbor, MI: Pierian Press, 1982.

5. Herbert, Trevor. *Music in Words: A Guide to Researching and Writing about Music*. 2nd ed. London: ABRSM, 2012.

5. Wingell, Richard. *Writing about Music: An Introductory Guide*. 4th ed. Upper Saddle River, NJ: Pearson Prentice Hall, 2009.

6. Bellman, Jonathan. *A Short Guide to Writing about Music*. 2nd ed. New York: Pearson Longman, 2006.

6. Holoman, D. Kern. *Writing about Music: A Style Sheet*. 3rd ed. Berkeley: University of California Press, 2014.

PHILOSOPHY

1. Blackburn, Simon. *The Oxford Dictionary of Philosophy*. 2nd ed. rev. Oxford: Oxford University Press, 2008. Also at http://www.oxfordreference.com/.

1. Wellington, Jean Susorney. *Dictionary of Bibliographic Abbreviations Found in the Scholarship of Classical Studies and Related Disciplines*. Rev. ed. Westport, CT: Praeger, 2004.

2. Borchert, Donald, ed. *The Encyclopedia of Philosophy*. 8 vols. 2nd ed. Detroit: Macmillan Reference USA, 2006.

2. Craig, Edward, ed. *Routledge Encyclopedia of Philosophy*. 10 vols. New York: Routledge, 1998. Also at http://www.rep.routledge.com/.

2. Parkinson, George H. R. *The Handbook of Western Philosophy*. New York: Macmillan, 1988.

2. Schrift, Alan D., ed. *The History of Continental Philosophy*. 8 vols. Chicago: University of Chicago Press, 2010.

2. Urmson, J. O., and Jonathan Rée, eds. *The Concise Encyclopedia of Western Philosophy and Philosophers*. 3rd ed. London: Routledge, 2005.

2. Zalta, Edward N. *Stanford Encyclopedia of Philosophy*. Stanford, CA: Stanford University, 1997–. http://plato.stanford.edu/.

3. List, Charles J., and Stephen H. Plum. *Library Research Guide to Philosophy*. Ann Arbor, MI: Pierian Press, 1990.

4. Bourget, David, and David Chalmers, eds. *PhilPapers*. London: Institute of Philosophy at the University of London, 2008–. Also at http://philpapers.org/.

4. *L'année philologique*. Paris: Belles Lettres, 1928–. Also at http://www.annee-philologique.com/.

4. *The Philosopher's Index*. Bowling Green, OH: Philosopher's Information Center, 1968–. Also at http://philindex.org/.

5. Martinich, A. P. *Philosophical Writing: An Introduction*. 3rd ed. Malden, MA: Blackwell, 2005.

5. Watson, Richard A. *Writing Philosophy: A Guide to Professional Writing and Publishing*. Carbondale: Southern Illinois University Press, 1992.

SOCIAL SCIENCES

GENERAL

1. Calhoun, Craig, ed. *Dictionary of the Social Sciences*. New York: Oxford University Press, 2002. Also at http://www.oxfordreference.com/.

1. *Statistical Abstract of the United States*. Washington, DC: US Census Bureau, 1878–. Also at http://www.census.gov/compendia/statab/.

2. Darity, William, ed. *International Encyclopedia of the Social Sciences*. 2nd ed. 9 vols. Detroit: Macmillan, 2008.

3. Herron, Nancy L., ed. *The Social Sciences: A Cross-Disciplinary Guide to Selected Sources*. 3rd ed. Englewood, CO: Libraries Unlimited, 2002.

3. Light, Richard J., and David B. Pillemer. *Summing Up: The Science of Reviewing Research*. Cambridge, MA: Harvard University Press, 1984.

3. Øyen, Else, ed. *Comparative Methodology: Theory and Practice in International Social Research*. London: Sage, 1990.

4. *Bibliography of Social Science Research and Writings on American Indians*. Compiled by Russell Thornton and Mary K. Grasmick. Minneapolis: Center for Urban and Regional Affairs, University of Minnesota, 1979.

4. *Book Review Index to Social Science Periodicals*. 4 vols. Ann Arbor, MI: Pierian Press, 1978–81.

4. *Communication and Mass Media Complete*. Ipswich, MA: EBSCO Publishing, 2004–. https://www.ebscohost.com/academic/communication-mass-media-complete/.

4. *C.R.I.S.: The Combined Retrospective Index Set to Journals in Sociology, 1895–1974*. With an introduction and user's guide by Evan I. Farber; executive editor, Annadel N. Wile; assistant editor, Deborah Purcell. Washington, DC: Carrollton Press, 1978.

4. *Current Contents: Social and Behavioral Sciences*. Philadelphia: Institute

for Scientific Information, 1974–. Also at http://ip-science.thomsonreuters.com/mjl/scope/scope_ccsbs/.

4. *Document Retrieval Index.* U.S. Dept. of Justice, Law Enforcement Assistance Administration, National Institute of Law Enforcement and Criminal Justice, 1978–. Microfiche.

4. Grossman, Jorge. *Índice general de publicaciones periódicas latinoamericanas: Humanidades y ciencias sociales / Index to Latin American Periodicals: Humanities and Social Sciences.* Metuchen, NJ: Scarecrow Press, 1961–70.

4. Harzfeld, Lois A. *Periodical Indexes in the Social Sciences and Humanities: A Subject Guide.* Metuchen, NJ: Scarecrow Press, 1978.

4. *Index of African Social Science Periodical Articles.* Dakar, Senegal: Council for the Development of Economic and Social Research in Africa, 1989–.

4. *Index to Social Sciences and Humanities Proceedings.* Philadelphia: Institute for Scientific Information, 1979–. Also at http://ip-science.thomsonreuters.com/mjl/scope/scope_cpci-ssh/.

4. Lester, Ray, ed. *The New Walford.* Vol. 2, *The Social Sciences.* London: Facet, 2008.

4. *PAIS International in Print.* New York: OCLC Public Affairs Information Service, 1991–. Also at http://www.csa.com/.

4. *Social Sciences Citation Index.* Philadelphia: Institute for Scientific Information, 1969–. Also at http://wokinfo.com/.

4. *Social Sciences Index.* New York: H. W. Wilson, 1974–. Also at http://www.ebscohost.com/wilson/ (as *Social Science Abstracts*).

5. Becker, Howard S. *Writing for Social Scientists: How to Start and Finish Your Thesis, Book, or Article.* 2nd ed. Chicago: University of Chicago Press, 2007.

5. Bell, Judith. *Doing Your Research Project: A Guide for First-Time Researchers in Education, Health, and Social Science.* 5th ed. Maidenhead, UK: McGraw-Hill Open University Press, 2010.

5. Krathwohl, David R., and Nick L. Smith. *How to Prepare a Dissertation Proposal: Suggestions for Students in Education and the Social and Behavioral Sciences.* Syracuse, NY: Syracuse University Press, 2005.

5. Northey, Margot, Lorne Tepperman, and Patrizia Albanese. *Making Sense: A Student's Guide to Research and Writing; Social Sciences.* 6th ed. Ontario: Oxford University Press, 2015.

ANTHROPOLOGY

1. Barfield, Thomas, ed. *The Dictionary of Anthropology.* 13th pr. Malden, MA: Blackwell, 2009.

1. Winthrop, Robert H. *Dictionary of Concepts in Cultural Anthropology.* New York: Greenwood Press, 1991.

2. Barnard, Alan, and Jonathan Spencer, eds. *Routledge Encyclopedia of Social and Cultural Anthropology.* 2nd ed. London: Routledge, 2012.

2. Ember, Melvin, Carol R. Ember, and Ian A. Skoggard, eds. *Encyclopedia of World Cultures: Supplement.* New York: Gale Group/Thomson Learning, 2002.

2. Ingold, Tim, ed. *Companion Encyclopedia of Anthropology: Humanity, Culture, and Social Life.* London: Routledge, 2007.

2. Levinson, David, ed. *Encyclopedia of World Cultures.* 10 vols. Boston: G. K. Hall, 1991–96.

2. Levinson, David, and Melvin Ember, eds. *Encyclopedia of Cultural Anthropology.* 4 vols. New York: Henry Holt, 1997.

3. Bernard, H. Russell. *Research Methods in Anthropology: Qualitative and Quantitative Approaches.* 5th ed. Lanham, MD: AltaMira Press, 2011.

3. Bernard, H. Russell, ed. *Handbook of Methods in Cultural Anthropology.* Walnut Creek, CA: AltaMira Press, 2000.

3. *Current Topics in Anthropology: Theory, Methods, and Content.* 8 vols. Reading, MA: Addison-Wesley, 1971–75.

3. Glenn, James R. *Guide to the National Anthropological Archives, Smithsonian Institution.* Rev. and enl. ed. Washington, DC: National Anthropological Archives, 1996. Also at http://www.nmnh.si.edu/naa/guides.htm/.

3. Poggie, John J., Jr., Billie R. DeWalt, and William W. Dressler, eds. *Anthropological Research: Process and Application.* Albany: State University of New York Press, 1992.

4. *Abstracts in Anthropology.* Amityville, NY: Baywood Publishing, 1970–. Also at http://anthropology.metapress.com/.

4. *Annual Review of Anthropology.* Palo Alto, CA: Annual Reviews Inc., 1972–. Also at http://www.annualreviews.org/journal/anthro.

4. *The Urban Portal.* Chicago: University of Chicago Urban Network. http://urban.uchicago.edu/.

BUSINESS

1. Friedman, Jack P. *Dictionary of Business Terms.* 4th ed. Hauppauge, NY: Barron's Educational Series, 2012.

1. Link, Albert N. *Link's International Dictionary of Business Economics.* Chicago: Probus, 1993.

1. Nisberg, Jay N. *The Random House Dictionary of Business Terms.* New York: Random House, 1992.

1. Wiechmann, Jack G., and Laurence Urdang, eds. *NTC's Dictionary of Advertising.* 2nd ed. Lincolnwood, IL: National Textbook, 1993.

2. Folsom, W. Davis, and Stacia N. VanDyne, eds. *Encyclopedia of American Business.* Rev. ed. 2 vols. New York: Facts on File, 2004.

2. *The Lifestyle Market Analyst: A Reference Guide for Consumer Market Analysis.* Wilmette, IL: Standard Rate and Data Service, 1989–2008.

2. McDonough, John, and Karen Egolf, eds. *The Advertising Age Encyclopedia of Advertising.* 3 vols. New York: Fitzroy Dearborn, 2003.

2. Vernon, Mark. *Business: The Key Concepts.* New York: Routledge, 2002.

2. Warner, Malcolm, and John P. Kotter, eds. *International Encyclopedia of Business and Management*. 2nd ed. 8 vols. London: Thomson Learning, 2002.

3. Bryman, Alan, and Emma Bell. *Business Research Methods*. 4th ed. New York: Oxford University Press, 2015.

3. Daniells, Lorna M. *Business Information Sources*. 3rd ed. Berkeley: University of California Press, 1993.

3. Moss, Rita W., and David G. Ernsthausen. *Strauss's Handbook of Business Information: A Guide for Librarians, Students, and Researchers*. 3rd ed. Westport, CT: Libraries Unlimited, 2012.

3. Sekaran, Uma, and Roger Bougie. *Research Methods for Business: A Skill Building Approach*. 6th ed. New York: John Wiley and Sons, 2013.

3. Woy, James B., ed. *Encyclopedia of Business Information Sources*. 32nd ed. 2 vols. Detroit: Gale Cengage Learning, 2015.

4. *Business Periodicals Index*. New York: H. W. Wilson, 1958–. Also at http://www.ebscohost.com/academic/ (as *Business Periodicals Index Retrospective*).

5. Farrell, Thomas J., and Charlotte Donabedian. *Writing the Business Research Paper: A Complete Guide*. Durham, NC: Carolina Academic Press, 1991.

6. Vetter, William. *Business Law, Legal Research, and Writing: Handbook*. Needham Heights, MA: Ginn Press, 1991.

6. Yelin, Andrea, and Hope Viner Samborn. *The Legal Research and Writing Handbook: A Basic Approach for Paralegals*. New York: Aspen Publishers, 2009.

COMMUNICATION, JOURNALISM, AND MEDIA STUDIES

1. Horak, Ray. *Webster's New World Telecom Dictionary*. Indianapolis: Wiley Technology, 2008.

1. Miller, Toby, ed. *Television: Critical Concepts in Media and Cultural Studies*. London: Routledge, 2003.

1. Newton, Harry. *Newton's Telecom Dictionary*. 26th ed. New York: Flatiron Books, 2011.

1. Watson, James, and Anne Hill. *A Dictionary of Communication and Media Studies*. 8th ed. New York: Bloomsbury Academic, 2012.

1. Weik, Martin H. *Communications Standard Dictionary*. 3rd ed. New York: Chapman and Hall, 1996.

2. Barnouw, Erik, ed. *International Encyclopedia of Communications*. 4 vols. New York: Oxford University Press, 1989.

2. Johnston, Donald H., ed. *Encyclopedia of International Media and Communications*. 4 vols. San Diego, CA: Academic Press, 2003.

2. Jones, Steve, ed. *Encyclopedia of New Media: An Essential Reference to Communication and Technology*. Thousand Oaks, CA: Sage, 2003.

2. Stern, Jane, and Michael Stern. *Jane and Michael Stern's Encyclopedia of Pop Culture: An A to Z Guide of Who's Who and What's What, from Aerobics and Bubble Gum to Valley of the Dolls and Moon Unit Zappa*. New York: HarperPerennial, 1992.

2. Vaughn, Stephen L. *Encyclopedia of American Journalism*. New York: Routledge, 2008.

3. Clark, Vivienne, James Baker, and Eileen Lewis. *Key Concepts and Skills for Media Studies*. London: Hodder and Stoughton, 2003.

3. Stokes, Jane. *How to Do Media and Cultural Studies*. 2nd ed. London: Sage, 2012.

3. Storey, John. *Cultural Studies and the Study of Popular Culture*. 3rd ed. Edinburgh: Edinburgh University Press, 2010.

4. Block, Eleanor S., and James K. Bracken. *Communication and the Mass Media: A Guide to the Reference Literature*. Englewood, CO: Libraries Unlimited, 1991.

4. Blum, Eleanor, and Frances Goins Wilhoit. *Mass Media Bibliography: An Annotated Guide to Books and Journals for Research and Reference*. 3rd ed. Urbana: University of Illinois Press, 1990.

4. Cates, Jo A. *Journalism: A Guide to the Reference Literature*. 3rd ed. Westport, CT: Libraries Unlimited, 2004.

4. *CD Review*. Hancock, NH: WGE Pub., 1989–96.

4. *Communications Abstracts*. Los Angeles: Dept. of Journalism, University of California, Los Angeles, 1960–. Also at http://www.ebscohost.com/academic/.

4. *Film Review Annual*. Englewood, NJ: J. S. Ozer, 1981–2002.

4. Matlon, Ronald J., and Sylvia P. Ortiz, eds. *Index to Journals in Communication Studies through 1995*. Annandale, VA: National Communication Association, 1997.

4. *Media Review Digest*. Ann Arbor, MI: Pierian Press, 1974–2006.

4. *New York Theatre Critics' Reviews*. New York: Critics' Theatre Reviews, 1943–95.

4. *New York Times Directory of the Film*. New York: Arno Press, 1971–.

4. *Records in Review*. Great Barrington, MA: Wyeth Press, 1957–.

4. Sterling, Christopher H., James K. Bracken, and Susan M. Hill, eds. *Mass Communications Research Resources: An Annotated Guide*. Mahwah, NJ: Erlbaum, 1998.

6. Christian, Darrell, Sally Jacobsen, and David Minthorn, eds. *Stylebook and Briefing on Media Law*. 46th ed. New York: Basic Books, 2011.

ECONOMICS

1. Pearce, David W., ed. *MIT Dictionary of Modern Economics*. 4th ed. Cambridge, MA: MIT Press, 1992.

2. Durlauf, Steven N., and Lawrence E. Blume, eds. *The New Palgrave Dictionary of Economics*. 8 vols. 2nd ed. New York: Palgrave Macmillan, 2008.

2. Greenwald, Douglas, ed. *The McGraw-Hill Encyclopedia of Economics*. 2nd ed. New York: McGraw-Hill, 1994.

2. Mokyr, Joel, ed. *The Oxford Encyclopedia of Economic History*. 5 vols. Oxford: Oxford University Press, 2003. Also at http://www.oxford-economichistory.com/.

3. Fletcher, John, ed. *Information Sources in Economics*. 2nd ed. London: Butterworths, 1984.

3. Johnson, Glenn L. *Research Methodology for Economists: Philosophy and Practice*. New York: Macmillan, 1986.

4. *Journal of Economic Literature*. Nashville: American Economic Association, 1969–. Also at http://www.jstor.org/.

5. McCloskey, Deirdre N. *Economical Writing*. 2nd ed. Prospect Heights, IL: Waveland Press, 2000.

5. Thomson, William. *A Guide for the Young Economist*. 2nd ed. Cambridge, MA: MIT Press, 2011.

EDUCATION

1. Barrow, Robin, and Geoffrey Milburn. *A Critical Dictionary of Educational Concepts: An Appraisal of Selected Ideas and Issues in Educational Theory and Practice*. 2nd ed. New York: Harvester Wheatsheaf, 1990.

1. Collins, John Williams, and Nancy P. O'Brien, eds. *The Greenwood Dictionary of Education*. 2nd ed. Santa Barbara, CA: Greenwood, 2011.

1. Gordon, Peter, and Denis Lawton. *Dictionary of British Education*. 3rd rev. ed. London: Woburn Press, 2004.

2. Alkin, Marvin C., ed. *Encyclopedia of Educational Research*. 6th ed. 4 vols. New York: Macmillan, 1992.

2. Guthrie, James W., ed. *Encyclopedia of Education*. 2nd ed. 8 vols. New York: Macmillan Reference USA, 2003.

2. Levinson, David L., Peter W. Cookson Jr., and Alan R. Sadovnik, eds. *Education and Sociology: An Encyclopedia*. New York: RoutledgeFalmer, 2002.

2. Peterson, Penelope, Eva Baker, and Barry McGaw, eds. *The International Encyclopedia of Education*. 3rd ed. 8 vols. Oxford: Elsevier, 2010.

2. Unger, Harlow G. *Encyclopedia of American Education*. 3rd ed. 3 vols. New York: Facts on File, 2007.

3. Bausell, R. Barker. *Advanced Research Methodology: An Annotated Guide to Sources*. Metuchen, NJ: Scarecrow Press, 1991.

3. Keeves, John P., ed. *Educational Research, Methodology, and Measurement: An International Handbook*. 2nd ed. New York: Pergamon, 1997.

3. Tuckman, Bruce W., and Brian E. Harper. *Conducting Educational Research*. 6th ed. Lanham, MD: Rowman and Littlefield, 2012.

4. *Education Index*. New York: H. W. Wilson, 1929–. Also at http://www.ebscohost.com/wilson/ (as *Education Index Retrospective* and *Education Abstracts*).

4. *ERIC Database*. Lanham, MD: Educational Resources Information Center, 2004–. http://www.eric.ed.gov/.

4. O'Brien, Nancy P., and Lois Buttlar. *Education: A Guide to Reference and Information Sources*. 2nd ed. Englewood, CO: Libraries Unlimited, 2000.

5. Carver, Ronald P. *Writing a Publishable Research Report: In Education, Psychology, and Related Disciplines*. Springfield, IL: C. C. Thomas, 1984.

GEOGRAPHY

1. Witherick, M. E., Simon Ross, and John Small. *A Modern Dictionary of Geography*. 4th ed. London: Arnold, 2001.

1. *The World Factbook*. Washington, DC: Central Intelligence Agency, 1990s–. https://www.cia.gov/library/publications/the-world-factbook/.

2. Dunbar, Gary S. *Modern Geography: An Encyclopedic Survey*. New York: Garland, 1991.

2. McCoy, John, ed. *Geo-Data: The World Geographical Encyclopedia*. 3rd ed. Detroit: Thomson/Gale, 2003. Also at http://www.gale.cengage.com/.

2. Parker, Sybil P., ed. *World Geographical Encyclopedia*. 5 vols. New York: McGraw-Hill, 1995.

3. *Historical GIS Clearinghouse and Forum*. Washington, DC: Association of American Geographers. http://www.aag.org/.

3. Walford, Nigel. *Geographical Data: Characteristics and Sources*. New York: John Wiley and Sons, 2002.

4. Conzen, Michael P., Thomas A. Rumney, and Graeme Wynn. *A Scholar's Guide to Geographical Writing on the American and Canadian Past*. Chicago: University of Chicago Press, 1993.

4. *Current Geographical Publications*. New York: American Geographical Society of New York, 1938–.

4. *Geographical Abstracts*. Norwich, UK: Geo Abstracts, 1966–.

4. Okuno, Takashi. *A World Bibliography of Geographical Bibliographies*. Japan: Institute of Geoscience, University of Tsukuba, 1992.

5. Durrenberger, Robert W., John K. Wright, and Elizabeth T. Platt. *Geographical Research and Writing*. New York: Crowell, 1985.

5. Northey, Margot, David B. Knight, and Dianne Draper. *Making Sense: A Student's Guide to Research and Writing; Geography and Environmental Sciences*. 5th ed. Don Mills, ON: Oxford University Press, 2012.

LAW

1. Garner, Bryan A., ed. *Black's Law Dictionary*. 9th ed. St. Paul, MN: Thomson/West, 2009.

1. Law, Jonathan, and Elizabeth A. Martin, eds. *A Dictionary of Law*. 8th ed. Oxford: Oxford University Press, 2015.

1. Richards, P. H., and L. B. Curzon. *The Longman Dictionary of Law*. 8th ed. New York: Pearson Longman, 2011.

2. Baker, Brian L., and Patrick J. Petit, eds. *Encyclopedia of Legal Information Sources*. 2nd ed. Detroit: Gale Research, 1993.

2. *Corpus Juris Secundum*. Brooklyn: American Law Book; St. Paul, MN: West, 1936–.

2. *Gale Encyclopedia of American Law*. 3rd ed. 14 vols. Detroit: Gale Cengage Learning, 2011. Also at http://www.gale.cengage.com/.

2. Hall, Kermit, and David Scott Clark, eds. *The Oxford Companion to American Law*. New York: Oxford University Press, 2002. Also at http://www.oxfordreference.com/.

2. Patterson, Dennis M., ed. *A Companion to Philosophy of Law and Legal Theory*. Oxford: Blackwell, 1999.

3. Campbell, Enid Mona, Lee Poh-York, and Joycey G. Tooher. *Legal Research: Materials and Methods*. 4th ed. North Ryde, Australia: LBC Information Services, 1996.

3. *Online Legal Research: Beyond LexisNexis and Westlaw*. Los Angeles: University of California. http://libguides.law.ucla.edu/onlinelegalresearch.

4. *Current Index to Legal Periodicals*. Seattle: University of Washington Law Library, 1948–. Also at http://lib.law.washington.edu/cilp/cilp.html/.

4. *Current Law Index*. Los Altos, CA: Information Access; Farmington Hills, MI: Gale Cengage Learning, 1980–.

4. *Index to Legal Periodicals and Books*. New York: H. W. Wilson, 1924–. Also at http://www.ebscohost.com/wilson/.

5. Bast, Carol M., and Margie Hawkins. *Foundations of Legal Research and Writing*. 5th ed. Clifton Park, NY: Delmar Cengage Learning, 2012.

5. Garner, Bryan A. *The Elements of Legal Style*. 2nd ed. New York: Oxford University Press, 2002.

6. *The Bluebook: A Uniform System of Citation*. 19th ed. Cambridge, MA: Harvard Law Review Association, 2010. Also at https://www.legalbluebook.com/.

6. *The Maroonbook: The University of Chicago Manual of Legal Citation*. Chicago: University of Chicago, 2013.

POLITICAL SCIENCE

1. Robertson, David. *A Dictionary of Modern Politics*. 4th ed. London: Routledge, 2007.

2. *The Almanac of American Politics*. Washington, DC: National Journal, 1972–. Also at http://nationaljournal.com/almanac.

2. Hawkesworth, Mary E., and Maurice Kogan, eds. *Encyclopedia of Government and Politics*. 2nd ed. 2 vols. London: Routledge, 2004.

2. Lal, Shiv, ed. *International Encyclopedia of Politics and Laws*. 17 vols. 5th ed. New Delhi: Election Archives, 1992.

2. Miller, David, ed. *The Blackwell Encyclopaedia of Political Thought*. Oxford: Blackwell, 2004.

3. Green, Stephen W., and Douglas J. Ernest, eds. *Information Sources of Political Science*. 5th ed. Santa Barbara, CA: ABC-Clio, 2005.

3. Johnson, Janet Buttolph, and H. T. Reynolds. *Political Science Research Methods*. 7th ed. Los Angeles: Congressional Quarterly Press, 2012.

4. *ABC Pol Sci*. Santa Barbara, CA: ABC-Clio, 1969–2000.

4. Hardy, Gayle J., and Judith Schiek Robinson. *Subject Guide to U.S. Government Reference Sources*. 2nd ed. Englewood, CO: Libraries Unlimited, 1996.

4. *PAIS International Journals Indexed*. New York: Public Affairs Information Service, 1972–. Also at http://www.csa.com/.

4. *United States Political Science Documents*. Pittsburgh: University of Pittsburgh, University Center for International Studies, 1975–91.

4. *Worldwide Political Science Abstracts*. Bethesda, MD: Cambridge Scientific Abstracts, 1976–. Also at http://www.csa.com/.

5. Biddle, Arthur W., Kenneth M. Holland, and Toby Fulwiler. *Writer's Guide: Political Science*. Lexington, MA: D. C. Heath, 1987.

5. Lovell, David W., and Rhonda Moore. *Essay Writing and Style Guide for Politics and the Social Sciences*. Rev. ed. Canberra: Australasian Politic Studies Association, 1993.

5. Schmidt, Diane E. *Writing in Political Science: A Practical Guide*. 4th ed. Boston: Longman, 2010.

5. Scott, Gregory M., and Stephen M. Garrison. *The Political Science Student Writer's Manual*. 7th ed. Boston: Pearson, 2012.

6. American Political Science Association. *APSA Style Manual for Political Science*. Rev. ed. Washington, DC: American Political Science Association, 2006. http://www.apsanet.org/files/APSAStyleManual2006.pdf.

PSYCHOLOGY

1. Colman, Andrew M. *A Dictionary of Psychology*. 4th ed. Oxford: Oxford University Press, 2015. Also at http://www.oxfordreference.com/.

1. Eysenck, Michael W., ed. *The Blackwell Dictionary of Cognitive Psychology*. Oxford: Blackwell, 1997.

1. Hayes, Nicky, and Peter Stratton. *A Student's Dictionary of Psychology*. 4th ed. London: Arnold, 2003.

1. Wolman, Benjamin B., ed. *Dictionary of Behavioral Science*. 2nd ed. San Diego, CA: Academic Press, 1989.

2. Colman, Andrew M., ed. *Companion Encyclopedia of Psychology*. 2 vols. London: Routledge, 1997.

2. Craighead, W. Edward, Charles B. Nemeroff, and Raymond J. Corsini, eds. *The Corsini Encyclopedia of Psychology and Behavioral Science*. 4th ed. 4 vols. New York: John Wiley and Sons, 2010.

2. Kazdin, Alan E., ed. *Encyclopedia of Psychology*. 8 vols. Washington, DC: American Psychological Association; Oxford: Oxford University Press, 2000.

2. Weiner, Irving B., and W. Edward Craighead, eds. *The Corsini Encyclopedia of Psychology*. 4th ed. 4 vols. Hoboken, NJ: Wiley, 2010.

3. Breakwell, Glynis M., Sean Hammond, Chris Fife-Schaw, and Jonathan A. Smith. *Research Methods in Psychology*. 4th ed. London: Sage, 2012.

3. Elmes, David G., Barry H. Kantowitz, and Henry L. Roediger III. *Research Methods in Psychology*. 9th ed. Belmont, CA: Wadsworth Cengage Learning, 2012.

3. Reed, Jeffrey G., and Pam M. Baxter. *Library Use: A Handbook for Psychology*. 3rd ed. Washington, DC: American Psychological Association, 2003.

3. Shaughnessy, John J., Eugene B. Zechmeister, and Jeanne S. Zechmeister. *Research Methods in Psychology*. 10th ed. Boston: McGraw-Hill, 2014.

3. Wilson, Christopher. *Research Methods in Psychology: An Introductory Laboratory Manual*. Dubuque, IA: Kendall-Hunt, 1990.

4. *Annual Review of Psychology*. Palo Alto, CA: Annual Reviews, 1950–. Also at http://arjournals.annualreviews.org/journal/psych.

4. *APA PsycNET*. Washington, DC: American Psychological Association, 1990s–. http://www.apa.org/pubs/databases/psycnet/.

4. *NASPSPA Abstracts*. Champaign, IL: Human Kinetics Publishers, 1990s–. Also at http://journals.humankinetics.com/.

4. *PubMed*. Bethesda, MD: US National Library of Medicine. http://www.ncbi.nlm.nih.gov/pubmed/.

4. *Science Citation Index*. Philadelphia: Institute for Scientific Information, 1961–. Also at http://wokinfo.com/.

5. Solomon, Paul R. *A Student's Guide to Research Report Writing in Psychology*. Glenview, IL: Scott Foresman, 1985.

5. Sternberg, Robert J., and Karin Sternberg. *The Psychologist's Companion: A Guide to Writing Scientific Papers for Students and Researchers*. 5th ed. Cambridge: Cambridge University Press, 2010.

6. *Publication Manual of the American Psychological Association*. 6th ed. Washington, DC: American Psychological Association, 2009.

RELIGION

1. Bowker, John, ed. *The Concise Oxford Dictionary of World Religions*. New ed. Oxford: Oxford University Press, 2007. Also at http://www.oxfordreference.com/.

1. Pye, Michael, ed. *Continuum Dictionary of Religion*. New York: Continuum, 1994.

2. Cesari, Jocelyne. *Encyclopedia of Islam in the United States*. London: Greenwood Press, 2007. eBook, 2012.

2. Freedman, David Noel, ed. *The Anchor Yale Bible Dictionary*. 6 vols. New Haven, CT: Yale University Press, 2008.

2. Jones, Lindsay, ed. *Encyclopedia of Religion*. 2nd ed. 15 vols. Detroit: Macmillan Reference USA, 2005.

2. Martin, Richard C., ed. *Encyclopedia of Islam and the Muslim World*. 2 vols. New York: Macmillan Reference USA, 2003.

2. Routledge Encyclopedias of Religion and Society (series). New York: Routledge.

2. Skolnik, Fred, and Michael Berenbaum, eds. *Encyclopaedia Judaica*. 2nd ed. 22 vols. Detroit: Macmillan Reference USA, 2007.

3. Kennedy, James R., Jr. *Library Research Guide to Religion and Theology: Illustrated Search Strategy and Sources*. 2nd ed., rev. Ann Arbor, MI: Pierian, 1984.

4. Brown, David, and Richard Swinburne. *A Selective Bibliography of the Philosophy of Religion*. Rev. ed. Oxford: Sub-faculty of Philosophy, 1995.

4. Chinyamu, Salms F. *An Annotated Bibliography on Religion*. [Lilongwe,] Malawi: Malawi Library Association, 1993.

4. *Guide to Social Science and Religion in Periodical Literature*. Flint, MI: National Library of Religious Periodicals, 1970–88.

4. *Index of Articles on Jewish Studies (RAMBI).* Jerusalem: Jewish National and University Library, 2002–. http://jnul.huji.ac.il/rambi/.

4. *Index to Book Reviews in Religion.* Chicago: American Theological Library Association, 1990–. Also at http://www.ovid/ (as *ATLA Religion Database*).

4. *Islamic Book Review Index.* Berlin: Adiyok, 1982–.

4. O'Brien, Betty A., and Elmer J. O'Brien, eds. *Religion Index Two: Festschriften, 1960–1969.* Chicago: American Theological Library Association, 1980. Also at http://www.ovid.com/ (as *ATLA Religion Database*).

4. *Religion Index One: Periodicals.* Chicago: American Theological Library Association, 1977–. Also at https://www.atla.com/products/catalog/pages/rdb-db.aspx (as *ATLA Religion Database*).

4. *Religion Index Two: Multi-author Works.* Chicago: American Theological Library Association, 1976–. Also at https://www.atla.com/products/catalog/pages/rdb-db.aspx (as *ATLA Religion Database*).

6. *CNS Stylebook on Religion: Reference Guide and Usage Manual.* 3rd ed. Washington, DC: Catholic News Service, 2006.

SOCIOLOGY

1. Abercrombie, Nicholas, Stephen Hill, and Bryan S. Turner. *The Penguin Dictionary of Sociology.* 5th ed. London: Penguin, 2006.

1. Johnson, Allan G. *The Blackwell Dictionary of Sociology: A User's Guide to Sociological Language.* 2nd ed. Oxford: Blackwell, 2002.

1. Scott, John, and Marshall Gordon, eds. *A Dictionary of Sociology.* 4th ed. rev. Oxford: Oxford University Press, 2009. Also at http://www.oxfordreference.com/.

2. Beckert, Jens, and Milan Zafirovksi, eds. *International Encyclopedia of Economic Sociology.* London: Routledge, 2006.

2. Borgatta, Edgar F., and Rhonda J. V. Montgomery, eds. *Encyclopedia of Sociology.* 2nd ed. 5 vols. New York: Macmillan Reference USA, 2000.

2. Levinson, David L., Peter W. Cookson, and Alan R. Sadovnik, eds. *Education and Sociology: An Encyclopedia.* New York: RoutledgeFalmer, 2014.

2. Ritzer, George, ed. *Encyclopedia of Social Theory.* 2 vols. Thousand Oaks, CA: Sage, 2005.

2. Smelser, Neil J., and Richard Swedberg, eds. 2nd ed. *The Handbook of Economic Sociology.* Princeton, NJ: Princeton University Press, 2005.

3. Aby, Stephen H., James Nalen, and Lori Fielding, eds. *Sociology: A Guide to Reference and Information Sources.* 3rd ed. Westport, CT: Libraries Unlimited, 2005.

3. Lieberson, Stanley. *Making It Count: The Improvement of Social Research and Theory.* Berkeley: University of California Press, 1987.

4. *Annual Review of Sociology.* Palo Alto, CA: Annual Reviews, 1975–. Also at http://www.annualreviews.org/journal/soc.

4. *Applied Social Sciences Index and Abstracts (ASSIA).* Bethesda, MD: Cambridge Scientific Abstracts, 1987–. Also at http://www.csa.com/.

4. *Social Science Research*. San Diego, CA: Academic Press, 1972–. Also at http://www.sciencedirect.com/science/journal/0049089X/.

4. *Sociological Abstracts*. Bethesda, MD: Sociological Abstracts, 1952–. Also at http://www.proquest.com/.

5. Sociology Writing Group. *A Guide to Writing Sociology Papers*. 7th ed. New York: Worth, 2013.

5. Tomovic, Vladislav A., ed. *Definitions in Sociology: Convergence, Conflict, and Alternative Vocabularies; A Manual for Writers of Term Papers, Research Reports, and Theses*. St. Catharines, ON: Diliton Publications, 1979.

WOMEN'S STUDIES

1. Bataille, Gretchen M., and Laurie Lisa, eds. *Native American Women: A Biographical Dictionary*. 2nd ed. New York: Routledge, 2001.

1. Hendry, Maggy, and Jennifer S. Uglow, eds. *The Palgrave Macmillan Dictionary of Women's Biography*. 4th ed. New York: Palgrave Macmillan, 2005.

1. Mills, Jane. *Womanwords: A Dictionary of Words about Women*. New York: H. Holt, 1993.

1. Salem, Dorothy C., ed. *African American Women: A Biographical Dictionary*. New York: Garland, 1993.

2. Hine, Darlene Clark, ed. *Black Women in America*. 2nd ed. 3 vols. New York: Oxford University Press, 2005.

2. Kramarae, Cheris, and Dale Spender, eds. *Routledge International Encyclopedia of Women: Global Women's Issues and Knowledge*. 4 vols. New York: Routledge, 2000.

2. Tierney, Helen, ed. *Women's Studies Encyclopedia*. Rev. ed. 3 vols. Westport, CT: Greenwood Press, 2007.

2. Willard, Frances E., and Mary A. Livermore, eds. *Great American Women of the 19th Century: A Biographical Encyclopedia*. Amherst, NY: Humanity Books, 2005.

3. Carter, Sarah, and Maureen Ritchie. *Women's Studies: A Guide to Information Sources*. Jefferson, NC: McFarland, 1991.

3. Searing, Susan E. *Introduction to Library Research in Women's Studies*. 2nd ed. Boulder, CO: Westview Press, 1998.

4. *Studies on Women and Gender Abstracts*. Abingdon, Oxfordshire, UK: Carfax, 1983–.

4. *ViVa: A Bibliography of Women's History in Historical and Women's Studies Journals*. Amsterdam: International Institute of Social History, 1995–. http://www.iisg.nl/womhist/vivahome.php/.

4. *Women's Review of Books*. Wellesley, MA: Wellesley College Center for Research on Women, 1983–. Also at http://www.oldcitypublishing.com/journals/wrb-home/.

4. *Women Studies Abstracts*. Rush, NY: Rush Publishing, 1972–. Also at http://www.ebscohost.com/academic/ (as *Women's Studies International*).

NATURAL SCIENCES

GENERAL

1. *McGraw-Hill Dictionary of Scientific and Technical Terms.* 6th ed. New York: McGraw-Hill, 2003. Also at http://www.accessscience.com/.

1. Morris, Christopher, ed. *Academic Press Dictionary of Science and Technology.* San Diego, CA: Academic, 1992.

1. Porter, Roy, and Marilyn Bailey Ogilvie, eds. *The Biographical Dictionary of Scientists.* 3rd ed. 2 vols. New York: Oxford University Press, 2000.

1. Walker, Peter M. B., ed. *Chambers Dictionary of Science and Technology.* London: Chambers, 2000.

2. Considine, Glenn D., and Peter H. Kulik, eds. *Van Nostrand's Scientific Encyclopedia.* 10th ed. 3 vols. Hoboken, NJ: Wiley, 2008. Also at http://dx.doi.org/10.1002/9780471743989.

2. Heilbron, J. L., ed. *The Oxford Companion to the History of Modern Science.* Oxford: Oxford University Press, 2003. Also at http://www.oxfordreference.com/.

2. *McGraw-Hill Encyclopedia of Science and Technology.* 11th ed. 20 vols. New York: McGraw-Hill, 2012. Also at http://www.accessscience.com/.

2. *Nature Encyclopedia: An A–Z Guide to Life on Earth.* New York: Oxford University Press, 2001.

3. *Directory of Technical and Scientific Directories: A World Bibliographic Guide to Medical, Agricultural, Industrial, and Natural Science Directories.* 6th ed. Phoenix: Oryx Press, 1989.

3. Hurt, Charlie Deuel. *Information Sources in Science and Technology.* 3rd ed. Englewood, CO: Libraries Unlimited, 1998.

3. Nielsen, Harry A. *Methods of Natural Science: An Introduction.* Englewood Cliffs, NJ: Prentice-Hall, 1967.

4. *Applied Science and Technology Index.* New York: H. W. Wilson, 1913–. Also at http://www.ebscohost.com/wilson/.

4. *Book Review Digest.* New York: H. W. Wilson, 1905–. Also at http://www.ebscohost.com/wilson/.

4. *British Technology Index.* London: Library Association, 1962–80.

4. *Compumath Citation Index.* Philadelphia: Institute for Scientific Information, 1981–2006.

4. *General Science Index.* New York: H. W. Wilson, 1978–. Also at http://www.ebscohost.com/wilson/ (as *General Science Full Text*).

4. *Genetics Citation Index: Experimental Citation Indexes to Genetics with Special Emphasis on Human Genetics.* Compiled by Eugene Garfield and Irving H. Sher. Philadelphia: Institute for Scientific Information, 1963.

4. *Index to Scientific Reviews: An International Interdisciplinary Index to the Review Literature of Science, Medicine, Agriculture, Technology, and the Behavioral Sciences.* Philadelphia: Institute for Scientific Information, 1974.

4. *Science and Technology Annual Reference Review.* Phoenix: Oryx Press, ca. 1989–.

4. *Science Citation Index*. Philadelphia: Institute for Scientific Information, 1961–. Also at http://wokinfo.com/.

4. *Technical Book Review Index*. New York: Special Libraries Association, 1935–88.

5. Booth, Vernon. *Communicating in Science: Writing a Scientific Paper and Speaking at Scientific Meetings*. 2nd ed. Cambridge: Cambridge University Press, 1993.

5. Montgomery, Scott L. *The Chicago Guide to Communicating Science*. Chicago: University of Chicago Press, 2003.

5. Valiela, Ivan. *Doing Science: Design, Analysis, and Communication of Scientific Research*. 2nd ed. Oxford: Oxford University Press, 2009.

5. Wilson, Anthony, et al. *Handbook of Science Communication*. Bristol, UK: Institute of Physics, 1998. Also at http://dx.doi.org/10.1201/9780849386855.

6. Rubens, Phillip, ed. *Science and Technical Writing: A Manual of Style*. 2nd ed. New York: Routledge, 2001.

BIOLOGY

1. Allaby, Michael, ed. *The Oxford Dictionary of Natural History*. Oxford: Oxford University Press, 1985.

1. Cammack, Richard et al., eds. *Oxford Dictionary of Biochemistry and Molecular Biology*. 2nd ed. Oxford: Oxford University Press, 2008. Also at http://www.oxfordreference.com/.

1. Lackie, John M., ed. *The Dictionary of Cell and Molecular Biology*. 5th ed. Amsterdam: Elsevier/AP, 2013.

1. Lawrence, Eleanor, ed. *Henderson's Dictionary of Biology*. 15th ed. New York: Benjamin Cummings, 2011.

1. Martin, Elizabeth, and Robert S. Hine, eds. *A Dictionary of Biology*. 6th ed. Oxford: Oxford University Press, 2008. Also at http://www.oxfordreference.com/.

1. Singleton, Paul, and Diana Sainsbury. *Dictionary of Microbiology and Molecular Biology*. 3rd ed. rev. New York: Wiley, 2006. Also at http://dx.doi.org/10.1002/9780470056981.

2. Creighton, Thomas E., ed. *Encyclopedia of Molecular Biology*. 4 vols. New York: John Wiley and Sons, 1999. Also at http://dx.doi.org/10.1002/047120918X.

2. Dulbecco, Renato, ed. *Encyclopedia of Human Biology*. 3rd ed. 10 vols. San Diego, CA: Academic Press, 2008.

2. Eldredge, Niles, ed. *Life on Earth: An Encyclopedia of Biodiversity, Ecology, and Evolution*. 2 vols. Santa Barbara, CA: ABC-Clio, 2002.

2. Hall, Brian Keith, and Wendy M. Olson, eds. *Keywords and Concepts in Evolutionary Developmental Biology*. Rev. ed. Cambridge, MA: Harvard University Press, 2006.

2. Huber, Jeffrey T., and Susan Swogger, eds. *Introduction to Reference Sources in the Health Sciences*. 6th ed. Chicago: ALA Neal-Schuman Publishers, 2014.

2. Pagel, Mark D., ed. *Encyclopedia of Evolution*. 2 vols. Oxford: Oxford University Press, 2002. Also at http://www.oxford-evolution.com/.

3. Wyatt, H. V., ed. *Information Sources in the Life Sciences*. 4th ed. London: Bowker-Saur, 1997.

4. *Biological Abstracts*. Philadelphia: BioSciences Information Service of Biological Abstracts, 1926–. Also at http://www.ebscohost.com/academic/biological-abstracts/.

4. *Biological and Agricultural Index*. New York: H. W. Wilson, 1964–. Also at http://www.ebscohost.com/wilson/.

4. *Environmental Sciences and Pollution Management*. Bethesda, MD: Cambridge Scientific Abstracts. Also at http://www.proquest.com/.

4. *Genetics Citation Index: Experimental Citation Indexes to Genetics with Special Emphasis on Human Genetics*. Compiled by Eugene Garfield and Irving H. Sher. Philadelphia: Institute for Scientific Information, 1963.

5. McMillan, Victoria E. *Writing Papers in the Biological Sciences*. 5th ed. Boston: Bedford/St. Martin's, 2012.

6. Council of Science Editors. *Scientific Style and Format: The CSE Manual for Authors, Editors, and Publishers*. 8th ed. Chicago: University of Chicago Press, 2014.

CHEMISTRY

1. Hawley, Gessner Goodrich, and Richard J. Lewis Sr. *Hawley's Condensed Chemical Dictionary*. 15th ed. New York: Wiley, 2007.

2. Haynes, William M., ed. *CRC Handbook of Chemistry and Physics*. 92nd ed. Boca Raton, FL: CRC Press, 2011.

2. *Kirk-Othmer Encyclopedia of Chemical Technology*. 5th ed. 2 vols. Hoboken, NJ: Wiley-Interscience, 2007. Also at http://dx.doi.org/10.1002/0471238961.

2. Meyers, Robert A., ed. *Encyclopedia of Physical Science and Technology*. 3rd ed. 18 vols. San Diego, CA: Academic, 2002. Also at http://www.sciencedirect.com/science/referenceworks/9780122274107/.

3. Leslie, Davies. *Efficiency in Research, Development, and Production: The Statistical Design and Analysis of Chemical Experiments*. Cambridge: Royal Society of Chemistry, 1993.

3. Wiggins, Gary. *Chemical Information Sources*. New York: McGraw-Hill, 1991. Also at http://en.wikibooks.org/wiki/Chemical_Information_Sources/.

4. *ACS Publications*. Columbus, OH: American Chemical Society. http://pubs.acs.org/.

4. *Chemical Abstracts*. Columbus, OH: American Chemical Society, 1907–. Also at http://www.cas.org/.

4. *Composite Index for CRC Handbooks*. 3rd ed. 3 vols. Boca Raton, FL: CRC Press, 1991.

4. *CrossFire Beilstein*. San Leandro, CA: MDL Information Systems, 1996–. Also at https://www.reaxys.com/.

4. *Reaxys*. New York: Elsevier Science. Also at http://www.elsevier.com/online-tools/reaxys.

4. *ScienceDirect*. New York: Elsevier Science, 1999–. http://www.sciencedirect.com/.

5. Davis, Holly B., Julian F. Tyson, and Jan A. Pechenik. *A Short Guide to Writing about Chemistry*. Boston: Longman, 2010.

5. Ebel, Hans Friedrich, Claus Bliefert, and William E. Russey. *The Art of Scientific Writing: From Student Reports to Professional Publications in Chemistry and Related Fields*. 2nd ed. Weinheim, Germany: Wiley-VCH, 2004.

5. Schoenfeld, Robert. *The Chemist's English, with "Say It in English, Please!"* 3rd rev. ed. New York: Wiley-VCH, 2001.

6. Dodd, Janet S., ed. *The ACS Style Guide: Effective Communication of Scientific Information*. 3rd ed. Washington, DC: American Chemical Society, 2006.

COMPUTER SCIENCES

1. Gattiker, Urs E. *The Information Security Dictionary: Defining the Terms That Define Security for E-Business, Internet, Information, and Wireless Technology*. Boston: Kluwer Academic, 2004.

1. LaPlante, Phillip A. *Dictionary of Computer Science, Engineering, and Technology*. Boca Raton, FL: CRC Press, 2001.

1. Pfaffenberger, Bryan. *Webster's New World Computer Dictionary*. 10th ed. Indianapolis: Wiley, 2003.

1. *Random House Concise Dictionary of Science and Computers*. New York: Random House Reference, 2004.

1. South, David W. *The Computer and Information Science and Technology Abbreviations and Acronyms Dictionary*. Boca Raton, FL: CRC Press, 1994.

2. Henderson, Harry. *Encyclopedia of Computer Science and Technology*. Rev. ed. New York: Facts on File, 2009.

2. Narins, Brigham, ed. *World of Computer Science*. 2 vols. Detroit: Gale Group/Thomson Learning, 2002.

2. Wah, Benjamin W., ed. *Wiley Encyclopedia of Computer Science and Engineering*. 5 vols. Hoboken, NJ: Wiley, 2009.

3. Ardis, Susan B., and Jean A. Poland. *A Guide to the Literature of Electrical and Electronics Engineering*. Littleton, CO: Libraries Unlimited, 1987.

4. *Directory of Library Automation Software, Systems, and Services*. Medford, NJ: Learned Information, 1993–2007.

5. Eckstein, C. J. *Style Manual for Use in Computer-Based Instruction*. Brooks Air Force Base, TX: Air Force Human Resources Laboratory, Air Force Systems Command, 1990. Also at http://www.dtic.mil/dtic/tr/fulltext/u2/a226959.pdf.

GEOLOGY AND EARTH SCIENCES

1. *McGraw-Hill Dictionary of Geology and Mineralogy*. 2nd ed. New York: McGraw-Hill, 2003.

1. Neuendorf, Klaus K. E., et al., eds. *Glossary of Geology*. 5th ed. rev. Alexandria, VA: American Geological Institute, 2011.

1. Smith, Jacqueline, ed. *The Facts on File Dictionary of Earth Science*. Rev. ed. New York: Facts on File, 2006. Also at http://www.factsonfile.com/.

2. Bishop, Arthur C., Alan R. Woolley, and William R. Hamilton. *Cambridge Guide to Minerals, Rocks, and Fossils*. Rev. ed. Cambridge: Cambridge University Press, 2001.

2. Bowes, Donald R., ed. *The Encyclopedia of Igneous and Metamorphic Petrology*. New York: Van Nostrand Reinhold, 1989.

2. Dasch, E. Julius, ed. *Macmillan Encyclopedia of Earth Sciences*. 2 vols. New York: Macmillan Reference USA, 1996.

2. Good, Gregory A., ed. *Sciences of the Earth: An Encyclopedia of Events, People, and Phenomena*. 2 vols. New York: Garland, 1998.

2. Hancock, Paul L., and Brian J. Skinner, eds. *The Oxford Companion to the Earth*. Oxford: Oxford University Press, 2000. Also at http://www.oxfordreference.com/.

2. Nierenberg, William A., ed. *Encyclopedia of Earth System Science*. 4 vols. San Diego, CA: Academic Press, 1992.

2. Selley, Richard C., et al., eds. *Encyclopedia of Geology*. 5 vols. Amsterdam: Elsevier Academic, 2005.

2. Seyfert, Carl K., ed. *The Encyclopedia of Structural Geology and Plate Tectonics*. New York: Van Nostrand Reinhold, 1987.

2. Singer, Ronald, ed. *Encyclopedia of Paleontology*. 2 vols. Chicago: Fitzroy Dearborn, 1999.

2. Steele, John H., S. A. Thorpe, and Karl K. Turekian, eds. *Encyclopedia of Ocean Sciences*. 2nd ed. 6 vols. Boston: Elsevier, 2009. Also at http://www.sciencedirect.com/science/referenceworks/9780122274305/.

4. *Bibliography and Index of Geology*. Alexandria, VA: American Geological Institute, 1966–2005. Also at http://www.proquest.com/ (as *GeoRef*).

4. *Geobase*. New York: Elsevier Science. Also at http://www.elsevier.com/online-tools/engineering-village/geobase/.

4. Wood, David N., Joan E. Hardy, and Anthony P. Harvey. *Information Sources in the Earth Sciences*. 2nd ed. London: Bowker-Saur, 1989.

5. Bates, Robert L., Marla D. Adkins-Heljeson, and Rex C. Buchanan, eds. *Geowriting: A Guide to Writing, Editing, and Printing in Earth Science*. Rev. 5th ed. Alexandria, VA: American Geological Institute, 2004.

5. Dunn, J., et al. *Organization and Content of a Typical Geologic Report*. Rev. ed. Arvada, CO: American Institute of Professional Geologists, 1993.

MATHEMATICS

1. Borowski, E. J., and J. M. Borwein, eds. *Collins Dictionary: Mathematics*. 2nd ed. Glasgow: HarperCollins, 2002.

1. Nelson, David, ed. *The Penguin Dictionary of Mathematics*. 4th ed. London: Penguin, 2008.

1. Nicholson, James. *The Concise Oxford Dictionary of Mathematics.* 5th ed. Oxford: Oxford University Press, 2014.

1. Schwartzman, Steven. *The Words of Mathematics: An Etymological Dictionary of Mathematical Terms Used in English.* Washington, DC: Mathematical Association of America, 1994.

2. Darling, David J. *The Universal Book of Mathematics: From Abracadabra to Zeno's Paradoxes.* Hoboken, NJ: Wiley, 2004.

2. Ito, Kiyosi, ed. *Encyclopedic Dictionary of Mathematics.* 2nd ed. 2 vols. Cambridge, MA: MIT Press, 1993.

2. Weisstein, Eric W. *CRC Concise Encyclopedia of Mathematics.* 2nd ed. Boca Raton, FL: Chapman and Hall/CRC, 2003.

3. Pemberton, John E. *How to Find Out in Mathematics: A Guide to Sources of Information.* 2nd rev. ed. Oxford: Pergamon, 1969.

4. *Mathematical Reviews: 50th Anniversary Celebration.* Providence, RI: American Mathematical Society, 1990.

4. *MathSci.* Providence, RI: American Mathematical Society. Also at http://www.ams.org/mathscinet/.

4. *USSR and East European Scientific Abstracts: Physics and Mathematics.* Arlington, VA: Joint Publications Research Service, 1973–78. Also at http://purl.fdlp.gov/GPO/gpo39529/.

5. *A Manual for Authors of Mathematical Papers.* Rev. ed. Providence, RI: American Mathematical Society, 1990.

5. Miller, Jane E. *The Chicago Guide to Writing about Multivariate Analysis.* 2nd ed. Chicago: University of Chicago Press, 2013.

PHYSICS

1. Basu, Dipak, ed. *Dictionary of Pure and Applied Physics.* Boca Raton, FL: CRC Press, 2001.

1. Daintith, John, ed. *A Dictionary of Physics.* 6th ed. Oxford: Oxford University Press, 2009. Also at http://www.oxfordreference.com/.

1. Sube, Ralf. *Dictionary: Physics Basic Terms; English-German.* Berlin: A. Hatier, 1994.

1. Thewlis, James. *Concise Dictionary of Physics and Related Subjects.* 2nd ed. rev. and enl. Oxford: Pergamon, 1979.

2. Lerner, Rita G., and George L. Trigg, eds. *Encyclopedia of Physics.* 3rd ed. Weinheim, Germany: Wiley-VCH, 2005.

2. *McGraw-Hill Concise Encyclopedia of Physics.* New York: McGraw-Hill, 2005.

2. Meyers, Robert A., ed. *Encyclopedia of Modern Physics.* San Diego, CA: Academic Press, 1990.

2. Trigg, George L., ed. *Encyclopedia of Applied Physics.* 23 vols. Weinheim, Germany: Wiley-VCH, 2004. Also at http://dx.doi.org/10.1002/3527600434/.

2. Woan, Graham. *The Cambridge Handbook of Physics Formulas.* 2003 ed. Cambridge: Cambridge University Press, 2003.

3. Shaw, Dennis F. *Information Sources in Physics*. 3rd ed. London: Bowker-Saur, 1994.

4. American Institute of Physics. Journals. College Park, MD: AIP. http://journals.aip.org/.

4. *Astronomy and Astrophysics Abstracts*. Berlin: Springer-Verlag, 1969–.

4. *Current Physics Index*. New York: American Institute of Physics, 1975–2005. Also at http://journals.aip.org/.

4. *IEEE Xplore*. New York: Institute of Electrical and Electronics Engineers. http://ieeexplore.ieee.org/Xplore/.

4. *Inspec*. Stevenage, UK: Institution of Electrical Engineers. Also at http://www.ebscohost.com/academic/.

4. Institute of Physics. Journals. London: IOP. http://iopscience.iop.org/journals/.

4. *Physics Abstracts*. London: Institution of Electrical Engineers, 1967–.

5. Katz, Michael J. *Elements of the Scientific Paper*. New Haven, CT: Yale University Press, 1985.

6. American Institute of Physics. *AIP Style Manual*. 4th ed. New York: American Institute of Physics, 1990. Also at http://www.aip.org/pubservs/style/4thed/toc.html.

Index

Page numbers in boldface indicate diagrams or illustrations.

abstractions, in writing, 253–57
abstracts, 197–99
acknowledgments and responses: definition and role in argument, 111, 114–19, **115**, **117**; placement in text, 182; to readers, 141–54; to sources, 92–93, 145; vocabulary of, 149–52
active voice, 260–62
agreements, creative, 89–90
analysis, vs. summaries, 184
anecdotes, 140, 143–44, 245
annotations: in bibliographies, 70, 102–3; of sources, 101–3
anxiety, managing, 104, 118, 188
APA-style citations, 206, 211–13
applied research, 57–60, 239
arguments, research: as conversation with readers, 107–9, 110–11, 141–54, 189, 193, 273; elements of, 111–21, 126; organization of, 181–83; planning, 107–9, 132–33, 142–45; in response to sources, 92–93, 145; revising, 191–93. *See also* acknowledgments and responses; claims; evidence; reasons; warrants
audience. *See* readers
author-date citations, 204–6, 211–13
author-title citations, 204–5, 211–13

bibliographies: annotated, 70, 102–3; in citation styles, 205–6, 211–13; and search for sources, 37, 47, 70, 73–74, 79
blogs, 35, 47, 76
books, as sources, 66–68, 71–73, 76, 77–80, 86

characters, subjects as, 251–62
charts, area, **229**, 231, **231**
charts, bar: design of, 217–20, 222–25, 230; effective use of, 215–16, 230; examples of, **216**, **223**, **224**, **225**, **228**, **230**
charts, bubble, 231, **231**
charts, image, 230, **230**
charts, pie, 225, 230, **230**
Chicago-style citations, 205, 206, 211–13
citation indexing, 74, 79–80
citations, source: contexts requiring, 206–10; reasons for, 203–4; recording information for, 86–87, 95; software for, 97, 204; styles of, 204–6, 211–13
claims: agreement and disagreement with sources, 89–92, 94; conceptual, 122–23, 143–44; definition and role in argument, 111–19, **114**, **115**, **117**, 122–31; evaluating, 124–26, 143; placement in text, 182–83, 192; practical, 122, 124, 143–44; qualifying, 129–31; significance of, 127–29; and warrants, 155, 160–64
clarity, revising for, 248–67
community of readers. *See* readers
conclusions: drafting, 62, 183; importance of, 190–91; relationship to introductions, 178–79, 190–91, 241–42, 245–46; structure and functions of, 245–46
context: in introductions, 232–37; in note-taking, 99–101; of research topic, 39–41, 197–98; in sentences, 258–60
contradictions, in research problems, 61, 90–92
Copernicus, Nicolaus, 128, 130–31

counterexamples, 146, 153, 168
Crick, Francis, 128, 238, 240

data, 30, 85; accuracy and precision of, 138–39, 192; from primary and secondary sources, 93–94, 135–37; visual representations of, 214–31. *See also* evidence
databases, online, 35–37, 70–71, 86–87
definitions, in argument, 17, 153–54, 180, 263
disagreements, creative, 90–92
dissertations, 32, 80–81
drafts: organization of, 181–83, 190–91; planning for, 5–6, 175–88; timing of, 185–86, 188. *See also* storyboards

elevator stories, 32
ellipses, 201–2
encyclopedias, 35–37, 66–67, 70, 75, 140
endnotes, 205, 212
ethics, research, 60, 271–74; in graphics, 227–29; plagiarism, 93, 203, 206–10, 271–74; using people as sources, 81–84
ethos, creating, 119, 203, 271
evidence, 29–31; definition and role in argument, 111–19, **114**, **115**, **117**, 132–40; evaluating, 137–40, 143–44, 192; placement in text, 182–83, 192, 202–3; and reports of evidence, 135–37; visual representations of, 214–31; and warrants, 171–72

facts: placement in text, 183, 192; verifying through research, 3, 9–10, 88
footnotes, 205, 212

Google Books, 76
Google Scholar, 36, 75
graphics: design of, 217–27; ethics of, 227–29; types of, 215–17, 230–31, **230**, **231**
graphs, line: design of, 217–20, 226–27, 231; effective use of, 215–16, 231; examples of, **216**, **218**, **226**, **227**, **228**, **231**; placement in text, 192

hedges, in argument, 130–31, 192
Hegel, Georg Wilhelm Friedrich, 249
Hemingway, Ernest, 183
histograms, 230, **230**
hypotheses. *See* claims

indexes, specialized, 36, 70–71
interests: and connecting with readers, 16–26, 35–36, 45–50; and topic selection, 34–37, 47–48
Internet, research on the. *See* online research
interviews, 81–84
introductions: drafting, 177–80; importance of, 141, 190–91, 232–34; keywords in, 180, 190–91; opening sentences of, 244–45; relationship to conclusions, 178–79, 190–91, 241–42, 245–46; structure and functions of, 179–80, 232–45

journals (personal), 31, 64
journals (scholarly): as sources, 66–68, 71–73, 77–80, 86–87; and topic selection, 36–37, 41–42

Kant, Immanuel, 249
keywords and key concepts: in abstracts, 199; and drafting, 180, 182, 186–87; in introductions, 180, 190–91; and note-taking, 95; placement in text, 180, 190–91, 193–95; searching on, 71–73, 75–77; in titles, 247

libraries, research in, 9, 68–74; archives, 37; book stacks, 73; catalogs, 69, 71–73, 97; librarians as resource, 69–70, 82; and topic selection, 35–37, 47–48
Library of Congress subject headings, 71–72
literature reviews, 70
logic: in claims, 125–26; in warrants, 115–17, 158–64

Maddow, Rachel, 3
McClintock, Barbara, 14
metaphors, in argument, 134
MLA-style citations, 205, 211–13

nominalizations, **253**, 255–57
note-taking, 31, 38, 88, 94–103; accuracy and context in, 98–101; electronic forms of, 94, 96–98, 102; organizing, 94–98; on paper, 94–96
nouns, effective use of, 251–62

Oliver, John, 3
online research, 9, 66–67, 68, 74–76; reli-

ability of information from, 75, 77–80; and topic selection, 35–37, 42, 47–48
originality, value of, 81, 93, 207
outlines, 5, 31, 32, 132, 185. *See also* storyboards

papers, parts of: body, 180–83; conclusion, 62, 178–80, 190–91, 241–42, 245–46; headings and section breaks, 186–87, 190, 194; introduction, 141, 177–80, 190–91, 232–46; and organization, 177–87, 190–91, 193–95; paragraphs, 195, 264–65; sections and subsections, 180–83, 192–95; titles, 247
paragraphs, revising, 195, 264–65
paraphrases: of draft, 196; placement in text, 192; and plagiarism, 206–10; vs. quotations and summaries, 95–96, 98–99, 100–101, 200–201, 207–8
passive voice, 260–62
peer review, and reliability of sources, 66, 76, 78
persona, in writing, 18
plagiarism, 93, 203, 206–10, 271–74
planning: argument, 107–9, 132–33, 142–45; draft, 5–6, 175–88; research, 5–6, 29–31
primary sources, 65–68, 76, 82, 85, 93–94
problems: conceptual, 51–52, 54–60, 122–23, 142–44; definition and role in research, 33–34, 49–64, 89–92; placement in text, 232–34, 237–42; practical, 10, 19–20, 50–51, 52–54, 62–63, 122, 124, 142–44
procrastination, 188
Project Gutenberg, 76
pure research, 57–60, 239

questions, 5, 20, 29–31; agreement and disagreement, 41, 89–92; examples of, 39–46; formulating, 33–34, 38–48; placement in text, 178–80; significance (*So what?*), 43–46, 49, 53–60, 178, 239–41, 245–46
quotations: accurate recording of, 93, 95–96, 98–99, 192; modifying, 201–2; vs. paraphrases and summaries, 95–96, 98–99, 100–101, 200–201, 207–8; placement in text, 192, 201–2, 244–45; and plagiarism, 206–10

readers: acknowledging and responding to, 111, 114–19, 141–54; anticipating the needs of, 12–15, 16–26, 35–36, 45–50, 108; and citations, 203–4; and clarity of style, 248–67; conversation with through argument, 107–9, 110–11, 141–54, 189, 193, 273; and ethics of research, 271–74; feedback from, 32, 104, 108, 142, 196; and need to state warrants, 164–65, 168–70; revising for, 189–96; and structure of paper, 178–79, 181–85, 232–46
reasons: definition and role in argument, 111–19, **114**, **115**, **117**, 132–40, 143–44; placement in text, 192; and warrants, 155, 160–64, 171–72
reference works, 35–37, 66–67, 70, 75, 140
research, definition and types of, 3–6, 9–15, 18–20, 57–60, 239
responses. *See* acknowledgments and responses
revising: argument, 191–93; organization, 190–91, 193–95; style, 248–67

scatterplots, 231, **231**
secondary sources, 65–68, 75; data from, 93–94; engaging with, 85–103, 145
sentences, revising, 248–67
sources: accurate representation of, 88–89, 98–101, 272; annotating, 101–3; citation of, 86–87, 203–13; critical reading of, 88–94; incorporating in text, 197–98, 200–13; in libraries, 68–74; narrowing selection of, 38–39, 65; online, 74–76; people as, 81–84; primary, secondary, and tertiary, 65–68; relevance of, 76–77; reliability of, 76, 77–80, 140; responding to, 41, 61–62, 89–94, 145; types of, 65–68, 80–84, 85
So what? (significance) question, 43–46, 49, 53–60, 178, 239–41, 245–46
storyboards, 132–33, **133**, 138; body of papers, 180–83; conclusions, 183; introductions, 177–78, 179–80; keywords, 180, 182, 186–87
style, components of, 248–67
subjects, of sentences, 251–62
summaries: vs. analysis, 184; of drafts, 196; placement in text, 177–78, 192; and plagiarism, 206–10; of problems, 32; vs. quotations and paraphrases, 95–96, 98–99, 100–101, 200–201, 207–8; of sources, 70, 88, 95–96, 98–99, 177–78, 184

tables: design of, 217–22; effective use of, 215; examples of, **214**, **215**, **219**, **221**, **222**; placement in text, 192
teachers: advice for, 275–80; as readers, 11–15, 18–19, 34, 104, 184–85, 196, 274; as researchers, 9, 60–61
terminology, use of, 17, 153–54, 180, 263
tertiary sources, 65–68, 70
theses (argument). *See* claims
theses (graduate), 32, 80–81
topics: and claims, 123, 127; and organization of paper, 181, 185, 195, 242, 259; vs. problems, 24, 49–52, 85, 110; selection of, 29–31, 33–48, 180; and sources, 67–79, 91; and thinking, 14–15, 64, 121
Turabian-style citations, 205, 206, 211–13

verbs, effective use of, 252–62
voice, active vs. passive, 260–62

warrants: challenging, 168–70; definition and role in argument, 111, 115–17, **116**, **117**, 155–72, **157**, **160**, **166**, **167**; need to state, 158, 164–65, 193; placement in text, 182–83; proverbs as, 156–57, 158–59, 169–70
Watson, James D., 128, 130–31, 238, 240
Wikipedia, 35, 66–67, 75, 140
writer's block, 188
writing, role of in research, 11–15, 185–86. *See also* drafts; revising
writing groups, 32

39287425R00200

Made in the USA
Middletown, DE
10 January 2017